Property of :   Tim Newcomb
PO Box 7
Laramie, Wyoming 82073

SUPREME INJUSTICE

Also by Alan M. Dershowitz

Psychoanalysis, Psychiatry, and Law
(with Jay Katz and Joseph Goldstein)

Criminal Law: Theory and Practice
(with Joseph Goldstein and Richard D. Schwartz)

The Best Defense

Reversal of Fortune: Inside the von Bülow Case

*Taking Liberties: A Decade of Hard Cases,
Bad Laws, and Bum Raps*

Chutzpah

Contrary to Popular Opinion

The Advocate's Devil

*The Abuse Excuse: And Other Cop-Outs, Sob Stories,
and Evasions of Responsibility*

Reasonable Doubts

*The Vanishing American Jew:
In Search of Jewish Identity for the Next Century*

*Sexual McCarthyism:
Clinton, Starr, and the Emerging Constitutional Crisis*

Just Revenge

*The Genesis of Justice: Ten Stories of Biblical Injustice That Led
to the Ten Commandments and Modern Morality and Law*

SUPREME
INJUSTICE

How the High Court
Hijacked Election 2000

Alan M. Dershowitz

OXFORD
UNIVERSITY PRESS
2001

OXFORD
UNIVERSITY PRESS

Oxford New York
Athens Auckland Bangkok Bogotá Buenos Aires
Cape Town Chennai Dar es Salaam Delhi Florence Hong Kong Istanbul
Karachi Kolkata Kuala Lumpur Madrid Melbourne Mexico City Mumbai
Nairobi Paris São Paulo Shanghai Singapore Taipei Tokyo Toronto Warsaw

and associated companies in
Berlin Ibadan

Published by Oxford University Press, Inc.
198 Madison Avenue, New York, New York 10016

Oxford is a registered trademark of Oxford University Press

Library of Congress Cataloging-in-Publication Data
Dershowitz, Alan M.
    Supreme injustice: how the high court hijacked
election 2000 / Alan M. Dershowitz.
        p.   cm.   Includes bibliographical references and index.
    ISBN 0-19-514827-4
    1. Bush, George W. (George Walker), 1946—Trials, litigation, etc.
    2. Gore, Albert, 1948—Trials, litigation, etc.
    3. Contested elections—United States.
    4. Contested elections—Florida.
    5. Presidents—United States—Election—2000.   I. Title.

    KF5074.2.D47 2001   324.973'0929—dc21   2001032193

Book designed by Susan Day.
Indexed by Peter Brigaitis and Marie Nuchols.
Typeset by Rainsford Type.
Printed by Quebecor Printing Book Group.

9 8 7 6 5 4 3 2

Printed in the United States of America
on acid-free paper

This book is lovingly dedicated to the memory
of my late father-in-law, Mordecai (Mortie) Cohen,
to whom justice and compassion came naturally.

And

to my mother-in-law, Dorothy (Dutch) Cohen,
who inspires by her example and caring insights.

Others say, Law is our Fate;
Others say, Law is our State;
Others say, others say
Law is no more,
Law has gone away.

—From "Law Like Love," by W. H. Auden (1939)

Contents

Acknowledgments

This book could not have been produced so quickly without the much-appreciated assistance of so many people. First, my primary assistant, Howard Anglin, coordinated the extensive research. Though the task was daunting, Howard was always pleasant and enthusiastic. He was ably assisted by David Yocis, Daniel Schwartz, Lee Fink, and especially John Orsini, on whom I can always count.

Maura Kelley typed much of this manuscript, as she has so many others over the years, and her 24/7 availability is sincerely appreciated. Manny Lim coordinated the typing and retyping effort and kept my office going during the turmoil of finishing this project. Thanks and much appreciation.

My appreciation to the dean, faculty, and staff of New York University School of Law for hosting me during my sabbatical year, and especially to Professors Richard Pildes, Jim Jacobs, and Yochai Binkler for sharing insights with me about the election cases.

My greatest debt is to my family, especially my wife, Carolyn, who read my drafts and made them better, and my daughter, Ella, who gave me some great ideas. My appreciation to them also for allowing me to turn our small apartment into a library, archive, and office during the months I labored over this book. My brother, Nathan, reviewed the drafts and helped improve them. My son, Elon, as usual, coached me on how to make my ideas clearer and more accessible. Other family members encouraged, kibitzed, and tolerated my *mishagas*.

At Oxford University Press, I thank copyeditor Sue Warga for an excellent job of making the book clearer and more readable; editorial director Peter Ginna for very helpful comments on several drafts of the manuscript and for coming up with the book's subtitle; editorial assistant Farahnaz Maroof for a tremendous amount of all-around assistance, including useful comments on early drafts; production editor Helen Mules for carefully and cheerfully shepherding the manuscript through production; managing editor Ruth Mannes for keeping us to a very tight schedule with aplomb; publicists Sarah Hemphill and Sara Leopold for setting up a wonderful group of events for the book; and Tom Willshire and Vera Plummer for getting so many copies into the bookstores.

A special word of gratitude to Tim Bartlett, who came to me with the idea for this book and guided it from beginning to end. All of his suggestions improved the book. A final word of appreciation to my friend Floyd Abrams, for his input on the title.

SUPREME
INJUSTICE

Although we may never know with complete certainty the identity of the winner of this year's Presidential election, the identity of the loser is perfectly clear.

—*Justice John Paul Stevens in his dissenting opinion in* Bush v. Gore

Introduction

The five justices who ended Election 2000 by stopping the Florida hand recount have damaged the credibility of the U.S. Supreme Court, and their lawless decision in *Bush v. Gore* promises to have a more enduring impact on Americans than the outcome of the election itself. The nation has accepted the election of George W. Bush, as it must under the rule of law. It will have an opportunity to reassess this result in 2004. But the unprecedented decision of the five justices to substitute their political judgment for that of the people threatens to undermine the moral authority of the high court for generations to come.

The Supreme Court, which consists of only nine relatively unknown justices with small staffs, has wielded an enormous influence on the history of our nation. It is the most powerful court in the world—the envy of judges in every other country. Presidents accept its rulings, even when disagreeing. The public eventually embraces much of what the justices say in their judgments. Legislatures rarely seek to overrule their decisions. Though only one part of our delicate system of checks and balances, the high court speaks the final word on many of the most divisive and important issues of the day.* This enormous power has always been viewed as legitimate because of the unique status of the justices as transcending partisan politics, eschewing personal advantage and pronouncing the enduring constitutional values of our nation. We defer to them because we respect them.

Now in one fell swoop, five partisan judges have caused many Americans to question each of the assumptions undergirding the special status accorded these nine robed human beings. *Bush v. Gore* showed them to be little difference from ordinary politicians. Their votes reflected not any enduring constitutional values rooted in the precedents of the ages, but rather the partisan quest for immediate political victory. In so voting, they shamed themselves and the Court on which they serve, and they defiled their places in history.

Because the Supreme Court lacks the legitimacy and accountability that come with election and the power that derives from the sword and the purse, its authority rests on public acceptance of its status as a nonpartisan arbiter of the law. This moral authority is essential to its continued effectiveness as an important guarantor of our constitutional liberties. Unless steps are taken to mitigate the damage inflicted on the Court by these five justices, the balance struck by our Constitution between popular democracy and judicial oligarchy will remain askew.

------

*The awesome power of the United States Supreme Court to declare unconstitutional the actions of the other branches of government is nowhere explicitly granted by the Constitution itself. It was asserted by the justices in *Marbury v. Madison* (1803).

Preserving this delicate balance is essential to our liberties and to our system of checks and balances. That is why I have written a book about the Supreme Court decision rather than about the election. Here I offer a critical assessment of the decision itself as well as the motivations of the justices who rendered it. I provide both direct and circumstantial evidence that some of them were motivated by partisan advantage, while others were motivated by expectation of personal gain. I explore the dangerous implications of the decision in *Bush v. Gore* for all Americans, regardless of party affiliation or ideology, especially since the Supreme Court—prior to this case—was among the last institutions whose integrity remained above reproach. Finally, I propose steps that can be taken to avoid any repetition of this supreme injustice.

The majority ruling in *Bush v. Gore* marked a number of significant firsts. Never before in American history has a presidential election been decided by the Supreme Court.[1] Never before in American history have so many law professors, historians, political scientists, Supreme Court litigators, journalists who cover the high court, and other experts—at all points along the political spectrum—been in agreement that the majority decision of the Court was not only "bad constitutional law"[2] but "lawless,"[3] "illegitimate,"[4] "unprincipled," "partisan,"[5] "fraudulent," "disingenuous," and motivated by improper considerations.[6] In addition to the remarkable expert consensus regarding this case, there is also widespread popular outrage at what the high court did. Though the level of this outrage tends to mirror party affiliation, it is safe to say that the degree of confusion over what actually happened is not limited to one party. There are millions of Americans who do not strongly identify with the Democratic Party—indeed, even some who voted for George W. Bush—but who cannot understand how five justices could determine the outcome of a presidential election. Moreover, the furor within the Supreme Court itself—among some justices and law clerks—is unprecedented in the annals of this usually harmonious institution.

In light of these factors, many Americans who believed that the Court was an institution that could be trusted to remain above partisan politics are now experiencing a genuine loss of confidence in the impartiality of the judicial branch of our government. This widespread loss of confidence, reaching to the pinnacle of our judiciary, should be the concern of all Americans, because the Supreme Court has played such a critical role in the history of our nation. Without its moral authority, we would be a less tolerant, less vibrant, and less free democracy. The high court, throughout its long and distinguished history, has helped us—not always perfectly or swiftly—through crises of institutional racism, religious intolerance, McCarthyism, systematic malapportionment, presidents who deemed themselves above the law, and governors who defied the Constitution. The Court stepped in when the other branches of government were unwilling or unable to enforce the constitutional rights of unpopular minorities. The justices were always at their greatest when they could act unanimously and on principles that could be easily justified and widely accepted. When they act in an unprincipled and partisan manner—as they did in *Bush v. Gore*—they risk losing respect and frittering away the moral capital accumulated by their predecessors over generations. That is what Justice Stephen Breyer was referring to when he wrote in his dissent in *Bush v. Gore:*

> [I]n this highly politicized matter, the appearance of a split decision runs the risk of undermining the public's confidence in the Court itself. That confidence is a public treasure. It has been built slowly over many years. . . . It is a vitally necessary ingredient of any successful effort to protect basic liberty and, indeed, the rule of law itself. . . . [We] risk a self-inflicted

wound—a wound that may harm not just the Court, but the Nation.

That is why all Americans must care about this case and must derive the appropriate lessons from it. The Supreme Court's moral capital will certainly again be needed in our future, and so it is a tragedy that it has been dissipated for short-term partisan gain in a case in which the Supreme Court had no proper role.

The Constitution, after all, places the power to elect our president in every institution of government but the judiciary. The people vote for electors.[7] The electors vote for the president. If this process produces no clear winner, then the Constitution (and the laws enacted pursuant to it) assigns varying roles to the Senate, the House of Representatives, the state legislatures, and even the governors.[8] No role, however, is explicitly given to the Supreme Court. James Madison, in recording his own views of the constitutional debate as to how the president should be elected, dismissed selection by the appointed judiciary as "out of the question."[9]

Indeed, the justices themselves seemed to initially recognize the absence of a judicial role when they unanimously remanded *Bush v. Gore* back to the Florida Supreme Court for that court to explain whether it had improperly changed the election law as enacted by the Florida legislature. The high court suggested that if the state supreme court had changed duly enacted state legislation, then it may have violated Article II of the Constitution, which vests in state legislatures the authority to select the manner by which electors should be chosen. It seems ironic that the U.S. Supreme Court would take upon itself a judicial function nowhere specified in the Constitution—effectively ending a presidential election—while seeming to deny to the Florida Supreme Court its traditional role in interpreting and reconciling conflicting statutes.

Some of the Court's defenders have argued that since, in their view, the Florida Supreme Court engaged in partisan judicial activism in support of Gore, it was permissible for the nation's highest court to "correct" the lower court and undo the harm it had done. Indeed, I am reliably informed that several of the majority justices were outraged at what they believed was crass partisanship by the Florida justices. I have been told that one of the dissenting U.S. Supreme Court justices characterized the mind-set of some of the majority justices as follows: "If the Florida Supreme Court is going to act like a bunch of Democratic political hacks, well, by God, we will act like a bunch of Republican political hacks." Even if it is true that some Florida justices acted in a partisan manner, that would not justify a retaliatory partisan decision by U.S. Supreme Court justices. Two partisan wrongs do not make a judicial right. Moreover, under the U.S. Constitution, a state court has the right to be wrong on matters of state law, and the Supreme Court has no power to correct it unless its mistake is a matter of federal constitutional or statutory law. Even then, the Supreme Court does not traditionally correct every error a state court makes. Citing death penalty cases, Justice Ruth Bader Ginsburg, in her dissenting opinion in *Bush v. Gore,* reminded her colleagues that "[n]ot uncommonly, we let stand state-court interpretations of *federal* law with which we might disagree." During oral argument, she put it even more directly to Bush's lawyer:

> "I do not know of any case where we have impugned a state supreme court the way you are doing in this case," Ginsburg scolded Olson. Florida's seven justices "may have been wrong; we might have interpreted it differently, but we are not the arbiters—they are."[10]

The very justices who typically allow state prisoners to be executed even if their conviction was based on a mistaken reading of federal constitutional law[11] jumped into this case on the ground that the Florida Supreme Court's decision violated the equal-protection clause of the U.S. Constitution in a manner never before suggested by any court. Even some scholars who supported Bush—Robert Bork, Harvey Mansfield, Michael McConnell, and Richard Epstein, among others—have found this conclusion unconvincing, troublesome, and wrongheaded.[12]

It also seemed baffling to many that these five justices, whose records on the high court showed them to be the least sensitive to claims of equal protection, determined a presidential election on such doubtful equal-protection grounds.[13]

These and many other questions have led many Americans to wonder whether the black-robed justices are really any less politically partisan than elected politicians. When Antonin Scalia—one of the architects of the majority decision—was still a law professor, he made an observation that aptly characterized the feelings of many scholars in regard to this decision:

> It is increasingly difficult to pretend to one's students that the decisions of the Supreme Court are tied together by threads of logic and analysis as opposed to what seems to be the fact that the decisions of each of the Justices on the Court are tied together by threads of social preference and predisposition.[14]

In dissenting from the Supreme Court's decision ending the hand count, Justice John Paul Stevens, the court's senior associate justice, echoed Professor Scalia in strong words that will be long remembered and often quoted by those who follow the Court. He warned that the majority's position "can only lend credence to the most cynical appraisal of the work of judges throughout the land. It is," said Justice Stevens, "confidence in the men and women who administer the judicial system that is the true backbone of the rule of law. Time will one day heal the wound to that confidence that will be inflicted by today's decision. One thing, however, is certain. Although we may never know with complete certainty the identity of the winner of this year's Presidential election, the identity of the loser is perfectly clear. It is the Nation's confidence in the judge as an impartial guardian of the rule of law."[15]

Justice Stevens is wrong in only one respect: Time will never heal this wound so long as it remains untreated by the strong disinfectant of sunlight. And heal it must if our system of checks and balances, with the unique role our Supreme Court has played throughout our history, is to remain strong.

A significant diminution of confidence in our Supreme Court, based on legitimate concerns, should not be covered up or minimized in the false hope that it will be forgotten over time. Nor should well-intentioned defenders of the justices hold back their criticism out of fear that it will be misused by those who would weaken the Supreme Court as an institution. Well-founded criticism, if it leads to proper healing, can only strengthen the Court.

In this book, I will try to cast a bright light on the Court's decision and the justices who engineered it. At the same time, I will try to explain how we could have come to the point where five unelected judges, appointed for life and accountable to no one, could have had so much influence—in so partisan a manner—on the political destiny of a nation that proclaims itself to be the world's protector of democracy.

It will come as no surprise that I, too, was a partisan in this election and in the postelection legal and political dispute. I am a Democrat (who occasionally votes for Republicans) who in this election voted for Al Gore. A few days after the election, two groups of voters in Palm Beach County asked me to represent them on a pro bono basis to oppose the Bush efforts to stop the mandatory hand recount requested by Gore and to obtain other legal relief. I appeared in court once on behalf of one of these groups and continued to maintain an interest throughout the litigation. I also appeared frequently in the media, not as a spokesman for the Democratic Party—indeed, I disagreed strongly with some of their tactics—but rather as a supporter of a statewide hand count that categorized each disputed ballot by its salient characteristics (how many were fully punched through; how many had one, two, or three hanging chads; how many had chads that were pierced or dimpled; and so on). I am also an academic who has practiced before the Supreme Court for many years and who has taught courses for even more years dealing extensively with Supreme Court decisions. I served as a law clerk to the late Justice Arthur Goldberg during the 1963–64 term of the Supreme Court. I think I understand the important and unique role our high court plays in our system of governance, and I revere the Court as an institution, though I have often been critical of its work. In this book, as in all my writings, I try to bring to bear a combination of my experience, advocacy, academic orientation, and principles. It is for others to judge whether I have struck the appropriate balance, but I try to give the reader all the information about my biases necessary to make that judgment.

I wanted Al Gore to be elected president, but it was not Gore's loss or Bush's win that motivated me to write this book. I care much more about the enduring impact of this case on the credibility of the Supreme Court than about the transient effects of a single presidential election. I am angry at the Supreme Court not so much because of whom it elected, but because it took it upon itself to elect anyone.

Nor is it relevant to the point of this book that had the Supreme Court not stopped the hand count, Bush might well have won—according to some accounts, by even more of a margin than the official count gave him.[16] The Supreme Court did not know what the result of the hand count would be when it stopped it. A hijacking occurs when someone unlawfully seeks to divert a vehicle from its course. The fact that the vehicle ultimately ends up at its intended destination does not mitigate the hijacker's culpability.

This book is about the culpability of those justices who hijacked Election 2000 by distorting the law, violating their own expressed principles, and using their robes to bring about a partisan result. I accuse them of failing what I call the shoe-on-the-other-foot test: I believe that they would not have stopped a hand recount if George W. Bush had been seeking it. This is an extremely serious charge, because deciding a case on the basis of the identity of the litigants is a fundamental violation of the judicial oath, to "administer justice without respect to persons. . . ." In this book, I marshal the evidence in support of this charge. In a larger sense, this book is also about the Supreme Court and its continuing importance to all Americans. Its purpose is to alert the American people to a serious problem in the hope that constructive criticism can help to avoid a crisis that could endanger our liberties.

It is a sad day for America and the Constitution when a court decides the outcome of an election.

—*James Baker, Bush's chief lawyer, after the Florida Supreme Court ruled in favor of a hand recount*

1: Five Justices Decide the Election

There's a story, almost certainly apocryphal, about a lawyer making his first argument before the Supreme Court. Justice Felix Frankfurter, a stickler for procedural regularity, asked the rookie advocate the question he commonly asked lawyers in cases of questionable federal jurisdiction: "How did you get here?" To which the flustered young man replied, "By taxi!"

How a case gets to the Supreme Court is often intriguing and sometimes confusing. Despite the common misperception that every citizen has a right to bring his grievances to our highest court, the reality is that the Supreme Court's jurisdiction—that, is, its power to consider a case—is relatively limited. In some countries (Israel is a notable example) anyone has the right to appear before the supreme court on specified days to seek justice.[1] In the United States, the power of the Supreme Court is circumscribed by the U.S. Constitution and federal statutes. For example, the Supreme Court may not offer "advisory opinions" about abstract or hypothetical questions of law; it may rule only in actual "cases or controversies" involving litigants with a real stake in the outcome. Nor may it decide issues of state law; under our system of federalism, the highest court of each state is the final arbiter in local matters lacking a federal interest, such as domestic relations, local crimes, contracts, torts, and similar issues. But pursuant to the supremacy clause of the U.S. Constitution[2]—and a series of cases interpreting that clause[3]— the U.S. Supreme Court has the final word on questions of federal law, including federal constitutional law.

Cases within the Supreme Court's jurisdiction get to the justices through several different routes. With a few very narrow and rarely used exceptions, cases do not come to the Supreme Court directly.[4] They must first pass through either the lower state courts or the lower federal courts. In the Florida election matter, cases were being litigated simultaneously in both the Florida state court system and the federal court system.[5] There were as many as fifty separate, but often overlapping, court cases growing out of the election in Florida.[6] Because of the looming deadlines, these cases were also necessarily on a fast track, thus compressing the time ordinarily taken by courts to render decisions. The result was a flurry of lawsuits, arguments, and legal decisions, which were often difficult to follow.

Before considering these cases and the manner by which they made their way up through the courts, let me first outline the constitutional and statutory framework within which presidential elections are conducted in this country, and provide a brief chronology and a few words about the election itself. While many readers will be familiar with much of this information, it is sufficiently important to an understanding of *Bush v. Gore* to warrant a brief recounting.

How We Elect Our President

Many Americans were surprised to learn that they have no constitutional right to vote for the president of the United States.[7] The framers of our Constitution did not trust all of the people to elect their president. Fearful of "mobocracy," they created a governmental structure under which elites would check and balance the rabble. These elites consisted of electors, chosen by whatever manner each state legislature designated, who would select the president and vice president; senators, who would be chosen by state legislatures; and judges, appointed for life. Only the members of the House of Representatives were to be elected directly by the voters. Moreover, a relatively small percentage of people were deemed qualified to vote in *any* elections.[8]

Challenges to this elitism soon began to emerge. Jacksonian democracy placed more trust in the people than in the elites.[9] The requirement that one had to be a taxpayer in order to vote was gradually eliminated; secret paper ballots largely replaced the old method of oral voting; and whereas in 1800 only two states provided for the popular selection of presidential electors, by 1836 only South Carolina still left the selection of electors to the legislature.[10]

Gradually the U.S. Constitution, and the constitutions of many states, changed to reflect this growing distrust of elites. Senators were elected directly by the people.[11] Universal suffrage was introduced. The voting age was lowered. Many state judges were elected. In Florida today, even public defenders are elected.

The only elite institution that remains close to what it was when our original Constitution was adopted is the federal judiciary, headed by the Supreme Court. If anything, the power of the Supreme Court has been enhanced. In 1803, in the transforming case of *Marbury v. Madison,* the Supreme Court allocated to itself the power to declare the actions of the other branches unconstitutional. This decision, which had no precedent anywhere in the world, made the Supreme Court the final arbiter on how the Constitution would be interpreted. As Justice Robert Jackson once quipped in regard to this awesome power: "We are not final because we are infallible, but we are infallible only because we are final."[12]

Following the democratization of all the other branches of government, the Supreme Court remained the only elite check on the perceived excesses of democracy. It was permitted to retain that power on the assumption that it would act differently than the popular branches and that its decisions would not be driven by partisan political considerations, self-interest, or the desire for immediate popular approval.

Now back to the way our Constitution and statutes determine how our presidents are to be elected.

Under Article II of the Constitution, electors decide who shall become president, and each state legislature may decide for itself the manner by which its electors are appointed. The legislature could appoint them, or it could—as every state legislature has now done—delegate that authority to the voters. In all but two states, the winner of the popular vote receives all of the state's electors,[13] who are committed—either by law or by tradition—to vote for the candidate who wins the state popular vote.[14] If there is a dispute over who has won the popular vote in a given state, the election law of that state, with its provision for recounts, governs—at least initially. Under a federal statute enacted after the disputed Tilden-Hays election of 1876, if a state makes "its final determination" of who its electors shall be "at least six days before" the Electoral College meets, that determination "shall govern."[15] This deadline is popularly known as the safe-harbor provision of federal law—a provision that came to play a pivotal role in the 2000 presidential election. There is, of course, no actual Electoral College, in the sense of a group that meets in a single location and deliberates on who shall become president. The electors from each state

Hayes

meet in the state capital and send their vote (or votes) to the United States Capitol in Washington, where all the votes are tabulated. If a majority of the electors vote for a given candidate, he becomes president, but if there is no majority, the election is thrown into the House of Representatives, where each state casts one vote. There, a majority of twenty-six votes is needed to win.[16]

The 2000 Election and Its Aftermath

It was within this constitutional and statutory framework that the 2000 election was held on November 7. Shortly before 8 P.M., the major television networks projected, based on exit polls, that Al Gore had won Florida. Within a few hours, they retracted this projection and declared the state too close to call. At approximately 2:15 A.M. on November 8, the networks declared that George W. Bush had won Florida by approximately fifty thousand votes and hence had won the presidency, despite Gore's lead in the national popular vote. Gore called Bush to concede, but less than an hour later, Gore learned that the actual count had shrunk Bush's lead to the point where, under Florida law, an automatic machine recount was required.[17] He again called Bush, this time to retract his private concession. At 4:15 A.M., the networks withdrew their projection that Bush had been elected. From this point on, confusion reigned, and the world turned its attention to Florida and to several key counties in particular. Within days, virtually every American had learned new terms such as "butterfly ballot,"* "chad,"† and

---

*The form of ballot used in Palm Beach County, consisting of two leaves in book form, with chads to be punched out from the center, using the Votomatic system.

†A chad is a small, perforated piece that is intended to detach from the ballot when it is punched with a stylus by a voter.

"Votomatic." We were introduced to new characters in the un-folding drama, such as Florida secretary of state Katherine Har-ris and Florida attorney general Bob Butterworth. Images of weary vote counters holding perforated ballots up to the light flashed around the world.

The thirty-six days between November 7, when Americans voted, and December 13, when Al Gore finally conceded the presidency to George W. Bush, were among the most confusing, exhilarating, nerve-wracking, educational, divisive, uplifting, and depressing in our political history as a nation. We were exposed to what many called a high-stakes civics lesson on a subject about which most Americans had strong feelings but little prior knowledge. It was a wild ride for the candidates, their supporters, and a fascinated world that hadn't seen any-thing quite like this struggle for an Electoral College victory, which would determine the leadership of the free world based on several hundred disputed ballots in counties few people had ever heard of prior to November 7.

Shortly after the polls closed, several things became apparent: Gore appeared to have won the national popular vote by a razor-slim margin, but whichever candidate secured Florida's twenty-five electoral votes would win in the Electoral College and become president. More Floridians probably *intended* to vote for Gore than for Bush, but if the machine count was an accurate reflection of votes properly cast, more had *actually* voted for Bush. Gore was going to challenge the machine vote unless the automatic machine recount put him over the top, and Bush was going to resist any such challenge. This was going to be a fight to the finish, with nei-ther candidate likely to concede until all hope was lost.

Both campaigns sent teams of lawyers, political operatives, and media mavens to Florida to conduct the anticipated liti-gation as the post–Election Day drama played itself out on sev-eral fronts: the legal, the political, the public relations, and the personal.

The Ground War in Florida

I was in Palm Beach and Miami for only a few days shortly after Election Day, and others who were there have written more detailed accounts of the ground war in Florida. I will focus instead on what the Supreme Court did in the five crucial decisions it rendered:[18]

1. It agreed to review one aspect of the initial decision of the Florida Supreme Court, which had ordered the manual recount to continue and which extended the deadline for certifying the election by twelve days.
2. It vacated that decision and sent the case back to the Florida Supreme Court for clarification regarding the grounds of its decision.
3. It stayed the Florida Supreme Court's second decision, which had mandated a statewide recount of all undervotes* and had ordered certain votes not counted by the machines but identified in the hand count to be included in the final certification.[19]
4. It agreed to review that decision on its merits.
5. It reversed that decision and permanently stopped all hand counting of undervotes, thereby ending the election in favor of George W. Bush.

In order to understand the context of these decisions and to assess their validity, we must briefly look at some background information regarding the ground war and the numerous over-

---

*An undervote is a ballot on which the voter did not choose a candidate for president (according to machine reading).

lapping battles—in both the courts of law and the courts of public opinion—that were raging throughout Florida and beyond between Election Day and the night of the Supreme Court's final decision.

The Butterfly Ballot

The first hint of trouble emerged even before the polls closed.[20] By midday on November 7, it was becoming obvious that Theresa LePore, the election supervisor of Palm Beach County, had made a dreadful error in designing the ballot for her constituents. What was not yet obvious was that her mistake would change the outcome of the presidential election. As the result of a little-noticed 1998 referendum, it had become easier for marginal third-party candidates to demand a place on the ballot. Ten candidates, instead of the usual three or four, had their names listed on the presidential ballot, and this crowding of the field required election officials to figure out a way of getting so many names on a single ballot. The most common solution was simply to use smaller print. LePore rejected this approach because the voters in her county tended to be older and might have difficulty with small print. She decided instead on a design that was described this way in a report in the *Washington Post:*

> The design LePore chose placed the names on two facing pages, with the punch holes running down the center. Arrows pointed from the names to the holes—but when the ballot cards were fed into the voting machines, the holes didn't always line up with the arrows. Not that the arrows were entirely clear, either: The hole for a minor third-party candidate, Patrick J. Buchanan, was higher on the card than the hole for Al Gore.[21]

The so-called butterfly ballot actually looked like this:

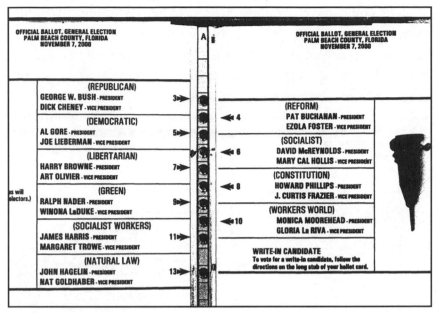

All through the day, complaints came in from voters who were confused by the ballot and worried that they had accidentally voted for the wrong candidate. This occurred before anyone had any idea how close the Florida election would turn out to be. The butterfly ballot caused so much confusion—almost all of it hurting Gore—that a widely reprinted editorial cartoon caricatured it as follows:

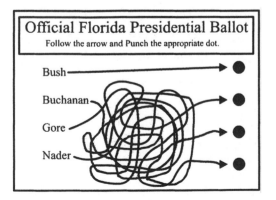

The tragedy is that any moderately intelligent elementary-school student could have avoided these problems without any additional cost. My then-ten-year-old daughter was asked by her teacher to redesign the ballot so as to avoid the confusion. She changed nothing other than to add a circle around each candidate and his correct hole, like this:

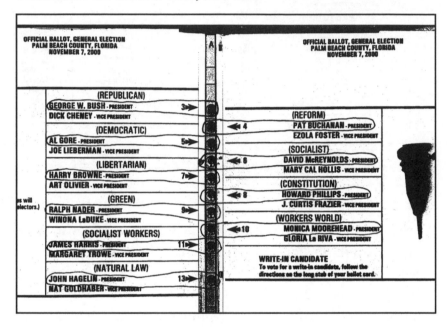

Had these circles or some other simple visual device been added, there is virtually no doubt that Gore would have been elected president, without any recount or challenge.

The *Palm Beach Post* later conducted a review of more than nineteen thousand double-punched ballots* that had been invalidated. The newspaper concluded that "Gore lost 6,607 votes when voters marked more than one name on the county's 'butterfly ballot.'"[22] This does not even include around three thousand individuals who may have intended to vote for Gore

---

*Also known as overvotes, on which voters chose more than one candidate for president.

but inadvertently cast a vote for Patrick Buchanan. As one elderly Jewish woman who believes she accidentally voted for Buchanan told me colorfully: "I would rather have had a colonoscopy than vote for that son of a bitch Buchanan." Buchanan himself acknowledged that very few of the votes he received in heavily Jewish and Democratic Palm Beach County were intended for him.[23]

The newspaper's review found that 5,330 voters punched chads for both Gore and Buchanan. An additional 2,908 voters punched chads for Gore and the Socialist candidate whose hole was just below Gore's; these voters apparently thought they were voting for Gore *and Lieberman*. As Palm Beach County resident Paul Berman told a reporter from the *Washington Post:* "I voted for Gore, but I also voted for the vice president. I punched two holes instead of one. . . . All I had to do was just punch Gore. . . . But I saw Lieberman—so I punched it too."[24]

Bush lost 1,631 votes as a result of people punching his name and Buchanan's. But the net loss for Gore was 6,607—more than ten times the number of votes he would have needed to overcome Bush's official 537-vote margin of victory.[25]

Initially, most of the legal attention was focused on the butterfly ballot, since the incompetently—and perhaps illegally[26]—designed ballot probably resulted in more lost Gore votes than any other potential legal issue. But ultimately the Gore legal team concluded that they were unlikely to prevail on this matter. There were two daunting hurdles to overcome. First, the person who had designed the ballot was a registered Democrat.[27] Theresa LePore—whom the media dubbed "Madame Butterfly"—had obviously not deliberately designed the butterfly ballot to help Bush, though anyone looking at it should have seen that it gave Bush a significant benefit. The problem for the Democrats was that *they* had looked at a sample ballot before the election and had not noticed the potential for confusion.

The other hurdle—this one even more difficult to overcome—
was that there was no apparent practical remedy that a court
would be willing to impose even if it concluded that the rights
of confused voters had been violated by the ballot. The Gore
legal team considered asking for a complete revote with a less
confusing ballot in Palm Beach County, but after reviewing previous election cases, it became apparent to them that no court
would order such a radical remedy. The law requires presidential elections to be held on a given day,[28] suggesting that a revote
on another day might raise legal concerns. As one Bush lawyer
put it: "There are no do-overs in a presidential election."[29] Indeed, when some Palm Beach voters sought this remedy, a circuit court judge rebuffed them, saying that he lacked the authority to order a revote.[30] Other remedies were suggested,
including an effort to determine the number of votes lost to
each candidate by using a probabilistic extrapolation of the
kind ultimately done by several newspapers with the help of
expert statisticians, but the consensus was, rightly, that no judge
would allow a presidential election to be decided by statisticians
or hypothetical extrapolations, and that the public would never
accept a president selected by experts.

According to an account published in the *Washington Post,*
Gore's campaign manager, William Daley, was among those
who argued strongly against seeking a remedy that he felt they
would never get. Daley acknowledged that Gore had been hurt
by the butterfly ballot, but he pointed out that "people get
screwed every day" and "they don't have a remedy." There was
"no way to solve this problem," he insisted, urging the Gore
legal team to focus on problems they could solve, such as the
county-by-county hand count provided for by Florida law.[31]
The decision was made to abandon the butterfly ballot issue
and try to count as many Gore votes as possible that were
missed by the machine counts.

The butterfly ballot, it was soon learned, was not the only

poorly designed part in the complex machinery of the Florida
election process. Interviews with poll workers disclosed that the
voting machines used in several counties failed to count a significant number of ballots that were validly cast under Florida
law. The Votomatic cards were "alarmingly unreliable," with
a failure rate of "4 percent or more,"[32] and in an election decided by a mere fraction of 1 percent of the votes cast, this is
highly significant. A Gore lawyer found a 1982 patent application by the man who helped design the Votomatic machine,
which read in part as follows:

> "If chips are permitted to accumulate . . . this can interfere
> with the punching operations, . . . and occasionally, it has
> been observed that a partially punched chip has been left
> hanging onto a card" resulting in the machine becoming "so
> clogged with chips as to prevent a clean punching operation.
> Incompletely punched cards can cause serious errors to occur
> in data processing operations utilizing such cards."[33]

Another Gore lawyer noted that "it has been eight years since
Miami-Dade County cleaned the chads from its machines."[34] A
poll worker said that she had "tried to shake out the chads
every few hours" but some machines "became clogged beyond
repair."[35]

Beyond the clogging problem, the machines themselves had
a design flaw that made them entirely inappropriate for use in
Florida and other states that, by law, require the counting of
every ballot from which the intent of the voter could be clearly
inferred. The Votomatic sometimes did and sometimes did not
count ballots whose chads were fully punched through (thus
demonstrating a clear intent to vote for that candidate) but on
which the chad was not fully detached. These "hanging chads,"
as they came to be called, generated considerable controversy.
Voters received written instructions at the polls to inspect

their ballots to be sure that no chads remained hanging, but thousands failed to do so.[36] No reasonable person could claim— though Justice O'Connor later appeared to—that this failure somehow reflected an intent *not* to cast a valid vote, any more than, for example, using a No. 1 pencil when the instructions called for using a No. 2 pencil. And unless a ballot could be interpreted as not intending to cast a vote, it had to be counted under Florida law. Yet the Votomatic machines failed to count many such votes—enough to change the outcome of a close election. They also failed to count other ballots that arguably showed an intent to vote for particular candidates. For example, some machines were clogged or misaligned so as to make it impossible or quite difficult to punch the chad through for any candidates. Some ballots that were uncounted by the machines showed clear indentations or pinholes for one candidate for *every* office, thus reflecting an effort to vote for those candidates. Those ballots can be distinguished from ballots on which there was only a slight indentation on one chad for a candidate for only one office, while the chads for candidates for every other office were fully punched through, thus leaving open the possibility that the voter changed his or her mind and decided not to cast a vote for that office. Under Florida law, the former ballots surely should have been counted, while the latter probably should not. Yet the Votomatic failed to distinguish between these ballots and did not count *any* of them. These "dimpled," "pregnant," and "penetrated" chads generated even more controversy than the hanging ones, and gave rise to much late-night and Internet humor ("Palm Beach is being called the Immaculate Conception county, because a chad can become pregnant without being penetrated").

It was against this confusing background that the Gore camp developed its strategy for turning the election in its favor.

"Count All the Votes"—or at Least the Ones That Favor Gore

The Gore camp's mantra was "count all the votes," but, of course, they were particularly interested in counting Gore votes, and so they used Florida law to fashion a challenge that would maximize their chance of winning. Florida law permits a candidate to seek a hand count in any county if he can demonstrate that a preliminary hand count of at least 1 percent of the votes in three precincts "indicates an error in the voter tabulation which could affect the outcome of the election."[37] Accordingly, they handpicked four Democratic counties in which to seek a recount, insisting on the broadest possible criteria for counting a vote, including dimpled, punched, pregnant, and scratched chads.[38] They were behind and needed all the votes they could muster—and they needed them quickly.

Time was of the essence because several deadlines loomed on the horizon. The first was the Florida statutory deadline for certification of the official vote.[39] This deadline—seven days after the election—carried with it both legal and political consequences, which seemed to point in opposite directions for Gore. Legally, certification marks the end of the period in which a candidate may protest an election and the beginning of the period in which the candidate may contest it.[40] If Gore was behind at the time of certification, he would benefit from a longer contest period, which would suggest that he should accept certification as soon as possible and then move to contest. Politically, however, it was important for Gore to delay official certification until he had a chance to pull ahead by having votes hand-counted. Timing was everything, and the Bush camp controlled the clock, because Florida's secretary of state, Katherine Harris, who was formally in charge of enforcing deadlines, was a Bush campaign official loyal to Governor Jeb Bush, George's brother.

Even before the Gore campaign's request for hand counts

could be acted on, the automatic machine recount mandated by law in close elections had shrunk Bush's lead, according to the Associated Press, to a mere 327 votes out of nearly 6 million cast.[41]

The Bush team became worried at the prospect of being overtaken in a hand count of the four Democratic counties Gore had selected. They considered seeking a federal injunction, but ideology clashed with politics. Many of them were diehard conservatives who had always eschewed federal court intervention into state matters, and the hand count was clearly a matter of Florida law. The principal ground on which they considered challenging the manual count was that the Florida standard for deciding whether to count a ballot—the clear intent of the voter—violated the equal-protection clause of the U.S. Constitution. That clause is part of the Fourteenth Amendment, added to the Constitution following the Civil War, which provides, in relevant part, that "[n]o State shall . . . deny to any person within its jurisdiction the equal protection of the laws."[42] The Fourteenth Amendment was passed explicitly to secure the rights of recently emancipated slaves[43] and to prevent official discrimination against blacks.[44] Despite its primary focus on the protection of blacks,[45] the Fourteenth Amendment was drafted in broad and inclusive language; there is no mention of race or any other defining characteristic in the amendment.[46] Because the legislators who supported the Fourteenth Amendment favored an announcement of the general principle of equality over a narrowly tailored, race-specific provision,[47] the amendment has been relied on to support a variety of non-race-based equal-protection claims. The Supreme Court has found equal-protection violations in cases involving discrimination on the basis of sex[48] or mental capacity[49] and in cases involving discriminatory interference with the right to reproduce,[50] the right to vote,[51] the right to travel,[52] and the right to equal access to the judicial process.[53]

Conservative justices have generally taken a narrow view of the equal-protection clause. In recent years, they have used it primarily to strike down affirmative-action programs that have provided benefits to blacks and other minorities.[54] The *Washington Post* reported, "So sensitive was the question of federal intervention among conservative lawyers that when word of the plan for an equal protection claim began to drift up to Washington, angry conservatives started 'telling Republican lawyers all over Washington that it was a terrible argument,'" as one recalled.[55] Several Bush lawyers were particularly concerned about Justice Scalia, who was known for the "hard line" he usually took about "who has the legal standing to bring an equal-protection claim"—that is, who exactly was denied the equal protection of the law.[56] Scalia believed that an alleged victim of discrimination must show "tangible injury and concrete harm," rather than merely a "perception of unfairness."[57] If Scalia were to ask Republican lawyers to identify who the victims were in this case, they would be hard pressed to come up with a persuasive answer. Some in the Bush camp urged that instead of going to court, they should fight recounts with recounts—by requesting them in selected Republican counties. In the end, the decision was made not to seek recounts, for they were viewed as too risky. Bush was ahead—and who could predict what any recount, even in Republican counties, would show? The best tactic was to try to preserve the status quo, even if that required a federal lawsuit to stop the hand recounts. The Bush legal team was given the green light to seek a federal injunction, regardless of how ideologically inconsistent such a move would be. This was war, and there would be plenty of time for ideological consistency after they won.

Bush Goes to Court

The stage was set for the first of many courtroom confrontations. This one was before federal judge Donald Middlebrooks on Monday, November 13. The Bush legal team, headed by Theodore Olson, sought to stop the hand counts, arguing that the Florida standard of clear voter intent[58] was subject to varying interpretations and thus violated the equal-protection clause of the U.S. Constitution.[59] Few experienced lawyers on either side believed they could win on this theory. According to the *Washington Post,* several of Bush's key lawyers characterized the equal-protection argument as "lame" and "extremely weak."[60]

I certainly thought it was underwhelming as I listened to Ted Olson deliver it to a packed courtroom that morning. I was there representing a group of Palm Beach voters who did not want the hand count to be stopped. When my turn came, I argued that if "it is constitutional for the state to have two different kinds of machines, one of which provides a 5 percent margin of error and the other of which provides a 2 percent margin of error, surely it is not a denial of equal protection for that very same state to seek to remedy problems caused by the machine." I also argued that "in the interest of the [people's] right to know . . . what the facts are," the count should proceed. My Harvard colleague Laurence Tribe, who was there on behalf of the Gore campaign, made a similar argument, though in somewhat more detail. After politely giving Olson the chance to get in the last word, the judge quickly ruled against him.[61]

Gore still had a barrier to overcome before his request for a hand count could be granted. As previously indicated, Florida law provides that a manual recount may be conducted only if a preliminary hand recount of at least 1 percent of the ballots cast indicates "an error in the vote tabulation which could affect the outcome of the election."[62] The Republicans took the position that the statutory phrase "error in the vote tabulation" meant a hand count was permissible only if the voting machines themselves had malfunctioned, not if voter error had caused the ballot not to be counted. Theresa LePore agreed, arguing that "the vote difference . . . was not due to machine error." It is only natural, of course, that some voting officials would prefer to shift the blame from the machines, for which they are responsible, to the voters, who are responsible for themselves. The reality is that there is no sharp distinction between machine malfunction and voter error when the machines that are used fail to count votes that are perfectly valid under Florida law.

The confusion resulted, in part, from the fact that the general Florida standard for counting a ballot—"no vote shall be declared invalid or void if there is a clear indication of the intent of the voter"—appears in a section of the voting law that deals specifically with damaged ballots.[63] But the Florida courts, including the Florida Supreme Court, have long ruled that the clear-intent standard governs in all situations, including those in which there is no damage to the ballot and no machine error. In 1917, the Florida Supreme Court ruled that "[w]here a ballot is so marked as to plainly indicate the voter's choice and intent in placing his mark thereon, it should be counted as marked unless some positive provision of the law would thereby be violated."[64] In 1975, that court reiterated the governing principle that "the primary consideration in an election contest is whether the will of the people has been affected."[65] And in 1998, Florida's highest court made it crystal clear that the voter intent standard was generally applicable even in cases of pure voter error, no machine malfunction, and no damaged ballot. Ruling in a case in which many voters had used the wrong type of pencil to mark ballots that were to be read by optical scanners, a unanimous Florida Supreme Court had ruled that "we construe 'defective ballot' to include a ballot which is marked in a manner such that it cannot be read by a scanner," regardless of whether the problem was caused by voter error.[66]

If the Florida legislature disagreed with this entirely reasonable reading of its statutes, it could have amended them. Instead, it effectively ratified the state supreme court's interpretation by changing the voting laws in *other* respects, while leaving the voter intent provisions unamended.

Failure to clear away a hanging chad may also be called voter error, analogous to using the wrong type of pencil. But since either a fully punched-through chad or a mark with the wrong pencil reflects a clear intent to vote for the candidate, that vote is legal in Florida, and if the machine fails to count it—even if the machine is not designed to count such a vote—that is machine malfunction *as a matter of law*. Any human error in not checking for hanging chads or in using the wrong pencil must, under Florida law, be deemed harmless if the intent of the voter is clear.[67] This is particularly so because these Votomatic machines sometimes do and sometimes do not count a ballot with a hanging chad; it may depend on which way the chad hangs and whether it covers the hole. To attribute such randomly uncounted imperfect ballots exclusively to voter error ignores Florida law. I have also been told of instances in which perfectly punched ballots with no attached chads are not counted, perhaps because a loose chad from another ballot blocked the hole or for another reason not attributable to voter error. No machines are perfect, especially the error-prone Votomatics, as evidenced by the fact that virtually every machine recount produces a somewhat different result. (See p. 226, note 11.)

Moreover, different types of machines produce significantly different rates of error and types of error, and there were allegations that the rates of error were highest in those areas where more blacks and other minorities lived.[68]

On November 13 and 14, conflicting advisory opinions were issued by the Republican-controlled secretary of state's office and the Democratic-controlled attorney general's office. Not surprisingly, the secretary of state ruled that only a machine malfunction, narrowly defined, warranted a hand count, while the attorney general said the failure of a machine to count a ballot that shows the intent of the voter should also trigger a hand count. This conflict was enough to stop the counting in Palm Beach County, because LePore's lawyer decided not to proceed with the hand count until the conflict was resolved by the courts.[69] The secretary of state, Katherine Harris, then announced that she would not accept any hand recounts submitted to her after the certification deadline on the seventh day following the election. This ruling set the stage for yet another lawsuit—the one that would eventually end up in the U.S. Supreme Court.

That lawsuit began in the courtroom of Judge Terry Lewis, a Democratic appointee, who ruled for Bush, concluding that Secretary Harris did have the authority to certify the election on the designated day. However, he also gave Gore a Pyrrhic victory, telling Harris that she could not refuse to accept late returns without a good reason. Harris immediately wrote to the county election supervisors, requiring them to provide, in advance, the reasons why they should be allowed to file late returns. This unprecedented demand caught them off guard, and they failed to offer the one argument that would have made it difficult for Harris to refuse late returns. Earlier, she had given as an example of a good reason a broken machine. Yet despite the trouble-plagued Votomatic machines, none of the supervisors offered this reason—which *was* the actual reason for the delays.[70] As the *Washington Post* subsequently reported:

> Two and a half weeks later, the Gore campaign would present evidence in court that aging Votomatic machines are plagued by problems—the rubber strips can harden, the punched chads can pile up, all sorts of things can happen to make it more difficult to vote properly. But at this point, no

one thought to allege a mechanical problem. Had they done so, in the words of Donna Blanton, a key lawyer for Harris: "It would have been a different story."[71]

On November 18, Harris was set to certify Bush as the winner, but the Florida Supreme Court intervened, deciding to preserve the status quo pending its decision on the merits of Gore's appeal. This meant that the secretary of state could not make any certification of a winner and that the hand count could continue. This was a victory for Gore. Before the Florida Supreme Court could hear and decide the case, Bush's lead increased to 930 votes, based on overseas absentee ballots. But there were questions about many of these votes—questions that would soon create a major dilemma for the Gore camp.

On November 21, the Florida Supreme Court reiterated its prior interpretation of Florida law as requiring the counting of all ballots in this election that reflected the clear intent of the voter, regardless of whether the failure to count the vote was the result of machine error or voter error. It also ruled that in order to give meaning to the statutory mandate, the deadlines for certifying the vote would have to be extended twelve days. This was a victory for Gore, but it also presented a daunting challenge: The Gore team had to find more than a thousand votes in less than a week. Their great hope lay in Miami-Dade County, where old machines had failed to count approximately ten thousand votes. The three-member Miami-Dade Canvassing Board originally decided against a hand count because of the difficulty of meeting the deadlines, but they soon changed their decision and the counting began. Then something unprecedented in American politics occurred.

Congressman John Sweeney, a Republican from New York, led a group of Republican operatives to the site of the counting, with the mission—in the words of Sweeney—to "shut it down." They banged on doors and windows of the building where the

Miami-Dade votes were being hand-counted and chased people into elevators, raising the specter of physical violence.

According to *Wall Street Journal* columnist Paul A. Gigot—who wrote an admiring article about what he called the "semi-spontaneous combustion" that produced a "bourgeois riot"—the Republican apparatchiks "let it be known that 1,000 local Cuban Republicans were on the way." That must surely have scared the hell out of the three "Anglo judges"—the canvassing board, who served in a quasi-judicial capacity—who thereupon "caved," as Gigot put it, reversing their previous determination to recount with the sudden decision to stop counting any more votes at all. This may have been the first time in modern American history that a mob succeeded in shutting down a quasi-judicial proceeding. Yet the Pulitzer Prize–winning Gigot praised the riot, asserting it "could end up saving the presidency for George W. Bush."[72] In an investigative report, the *New York Times* disclosed that, according to Gore's supporters, ending the Miami-Dade count "marked the real end of [Gore's] campaign for the White House."[73]

In the meantime, the Bush team, furious at the Florida Supreme Court decision extending the deadline for certification, decided to seek review by the U.S. Supreme Court, and on November 24, the Court shocked most experts by agreeing to hear the case. In granting review of the Bush petition, the justices limited the argument they would hear to the claim that the Florida Supreme Court had violated Article II of the U.S. Constitution by changing the law as enacted by the Florida legislature. It declined to review the Bush equal-protection claim. Two days later, Harris certified Bush as the winner by 537 votes. It had been a very good week for Bush—so good that his legal team actually considered withdrawing their appeal from the U.S. Supreme Court. It looked as if they were on track to win without any help from the justices, because with the protest period having ended with the certification, Gore had only sixteen days to contest the Bush victory before the next deadline kicked in.

This one, called the safe-harbor deadline, was to assume a critical role in the case. As noted previously, the safe-harbor provision holds that if a state makes its final determination of who its electors shall be at least six days before the Electoral College meets, that determination is conclusive. The Florida Supreme Court expressed concern over this deadline, and Gore's lawyer, David Boies, acknowledged during oral argument that it was a deadline that had to be taken seriously.[74] It would be awfully difficult for Gore to catch up to Bush before December 12—unless a court disqualified enough Bush overseas absentee votes. And there were problems with these votes, since the Seminole County Canvassing Board had allowed Republican Party volunteers to fill in missing data on absentee-ballot applications completed by registered Republicans—a violation of Florida law—and many overseas absentee ballots from members of the armed forces lacked the postmarks required by law.[75]

The Overseas Absentee Ballots

The Gore mantra of "count every vote" would be inconsistent with a Gore effort to challenge absentee votes on a legal technicality, especially since the intent of these voters was quite clear. Some Gore advisors took the position that if the Bush camp could violate its own principles by making liberal-activist arguments to the federal courts, why should the Gore camp have qualms about such a challenge? The difference, of course, was that only lawyers and Court watchers understood how inconsistent the Bush camp was being; judicial restraint is not a concept widely understood by the general public. "Count every vote," on the other hand, was a slogan intended for the general public, and it was having a positive effect. To abandon that salutary position in order to gain a tactical advantage would appear unprincipled. There was, however, a third way. The

Gore camp could announce that they remained committed to the principle of "count every vote," and so long as every vote was, in fact, being counted, they would not challenge any absentee ballots. But if the Bush camp persisted in challenging the hand counts, the Gore team would demand consistency: Either count them all or challenge your opponent. The Bush team should not be able to have it both ways. In the end, the Gore team took yet a fourth way: *They* did not challenge the overseas absentee ballots, but they did not try to stop Democratic voters from doing so. An African-American judge who had been appointed by a Democrat and passed over for promotion by Jeb Bush ruled for George W. Bush and refused to disqualify the absentee ballots.

The Supreme Court's Initial—Unanimous—Decision

The Bush team decided to go forward with its case in the U.S. Supreme Court, and on December 3, 2000, the justices issued a unanimous per curiam opinion* vacating the Florida Supreme Court's unanimous decision of November 21, which had ordered the manual recounts to continue and had extended the certification deadline by twelve days. The high court remanded the case back to the Florida Supreme Court for clarification of its opinion. The U.S. Supreme Court justices focused on Article II of the U.S. Constitution, which gives each state legislature the authority to determine how the state's electors shall be chosen. They were "unclear as to the extent to which the Florida Supreme Court saw the Florida Constitution as circumscribing the legislature's authority under Article II, Sec. 1, cl. 2 [of the United States Constitution]." In other words, the justices suggested that the

---

Per curiam means "by the court," and a per curiam opinion is generally a short, unanimous opinion that is not attributed to any single justice as the author.

Florida Supreme Court may have given too much weight to the Florida constitution in interpreting the statutes enacted by the Florida legislature. In fact, the Florida Supreme Court, in its "unclear" decision, had done exactly what courts—state courts, federal courts, and the Supreme Court—have done for centuries: It described a conflict it saw between two statutes and tried to resolve it by looking to the intent of the legislature, the text of the applicable constitution, and previous case law.

The conflict, which was apparent on the face of the statutes, was the following: One part of the Florida election law authorized a manual recount in any county challenged by a candidate if there was "an error in the vote tabulation which could affect the outcome of the election"; another part of the law required that the results must be submitted within a week of the election—a deadline that would make such a recount impossible in many cases.[76] Construing the Florida election "as a whole" and employing "traditional rules of statutory construction to resolve these ambiguities," the Florida Supreme Court issued a narrow ruling. (It expressly declined "to rule more expansively, for to do so would result in this Court substantially rewriting the Code." It left "that matter to the sound discretion of the body best equipped to address it—the Legislature.") It found that "the legislative intent evinced in the Florida election code" could be served only if the recount was given a reasonable time for completion, consistent with federal deadlines. It set the recount period to end on November 26, 2000—a full sixteen days before the safe-harbor provision of federal law kicked in.

It would be difficult to imagine a more traditional state court decision, and one that more consciously paid deference to the legislature. After all, *someone* had to resolve the conflict between two inconsistent pieces of legislation. The problem would not solve itself. And it has long been the role of state courts to resolve legislative ambiguities and conflicts.[77] Accordingly, almost no knowledgeable student of the U.S. Supreme Court expected the justices to intrude into this matter of state law.[78]

But intrude they did—not just the five who eventually gave the presidency to Bush, but all the justices. In doing so, the justices broadly hinted that the Florida Supreme Court had not deferred sufficiently to the legislature. We now know that the Supreme Court was sharply split even then and that it was the eventual majority five who drove the decision to intervene in the first place. According to Linda Greenhouse of the *New York Times,* the minority four "were startled to learn from a memorandum that circulated shortly before the justices met on the day after Thanksgiving to discuss the appeals that the votes were there to take the [Florida] case." In other words, the five-justice majority had already decided this matter behind the backs of their colleagues. The fact that this first decision was unanimous and per curiam "papered over" the actual division that existed among the justices. The four justices who did not want the Supreme Court to take the case apparently hoped that by joining the per curiam and remanding the case back to Florida, they might keep it from coming back; they assumed that because events were moving so quickly on the ground, "the election would be over before the case could come back to haunt the Supreme Court again."[79]

In retrospect, it appears that the minority four were duped, or at least outmaneuvered, by the majority five. Linda Greenhouse reported that "the view held in some quarters at the court"—which is a good reporter's way of saying that at least one minority justice told her in confidence—was that "the initial fateful decision to hear the first case made the eventual outcome all but inevitable, that a narrow majority had set the court on a path from which there was no logical exit unless the Florida Supreme Court itself backed down."

Whether or not this is true, it is perfectly clear that the unanimous per curiam opinion of the U.S. Supreme Court set a trap for the Florida Supreme Court from which it could not escape. Whether the minority justices, who joined in setting the trap, were aware of what they were doing is unclear. That at least some of the majority justices knew they were setting a trap now seems obvious.

In a strange reading of the U.S. Constitution, the Supreme Court per curiam opinion implied that Article II, section 1, clause 2 vests solely in the state legislature the authority to decide how electors shall be appointed, even if the state legislature enacts laws that conflict with each other or with the state constitution. Here is the text of that provision:

> Each State shall appoint, *in such Manner as the Legislature thereof may direct,* a Number of Electors, equal to the whole Number of Senators and Representatives to which the State may be entitled in the Congress: but no Senator or Representative, or Person holding an Office of Trust or Profit under the United States, shall be appointed an Elector. (Emphasis added)

The Court seemed to be suggesting that these words require the state supreme court to abdicate its usual responsibility to reconcile conflicting laws. Consider, for example, the following hypothetical case: A state legislature enacts a statute prohibiting the selection of any gay elector, in the face of a state constitutional provision forbidding discrimination on account of sexual orientation, and the state supreme court properly strikes down that statute as unconstitutional.[80] Under the rationale of the Supreme Court's December 3 per curiam opinion, the state supreme court might lack the power to impose its own constitutional requirements on its own legislature—which is a creation of the state's own constitution—in a presidential election case.

This view simply ignores the history of judicial review since shortly after the founding of our nation. When the U.S. Con-

stitution was ratified in 1788, there was no explicit mention of
the power of the courts, including the Supreme Court, to strike
down legislation that was inconsistent with the Constitution.
That power was explicitly recognized by the Supreme Court in
its 1803 decision in *Marbury v. Madison*—perhaps the most
significant decision in its history—which ruled that "if two laws
conflict with each other, the courts must decide on the operation of each," which is precisely what the Florida Supreme
Court did.[81]

More broadly, that foundational case recognized that all legislation must be consistent with the constitution that authorized
it, and that the courts are empowered either to impose that
consistency by interpreting statutes so as to bring them in line
with the relevant constitution or, if they cannot be interpreted
in a constitutional manner, to declare them unconstitutional. As
Chief Justice John Marshall put it: "It is emphatically the province and duty of the judicial department to say what the law
is." Indeed, "this is the essence of judicial duty." Nor is that
judicial duty limited to the U.S. Supreme Court; it inheres in all
courts. The *Marbury* Court went out of its way to emphasize
that it had based its broad ruling on general principles applicable to all courts that confront conflicting laws.

This has been the understanding of the role of courts for
nearly two hundred years—until the Supreme Court's preposterous suggestion in its per curiam opinion that Article II takes
away the power of a state supreme court in a presidential election to do in relation to its legislature exactly what the U.S.
Supreme Court is empowered to do in relation to the Congress,
namely, to reconcile conflicting statutes so as to bring them into
conformity with the Constitution. If the U.S. Supreme Court
read Article II in this most literal, ahistorical manner—that the
U.S. Constitution empowers the state legislature *alone* to decide
how electors are to be selected—then it would logically follow
that not only could the Florida Supreme Court not perform its

traditional judicial functions, but neither could the U.S. Supreme Court. Moreover, this would still not resolve the conflict between two irreconcilable state statutes. If the courts are stripped of their traditional role, who would decide which statute controls?

How the justices who later dissented could have brought themselves to join this per curiam opinion defies understanding—unless they, too, were playing a game, trying to prevent a result with which they disagreed by forestalling the possibility that the Court would have to overrule the state court. Perhaps they were seeking to show apparent unanimity, despite the reality of deep division.

In any event, because the per curiam opinion was unanimous and because its meaning was so unclear—far less clear than the Florida Supreme Court's opinion it asked to have clarified—it sent an ambiguous message to the Florida Supreme Court. First, it warned against tampering with Florida election law, even if some tampering was required to make it conform to the Constitution. And second, by not saying anything about the equal-protection clause—indeed, by explicitly denying review of the Bush claim that a manual recount employing different standards for counting questionable ballots denied him equal protection—the per curiam implied that the justices did not think that the use of such different standards created an equal-protection problem. The combined message of this confusing Supreme Court per curiam remand was that (1) even if the Florida Supreme Court could solve the problem of differing standards by interpreting the Florida statutes so as to require a uniform standard—say, that hanging chads count but dimpled chads don't—it should not do so, because if it did, it might run afoul of Article II; and (2) if it didn't, there would be no equal-protection problem.

Faced with these mixed messages, the Florida Supreme Court split, 4–3, in its next ruling.[82] That ruling came in an appeal from the order of Judge N. Sanders Sauls, which had stopped all hand counts on a number of legal grounds. The majority of the Florida Supreme Court reversed Judge Sauls and ordered an immediate hand tabulation of "the approximately 9,000 Miami-Dade ballots which the machine registered as non-votes, but which have never been manually reviewed." It also directed that all other "legal votes" that had been counted in Palm Beach County must be added to the final tabulation. And it ordered "all counties that have not conducted a manual recount or tabulation of the undervotes in this election to do so forthwith." Because it apparently felt disempowered by the Supreme Court's per curiam opinion to do otherwise, the Florida Supreme Court ruled that the standard to be applied in these recounts must be the one explicitly established by the Florida legislature:

> In tabulating the ballots and in making a determination of what is a "legal" vote, the standards to be employed is that established by the Legislature in our Election Code which is that the vote shall be counted as a "legal" vote if there is "clear indication of the intent of the voter."[83]

The Florida Supreme Court thus followed the advice implicit in the unanimous per curiam opinion: It applied the Florida legislative standard without trying to narrow it further so as to eliminate any possible equal-protection concerns. Little did it know that the advice it was following was a catch-22.

This Florida Supreme Court decision was issued a little before 4:00 P.M. on Friday, December 8, 2000, and the counting began shortly thereafter. But at 2:40 P.M. on Saturday, December 9, 2000, the U.S. Supreme Court, in a 5–4 ruling, sprang its equal-protection trap. It granted a Bush application for a stay, thereby stopping the counting. That decision effectively ended the election and gave it to Bush. No vote was ever again officially counted in the Florida presidential election after the stay was issued. In its eventual decision on the merits, the majority ruled that the Florida justices did have "the power to assure uniformity," and if that court had simply imposed a uniform standard for the recount, there would have been no equal-protection problem.[84] But they had earlier—in the per curiam opinion— warned against any such tampering with Florida election law. Gotcha!

The Supreme Court Stay

Of all the judicial decisions rendered in this case, none was more surprising and controversial than the 5–4 ruling to stop the counting even before hearing argument. The Supreme Court issues stays very rarely, and when it does, it is because the harm in not doing so would be irreparable and extraordinary, such as with executions. Even when it comes to executions, however, this Court has been reluctant to stay scheduled state executions. For example, in cases in which four justices voted to review an inmate's death sentence,* none of the justices who voted for a stay in the Florida election case voted to stay the execution pending full briefing and argument.[85] In these cases, the majority justices voted to allow the execution to proceed even though the case was scheduled for argument in front of nine justices who were all supposed to have open minds on the merits of the case and who might therefore be persuaded that the defendant should not be executed.[86] Unlike in *Bush v. Gore*, Justice

---

*The decision to grant certiorari (full review of a case) and the decision to grant a stay are separate. It takes only four votes for the former, but five for the latter. Traditionally, when four justices voted to hear a capital case, one of the other justices would, in deference to his colleagues, add his vote to the four in order to grant the stay. But in recent years, this tradition has ended and the five justices who oppose review also oppose the stay.

Scalia did not bother to explain his vote in those cases, despite ringing dissents signed by several justices. In *Watson v. Butler,* in which four justices voted to "hold" the case—that is, to withhold judgment about whether or not to review this case until a decision was rendered in another case that raised the same issue—Justice Brennan wrote the following unanswered dissent:

> Four members of this Court consider the above view sufficiently compelling to have voted to hold this case until *Lowenfield* [another case scheduled for argument that raises the same issue as this case] is decided. . . . [B]ut it takes five votes to stay an execution. The Court today thus permits Mr. Watson's legal claim to stay alive while condemning Watson himself to die under a sentencing scheme that within a matter of months the Court may conclude is unconstitutional. Half the Members of this Court believe that Watson's claim might be indistinguishable from Lowenfield's, yet tonight Watson will be executed while Lowenfield may prevail and be spared. This prospect is the ultimate derogation of the Court's duty to provide equal justice under law.[87]

Yet despite this compelling claim of equal protection and irremediable harm, the Supreme Court majority allowed Watson to be executed.

In a subsequent case, *Hamilton v. Texas,* the Court actually voted to hear the defendant's case—it granted full review—but the majority voted to deny a stay, prompting Justice Brennan to observe that "for the first time in recent memory, a man will be executed after the Court has decided to hear his claim."[88]

The very idea of allowing a man to be executed before his case has been argued and decided by the Court, whose own rules require the case to be heard and decided on its merits, is barbaric, whatever one may think of capital punishment. Yet four of the same justices—Rehnquist, O'Connor, Scalia, and

Kennedy—who were so anxious to grant the stay in the Florida election case, voted to deny the stay in *Hamilton.* The defendant in this case was executed before his case could be briefed or argued.[89] His case was then dismissed as moot! Dead men have no rights, even if their death was caused by the action of the Supreme Court in denying a stay of execution.

In contrast to the irremediable harm in a capital punishment case, what was the harm in the Florida election case? What possible harm could result from merely counting ballots by hand? If the Supreme Court ultimately ruled that these ballots should not have been counted, they could simply be eliminated from the tally. Moreover, in the process of counting, new and relevant information might be learned. For example, it might have turned out that, contrary to claims made by the Bush camp, most counters actually employed the same standards in discerning the intent of the voters.[90] It might have turned out that one candidate or another had a sufficient margin of victory without counting any ballots with dimpled or perforated chads. Or it might have turned out that the situation was more complex, with some new information favoring the Bush position and some favoring the Gore position. But with the counting stopped, the justices could focus—as they did—on the worst-case scenarios, all of which favored Bush's constitutional arguments.[91]

Realizing that there would be an outcry against stopping the count before any argument, Justice Scalia decided to write an unusual opinion explaining why he voted for the stay[92] and why Justice Stevens, who wrote a short opinion for the four dissenters, was wrong. On the issue of irreparable harm, Scalia wrote:

> The counting of votes that are of questionable legality does, in my view, threaten irreparable harm to petitioner [Bush] and to the country, by casting a cloud upon what he claims

to be the legality of his election. Count first, and rule upon legality afterwards, is not a recipe for producing election results that have the public acceptance democratic stability requires.

But disputed ballots are generally counted before they are challenged and their legality is ruled upon. Indeed, that chronology is explicitly mandated by Florida law—enacted by the very state legislature that Scalia believes has the power to make these decisions.[93]

In any event, unless the questionable ballots were to be burned—which some Republican partisans actually proposed—they would eventually be counted by the media, and if it turned out that there had been enough unquestionable votes for Gore (without counting dimpled chads, for example) to give him a victory, then a cloud certainly would have been placed over Bush's victory. At the time the majority issued the stay, it could not know whether the result of continuing the recount would be a victory for Gore or Bush. Its logic suggests that it assumed that the recount might well have produced more votes for Gore.

The difference between "count first," which Scalia rejected, and "stop the count before deciding the case," which he accepted, is that if the official hand count was stopped and Bush became president, and the media count then eventually proved that a plurality of all the legal votes had been cast in favor of Gore, there would be nothing anyone could do—Bush would still be president even though by right he should not have been. That would truly be irreparable harm. But Scalia never mentioned that possibility, because to *him*, it apparently would *not* be a harm. No wonder the columnist Mary McGrory said that "Antonin Scalia . . . might as well have been wearing a Bush button on his robes."[94] As one long-term Court watcher, who did not want his name used, told me: "Scalia's stay opinion was the single most disingenuous opinion by a justice I have ever read."

One commentator, Ronald Brownstein, writing for the *Los Angeles Times,* may have been on target when he observed, immediately after the stay was granted, that "the more disturbing possibility is that Scalia and his allies were worried less about Bush's legitimacy than their own." At the time, it seemed likely that a recount would put Gore ahead in Florida's popular vote, and Brownstein's point was that the majority justices may have been concerned about the repercussions *for themselves* of overturning the state court's ruling after the recount and hence disregarding the actual vote totals. Stopping the counting would ensure that the justices would not have to confront this situation. It "appears," he concluded, that "the majority may have tried to reduce its own short-term political exposure—even at the price of increasing the long-term uncertainty about who really won Florida."[95] This analysis, of course, presupposes that the majority knew all along that their eventual decision would favor Bush.

The *New York Times* agreed with Brownstein's analysis, suggesting that the stay gave the appearance of "racing to beat the clock before an unwelcome truth could come out." Terrance Sandalow, former dean of the University of Michigan Law School and a judicial conservative who supported the nomination of Robert Bork to the Supreme Court, concluded that "the balance of harms so unmistakably were on the side of Gore" that the majority's decision to grant the stay was "incomprehensible" and that it was an "unmistakably partisan decision, without any foundation in law."[96]

Justice Stevens, who was appointed by President Gerald Ford, a Republican, and who dissented from the stay, got it exactly right:

> Counting every legally cast vote cannot constitute irreparable harm. On the other hand, there is a danger that a stay may cause irreparable harm to [Gore]—and, more importantly,

the public at large—because of the risk that "the entry of the stay would be tantamount to a decision on the merits in favor of [Bush]." . . . Preventing the recount from being completed will inevitably cast a cloud on the legitimacy of the election.[97]

One reason why courts are generally reluctant to grant stays before full briefing and oral argument is that the justices are supposed to remain open-minded about the result until both sides have had the opportunity to present their arguments. But in this case, as in the capital cases in which stays were refused after certiorari was granted, five justices had already made up their minds. I am reliably informed that work had already begun on the opinion giving the election to Bush *before* any briefs were received or any arguments heard. Scalia virtually acknowledged that the case had already been decided when he wrote in his stay opinion that Bush was likely to prevail.[98]

All the debate over whether Gore's lawyers did or did not do a good job is massively beside the point. No one could have persuaded these five justices to change their decision, because the only fact relevant to their decision was not subject to reasoned argument: If the counting was stopped, Bush would win. It is, of course, possible that if the Supreme Court had not stopped the recount, Bush might have won anyway (putting aside the butterfly ballots, the misaligned ballots, the barriers to black voting, the irregularities with absentee voting, and other issues that were not before the Supreme Court). In assessing the integrity of the majority's ruling, this possibility is, of course, beside the point. The crucial point is that at the time they ruled, the justices had absolutely no idea which way the counting would have come out. Indeed, their finding of "irreparable harm" suggests that they anticipated the real possibility, if not probability, that Gore would have gotten more votes, thereby "casting a cloud" on the victory Bush would eventually achieve after the Court ruled that those votes were invalid. But if the Court had refused to grant the stay and Bush had gotten more votes, his election would not have been tainted by doubt, and the Supreme Court's credibility would not have been tarnished by partisanship. Apparently, the justices were so determined to ensure a Republican victory that they engineered a short-term resolution locking in that victory—at the risk of considerable long-term costs to the Bush presidency and the credibility of the Supreme Court.

But we do risk a self-inflicted wound—a wound that may harm not just the Court, but the Nation.

—*Justice Stephen G. Breyer, dissenting, in* Bush v. Gore

2: The Final Decision

As television reporters scrambled under live coverage to decipher the decision that was rendered shortly before 10 P.M. on December 12, 2000, the nation waited to hear whether the election was finally over. They would quickly learn that it was, and within minutes the Court's decision was subject to more intense instant scrutiny than perhaps any other court decision in our nation's history.

The majority opinion was once again per curiam, but this time the Court was anything but unanimous. The breakdown was as follows:

- Five justices concluded that the Supreme Court should review the case. The other four justices believed that, in the words of Justice Breyer, "the Court was wrong to take this case."[1]

- Three justices—a minority consisting of Chief Justice
  Rehnquist and Justices Scalia and Thomas—concluded
  that the Florida Supreme Court had violated Article II
  of the U.S. Constitution by infringing on the authority
  of the Florida legislature to decide the manner in which
  presidential electors should be appointed. Six justices,
  presumably, disagreed with that conclusion, although it
  is possible, as I will explain in a later chapter, that if
  there had not been a majority for reversing the Florida
  decision on equal-protection grounds, Justice O'Connor
  and/or Justice Kennedy might have come to concur
  with the Article II opinion.

- Five justices concluded that the Florida Supreme Court
  had violated the equal-protection clause of the federal
  Constitution when it authorized a manual recount based
  on the legislative standard of clear voter intent, because
  that general standard was subject to different interpretations by different vote counters. The majority also ruled
  that no constitutionally acceptable recount could now be
  conducted within the safe-harbor provisions of federal
  law,[2] since that deadline was only two hours away and
  the Florida Supreme Court had implied that Florida law
  mandated that the safe-harbor deadline should be met.
  Four justices dissented from this latter conclusion, with
  two of them—Breyer and Souter—agreeing that the Florida decision presented serious equal-protection problems
  that the Florida Supreme Court might well have been
  able to fix had it not been warned away from trying to
  impose a uniform standard by the Court's original per
  curiam remand.[3]

- Two justices—Stevens and Ginsburg—filed separate
  opinions, dissenting as to every conclusion reached by
  the majority.

Six separate opinions were required in order to convey this lack of agreement among the justices. The only justices whose names appear on none of the opinions are Justices Kennedy and O'Connor, who, it has been reported, were responsible for cobbling together the per curiam majority opinion, most of which was reportedly written by Kennedy (see page 163).

Imperfect Ballots and the Misuse of the Equal-Protection Clause

The majority opinion held that "the recount process [established by Florida law] is inconsistent with the minimum procedures necessary to protect the fundamental right of each voter in the special instance of a statewide recount under the authority of a single state judicial officer." It concluded that the state may not, by "arbitrary and disparate treatment, value one person's vote over that of another"[4] and that "the right of suffrage can be denied by a debasement or dilution of the weight of a citizen's vote just as effectively as by wholly prohibiting the free exercise of the franchise."[5]

The legal analysis presented by the majority began with the following factual assertion: "Nationwide statistics reveal that an estimated 2% of ballots cast do not register a vote for President for whatever reason, including deliberately *choosing no candidate* at all or some *voter error,* such as voting for two candidates or insufficiently marking a ballot" (emphasis added).[6] It cited an article entitled "More than 2M Ballots Uncounted" (nationwide)[7] and then said, "In certifying election results, the votes eligible for inclusion in the certification are the votes meeting the properly established legal requirements." However, the Court's description is incomplete and misleading, because it omits a major cause of ballots not being counted: machine error. By limiting the reasons for the problem to vot-

ers' deliberate decisions and avoidable errors, the majority ignores the voters who intend to cast a ballot for a presidential
candidate and do everything they are instructed to do, yet
whose vote the machine nevertheless fails to count.

By ignoring this category of uncounted voters, the majority
sets up the case in a skewed manner: It rests its decision on the
false premise that all the properly cast votes were counted in
the machine tally and that the only votes that could be added
in a manual recount were improperly cast votes, which have a
lesser constitutional status than the properly cast ones that have
already been counted. There was nothing in the record before
the Court to support this view, nor anything that would allow
the Court to determine precisely how many properly cast votes
were never counted.

Nor did the Court consider in its equal-protection ruling the
rights of voters who may indeed have made a mistake by not
punching the chads all the way through or by not inspecting
their ballot for hanging chads. Any voter error that clearly
shows the voter's intent is harmless as a matter of Florida law
and should have been so regarded by the U.S. Supreme Court.
The Florida legislature had decided—as it clearly had the power
to do—that "no vote shall be declared invalid or void if there
is a clear indication of the intent of the voter as determined by
the Canvassing Board."[8] This statute had for many years been
reasonably interpreted as bestowing on every voter the right to
have his or her ballot counted, regardless of voter error, so long
as the intent to vote for a particular candidate could be discerned clearly. This meant that in this case voters had the right
to have their ballots counted if they left a hanging chad or if
they failed to punch their chad all the way through—even if it
was their fault, not the machine's.

The Florida legislature could presumably have denied voters
who made such errors the right to have their ballots counted,

but it chose otherwise, perhaps because it understood that many who make these kinds of voting mistake are inexperienced voters—young men and women, minority voters, new citizens—or elderly voters. Yet the Supreme Court majority improperly ignored the statutory right of these voters to have their ballots counted—a right given to these voters by the very state legislature that three of the majority justices believe must have the final word on which votes should be counted in a presidential election. Indeed, it took the statutory right of these voters away from them in order not to "dilute" the votes of others, even though under the Florida statute these voters have an equal right to have their ballots counted so long as "there is a clear indication of [their] intent."

Two years before this election, the Florida Supreme Court had ruled that Florida law required counting the ballots of several thousand voters who had committed voter error by not following the clear instruction to "fill in with a No. 2 pencil."[9] These voters had used pens and other kinds of pencils, and the optical scanners could not read their marks. The machines worked as they were supposed to; it was the voters who made mistakes. But their intent was clear, even though it could be determined only by hand. Moreover, the Florida Supreme Court ruled that the term "defective ballot" includes "a ballot which is marked in a manner such that it cannot be read by a scanner," even if the reason is voter error in using the wrong pencil. This was the Florida law at the time of the 2000 presidential election. Yet the majority ignored this established law in its decision, apparently believing that a ballot that is imperfect because of voter error is invalid, regardless of whether the voter's intent can be clearly discerned.

Justice O'Connor revealed this mistaken premise during oral argument when she made the following insensitive comment during a colloquy with Gore attorney David Boies:

JUSTICE O'CONNOR: Well, why isn't the standard the one that voters are instructed to follow, for goodness sakes? I mean, it couldn't be clearer. I mean, why don't we go to that standard?

MR. BOIES: Well, Your Honor, because in Florida law since 1917, *Darby Against State,* the Florida Supreme Court has held that where a voter's intent can be discerned, even if they don't do what they're told, that's supposed to be counted.

Boies continued by referring to the wrong-pencil case.

And the thing I wanted to say about the Beckstrom case is— that was a case that used optical ballots—voters were told, "Fill it in with a No. 2 pencil." Several thousand didn't. They used everything else, but not a No. 2 pencil, and so the machine wouldn't read it. It was voter error. The [state] Supreme Court in 1998, well before this election, said, "You've got to count those votes." And, in fact, they counted those votes, even though the way the canvassing board dealt with them was to go back and mark them over with a big black marker, which made it impossible to check whether the canvassing board had really just marked over the ballot or had put a new mark on the ballot.[10]

The majority opinion ignored this case and relied on the false premise that under Florida law, a ballot that is imperfect because of voter error but which clearly shows the voter's intent is an invalid vote. That premise became the foundation for the majority's implicit conclusion that if the so-called undervotes (the improperly cast votes) were to be counted in the absence of a uniform standard, the votes of those whose ballots were originally counted (the properly cast votes) would be diluted. But to ignore uncounted votes that were properly cast or otherwise valid under Florida law artificially *inflates* the votes of those whose ballots were counted by the machine. And those whose votes were not counted because of machine error suffered a fate far worse than having their votes diluted by some unknowable fraction—their votes were not counted *at all*. Such voters would stand to suffer much more serious violations of their equal-protection rights if there was no recount than would those voters whose ballots were counted by the machines if there was a recount. But the equal-protection right of those voters whose ballots were never counted was simply ignored by the majority.

Moreover, the majority failed to deal with the undisputed disparity between different kinds of machines then in use throughout Florida. Identical ballots—those with hanging chads, for example—were counted by some machines and not by others. Accordingly, some votes that Justice O'Connor deemed improperly cast—those on which chads remained because the voter did not follow the instruction to check for hanging chads—*were* counted by the machines. Under the majority's rationale, it would also violate equal protection for those improperly cast ballots to be counted while other identical ballots remained uncounted.

In order to put the majority opinion in a realistic context, it is important to understand that these voters whose ballots were not counted fall into several different categories:

1. Those who voted properly—punched the chad all the way through and checked the ballot for hanging chads— but failed to have their votes counted because of machine error.[11]
2. Those who could not punch the chad all the way because of machine error.[12]
3. Those who punched the chad all the way through but failed to notice that it remained attached to the ballot by one corner.

4. Those who punched the chad but detached only two of the corners.

5. Those who punched the chad but detached only one of the corners.

6. Those who punched the stylus through the chad, producing a pinprick through which light could be seen, but without having dislodged any of its corners. The first subcategory of such votes produced this sort of pinprick for every office, the second only for president.

7. Those who dimpled the chads, making a noticeable impression on the chad but without punching through it or dislodging any corner. The first subcategory includes those who dimpled the chads for every office; the second includes those who dimpled the chad in voting for president but not for any other office.

8. Those who wrote the name of their preferred candidate on the ballot instead of punching through the chad.

9. Those who voted for two candidates for president. This category of overvote has several variations comparable to those of the undervote—one vote is perfect and the second one is dimpled or hanging, etc.

This is the kind of categorization I called for immediately after the election. It would have permitted rational distinctions to be made between ballots that clearly show the intent of the voter and those that are less clear. By lumping them all together and focusing on those that were least likely to show voter intent— for example, an isolated dimpled chad on an otherwise punched-through ballot—the Republicans scored a public-relations coup and even seemed to influence some of the justices who apparently got their facts more from CNN than from the evidentiary record in the case.

As to the undervotes, it would seem clear that under any reasonable interpretation of the Florida statutory standard—clear indication of voter intent—all the punched-through ballots *must* be counted as valid votes. This includes ballots that were fully punched through but not counted because of machine error and those with hanging chads.[13] It should also include all ballots with a hole through the chad caused by the stylus. It would seem beyond dispute that all ballots on which the name of one candidate is written reflect clear intent; these votes are every bit as clear as those marked with the wrong type of pencil. The only category that remains open to question is the dimpled chad. The first of this category's two subcategories (in which the ballot contained a dimpled chad for each office) seems clearly to reflect the intent of the voter, especially if it resulted from a defective machine, while the second would appear not to, unless there was some other manifestation of intent on the ballot. When it made its decision, the Court had no idea how many ballots fell into this last category—or indeed, into any of the categories.[14] Because it had stopped the counting, it was operating in the dark—or by the light of the television.

Even if there was some reasonable disagreement as to one subcategory of ballots, how could that possibly justify denying all the voters in all the other categories their statutory (and hence constitutional) right to have their votes counted? Yet that is precisely what the majority did. Without even identifying precisely whose equal-protection rights it was protecting, it denied a large number of voters—some of whom cast perfect votes that were not counted by the machine, others of whom cast imperfect votes that reflected their intent and were thus valid under the Florida statute—*their* statutory (and hence constitutional) right to have *their* votes counted. This is the most perverse misuse of the equal-protection clause I have seen in my forty years as a lawyer, especially since the uncounted votes almost certainly were cast disproportionately by precisely those citizens whom the equal-protection clause was originally designed to protect—racial minorities.[15] A supreme injustice indeed.

Discerning Intent

The majority of justices knew that in many contexts a standard of clear intent has passed constitutional muster. Indeed, as I will show in Chapter 4, several of the majority justices had themselves written opinions upholding general standards that inevitably produce nonuniform results. Accordingly, it sought to distinguish the finding of voter intent in the counting of ballots from other contexts in which the law seeks to find intent:

> The law does not refrain from searching for the intent of the actor in a multitude of circumstances; and in some cases the general command to ascertain intent is not susceptible to much further refinement. In this instance, however, the question is not whether to believe a witness but how to interpret the marks or holes or scratches on an inanimate object, a piece of cardboard or paper which, it is said, might not have registered as a vote during the machine count. The factfinder confronts a thing, not a person. The search for intent can be confined by specific rules designed to ensure uniform treatment.

There is, of course, a valid distinction between people and things when it comes to discerning intent, but the majority overstates it by making it appear black and white. It is one of degree rather than kind. In many instances in which the law authorizes judges or juries to find the intent of a person without further defining the term *intent*, it would be feasible to refine the matter further. As Professor Richard Pildes, an expert on election law, has observed: "In theory, a norm can always be made more specific if the enacting body [the legislature, in most instances] is willing or required to provide greater determinate content *ex ante* as to how that norm is to be applied in a range of contexts, at least to the extent those contexts are foreseeable."[16]

For example, in distinguishing between first- and second-degree murder—often a life-or-death determination—some states are much more specific than others in defining the intent necessary to make a defendant eligible for the death penalty.[17] Yet the Supreme Court has never required all states to adopt these more specific definitions, thus allowing some judges and juries to sentence a defendant to die, while other judges and juries sentence defendants with the same level of intent to a prison term. (Moreover, this broad discretion often produces racially invidious results.) There are other contexts as well in which courts permit standardless determinations of intent—or of other vague concepts, such as negligence, reasonableness, and the best interest of a child—although it would be feasible to refine the concept further.

In *Bush v. Gore,* the majority seems to acknowledge that in certain contexts further refinement *is* feasible, saying that "in *some* cases the general command to ascertain intent is not susceptible to much further refinement" (emphasis added). Yet even when further refinement is feasible, the Court has not found an equal-protection violation on the ground that this refinement was not made. Why pick out the Florida election and declare that only in that context will a failure to refine the concept of intent create an equal-protection problem? It is especially difficult to justify this selective use of the equal-protection clause in a case where the remedy is to disenfranchise thousands of voters who had expressed a clear intent to vote for a specific candidate.

The majority's answer was that the "factfinder confronts a thing, not a person." The "thing," of course, is a ballot cast by a person, and another person must determine whether that ballot shows the clear intent of the voter. The distinction between a "thing" and a "person" is nowhere near as sharp as the majority suggested. First of all, in many other contexts, the factfinder "confronts a thing"—a contract, a will, a ballistics result, a fingerprint, a skid mark. In the second place, the "thing" confronted in the Florida case may also not be "susceptible to much further refinement." Consider, for example, a dimpled chad on a ballot on which the chads for all other offices are punched through. There may be dozens of subtle variations among such chads. Some are dimpled deeply, others more superficially. It would not be so easy to further categorize these ballots—beyond distinguishing between those found to reflect the clear intent of the voters and those that do not. Of course, some subjectivity is inevitable, but that is equally true of any situation requiring a finding of intent.

In all such decisions, mistakes will be made and inconsistencies will occur. As William O. Douglas, perhaps the most egalitarian justice in the Court's history and the justice whose opinion was relied on by the majority, observed: "Exact equality is no prerequisite of equal protection."[18] Or as the Supreme Judicial Court of Massachusetts ruled in a unanimous 1996 decision joined (though not written) by former Massachusetts justice Charles Fried (who himself filed a brief four years later arguing that Florida acted in violation of the equal-protection clause):

> The critical question in this case is whether a discernible indentation made *on* or *near* a chad should be recorded as a vote for the person to whom the chad is assigned. . . . The cardinal rule for guidance of election officers and courts in cases of this nature is that if the *intent* of the voter can be determined with *reasonable certainty* from an inspection of the ballot, in the light of the generally known conditions attendant upon the election, effect must be given to that intent and the vote counted in accordance therewith, provided the

voter has substantially complied with the requisites of the election law; if that intent cannot thus be fairly and satisfactorily ascertained, the ballot cannot rightly be counted. . . .

It is, of course, true that a voter who failed to push a stylus through the ballot and thereby create a hole in it could have done a better job of expressing his or her intent. Such a voter should not automatically be disqualified, however, like a litigant or one seeking favors from the government, because he or she failed to comply strictly with announced procedures. *The voters are the owners of the government, and our rule that we seek to discern the voter's intention and to give it effect reflects the proper relation between government and those to whom it is responsible.* (Emphasis added)[19]

Fried and his colleagues found no equal-protection violation in that case, despite the fact that it was a thing—a chad—from which the voter's intent was to be discerned. The Florida standard is, if anything, more uniform and less subject to individual variation than the Massachusetts standard: The former requires *clear* intent, while the latter permits "reasonable certainty." Yet Fried, now a lawyer for the Republicans, justified the U.S. Supreme Court majority opinion in a postelection debate with Ronald Dworkin:

The Florida court had explicitly ordered a procedure to take place which treated persons' votes in a senselessly variable manner, [deciding] whether each ballot, taken as a whole, showed a clear intent to vote for one or another of the candidates for president. Discerning intent from a will or contract, a statute, or even the Constitution, taken as a whole, is a familiar and appropriate task for legal interpretation. . . . Applied by many scores of variously trained, instructed, and supervised ballot counters to punched pieces of cardboard, such a concept is manifestly out of place, to say the least. In such stylized settings only a stylized system will do, and that system can and therefore should be uniform.[20]

Except, apparently, in Massachusetts and several other states where the standard is even less "stylized" than it was in Florida and where state court justices—including Fried, then a justice—found no equal-protection problem. What was good enough for Massachusetts in 1996 should have been good enough for Florida in 2000.[21]

Even if it were true that counting the ballots, missed in the machine count, by nonuniform standards would constitute a prima facie violation of equal protection, that conclusion could not survive if the only remedy for that violation itself created a far more serious equal-protection violation, as it did in this case.[22] What, after all, is the alleged violation of equal protection if all of the ballots missed by the machine are counted by hand and subjected to the Florida statutory test of clear voter intent? The only harm would be that, because of counter error, *some* votes that should not have been counted were in fact counted, thus diluting everyone else's votes by some tiny and unknowable percentage. Contrast that marginal and speculative harm with the far more serious and real harm done to those voters who cast proper ballots—perfect ballots or imperfect ballots from which intent could clearly be discerned—that would never be counted because of the Supreme Court's "remedy." These voters would not have their votes merely diluted; they would have their votes *completely ignored*. When the judicial "remedy" causes a far greater denial of equal protection than the prima facie problem, the Supreme Court should not strike down the statute on equal-protection grounds. This would seem particularly inappropriate when the equal-protection remedy denies voting rights disproportionately to racial minorities—precisely those voters for whom the equal-protection clause was added to our Constitution.

Our Constitution has been interpreted in criminal cases to mandate the principle that it is better for ten guilty defendants to go free than for even one innocent defendant to be wrongly condemned.[23] This means that, as a nation, we prefer one type of error (freeing the possibly guilty) over another type (convicting the possibly innocent). Although analogies from other areas are never perfect, it is possible to apply this general principle to voting: We should prefer the error of counting a possibly invalid ballot than of discounting a probably valid ballot. In the view of the Florida legislature and the state supreme court, a similar rule should apply in voting cases: It is far better that some questionable votes be counted than that a significant number of valid votes be ignored.

That certainly appears to be the view reflected in the Florida law that requires the counting of all votes in which the clear intent of the voter can be determined, and that was the principle applied by the Florida Supreme Court not only in this case but in prior cases as well (see pages 86–87). That was also the view advocated by the Bush lawyers and adopted by the Florida courts in *this election* in regard to questionable absentee ballots. It is the principle in many other states as well. Yet the Supreme Court turned this salutary principle on its head, preferring that many valid votes be ignored in order to prevent some arguably improper votes from being counted. The end result was that a large number of voters who cast proper votes under Florida law but whose votes were not counted were denied their statutory (and hence constitutional) right to vote for president in order to ensure that the votes of others would not be diluted by the improper inclusion of ballots that might be invalid.

When the majority justices imposed this topsy-turvy equal-protection "remedy" on the Florida voters, they had absolutely no idea how many voters would fall into each category if a recount was done. For all they knew, there may have been thousands of valid ballots—perfect or with hanging chads—

that had not yet been counted, and only hundreds (or dozens) of questionable ballots—dimpled chads only for president.[24] And numbers do matter in equal-protection cases. Yet because they stopped the count, the majority justices were forced to decide the case on the basis of speculative worst-case scenarios, selectively chosen anecdotes, and media accounts showing perplexed vote counters holding ballots up to the light. This was neither good science nor good constitutional law.

The Majority's Curious Use of Precedent to Reach Its Result

It is not surprising that the majority was unable to point to a single case that supported its highly questionable interpretation of the equal-protection clause. This lack of precedent is especially troubling, since standards similar to the Florida clear-intent standard have been employed over many years and in many places without challenge. What is even more disturbing is that the cases on which they rested their decision are not only far afield from the issue in this case, but seem to reflect a philosophy dramatically at odds with the result in this case.[25] *Harper v. Virginia Board of Elections* (383 U.S. 665) is a 1966 decision written by Justice William O. Douglas during the height of the civil rights era, which struck down the poll tax as an impermissible burden on the right to vote. The poll tax, which was traditional in many parts of the country and especially in the South, was designed to discourage poor people, and especially poor black people, from voting. If an otherwise eligible voter could not afford to pay the tax—or simply chose not to spend his hard-earned money to vote—he would not be permitted to cast a ballot. The Supreme Court, over vigorous dissents by Justices Harlan, Stewart, and Black, ruled that since "wealth or fee-paying" bears no "relation to voting qualifications," the poll tax "invidiously discriminate[s]" and thus vio-

lates the equal-protection clause. The effect of this decision was
to count the votes of many poor and black voters who had not
previously voted. The court's remedy, to strike down the poll
tax, did not deny anyone else the right to vote; it merely added
new voters to the voting lists (thus diluting the votes of those
who had been willing and able to pay the poll tax). The very
idea of using *this* case as a precedent for *denying* thousands of
voters—many of whom were poor and black—the right to have
their ballots counted because other voters might have their votes
diluted is preposterous. What makes it even more galling is that
there is little doubt in my mind that at least some of the majority justices in *Bush v. Gore* would have dissented from the
decision in *Harper*.

The same can be said about *Reynolds v. Sims,* 377 U.S. 533
(1964), a classic reapportionment case. The effect of that ruling
was to increase the voting power of blacks and urban dwellers
and to dilute the voting power primarily of rural whites, whose
votes had been inflated by malapportioned voting districts. No
one's votes were entirely discounted or ignored by this decision.
Yet it was cited in support of a decision that completely discounted the valid votes of thousands of voters, many of whom
were black, in order not to dilute the votes of others.

The majority also failed to cite an equal-protection decision
more closely related to this case than the ones they did cite. The
case is *Lassiter v. Northampton Election Board,* 360 U.S. 45
(1959), a decision also rendered by Justice Douglas for a unanimous Court, which included some of the Court's most equality-
minded justices, such as William Brennan and Earl Warren. The
Court, in *Lassiter,* upheld a standardless literacy test for voting
in North Carolina that required every voter to be able "to read
and write any section of the Constitution in the English language." It did not further define the ability to "read and write"
(by, for example, specifying the number of errors that would
signify failure), leaving that important definitional decision to

the discretion of voting registrars. As Professor Frank Michelman has observed in regard to the North Carolina literacy test, there is the "obvious possibility that different testers in the very same room might, under *that* standard, pass opposite judgments on submissions from different applicants, responding to the very same *dictée*, containing the very same mistakes or number of mistakes."[26] Yet despite the feasibility of further refining the vague standards for determining literacy, and the realistic possibility—indeed, the probability—that voters with the same level of literacy might be treated differently by different registrars, the Court unanimously upheld the North Carolina law against an equal-protection challenge. It concluded that since there was no evidence that the test was actually being administered in a racially discriminatory manner, a state had the right to require the test. Although literacy tests are now banned by federal statute, the equal-protection principle articulated in *Lassiter*—that absent racial discrimination, a state has broad powers to establish voting qualifications—was cited with approval in subsequent cases (including *Harper*) and has never been overruled.[27] Yet the majority in the Florida case, citing cases they would almost certainly have dissented from, failed to cite this relevant equal-protection election case they would almost certainly have agreed with, because it pointed away from the conclusion they wanted to reach.[28]

Nor did the majority address the dozens of federal appellate court decisions flatly contrary to their ruling. In their casebook on election law, Professors Samuel Issacharoff, Pamela Karlan, and Richard Pildes cite the following "typical" result reached by a "highly respected" judge:

> Because the constitutional framework leaves the conduct of state elections to the states, the Fifth Circuit, 619 F.2d at 453, concluded that federal law must:
>
> ... recognize a distinction between state laws and

patterns of state action that systematically deny equality in voting, and episodic events that, despite non-discriminatory laws, may result in the dilution of an individual's vote. Unlike systematically discriminatory laws, isolated events that adversely affect individuals are not presumed to be a violation of the equal protection clause. The unlawful administration by state officers of a non-discriminatory state law, "resulting in its unequal application to those who are entitled to be treated alike, is not a denial of equal protection unless there is shown to be present in it an element of intentional or purposeful discrimination."

If every state election irregularity were considered a federal constitutional deprivation, federal courts would adjudicate every state election dispute. . . . [Constitutional law does] not authorize federal courts to be state election monitors.[29]

This description could have been written about the Florida election, but the court in that case found no violation of equal protection. The authors also cited a similar case in which

voters claimed constitutional voting rights had been denied because electronic voting machines, which allegedly did not meet state-law standards, had malfunctioned and election officials had failed to respond as state law purportedly required. The Seventh Circuit rejected these claims, noting that not every election irregularity rose to the level of a constitutional violation—and that mere violation of a state statute by an election official was not, in itself, such a violation. *Hennings v. Grafton*, 523 F.2d 861 (7th Cir. 1975). As that court put it: "The work of conducting elections in our society is typically carried on by volunteers and recruits for whom it is at most an avocation and whose experience and intelligence vary widely. Given these conditions, errors and irregularities, including the kind of conduct proved here, are inevitable, and no constitutional guarantee exists to remedy them. Rather, state election laws must be relied upon to provide the proper remedy."

Again, this reads like a description of the situation in Florida, yet that court found no equal-protection violation.[30]

Also conveniently overlooked were the many capital punishment cases in which the very justices who found an equal-protection violation in this case had refused to find equal-protection violations in far more compelling cases of statistically demonstrable racial disparity in the imposition of the death penalty. The paradigm case is *McCleskey v. Kemp,* in which a condemned black man introduced statistical evidence, *which the Court assumed to be valid,* that in the state of Georgia, black defendants convicted of killing white victims are far more likely to be sentenced to death than white defendants convicted of killing black victims.[31]

Yet four of the five justices[32] who found an equal-protection violation in *Bush v. Gore* joined another justice, who is no longer on the Court, in ruling that this fact was irrelevant, because it failed to prove a discriminatory purpose. The majority ruled that in order to prevail under an equal-protection challenge, the particular person making the challenge "must prove that the decision-makers in *his* [italics in the original] case acted with a discriminatory purpose"—an almost impossible burden to meet.[33]

The 5–4 majority in *McCleskey* further emphasized the fact that because each properly chosen jury was unique, it was unrealistic to expect uniformity or even consistency from juries, especially since "discretion" is inevitable in the criminal process.

Now contrast the reasoning and ruling in the life-and-death case of *McCleskey v. Kemp* with the reasoning and ruling in the

Florida election case. In the election case, no one even alleged that there was a discriminatory purpose behind the Florida recount standard. It had been enacted years earlier and had produced victories for Republicans as well as Democrats. The statutory standard—the clear intent of the voter—was far more specific than the standards used in Georgia to decide who would get the death penalty. The election officials in Florida, like the jurors in Georgia, were properly selected and instructed to apply general standards in accordance with their best judgment. Moreover, there was no statistical or other evidence to suggest any pattern of discriminatory effect in the past or present.[34]

Of Fundamental Rights, Equal Protection, and Victims

The cases cited by the majority justices in *Bush v. Gore* suggest that they would have the Court distinguish voting cases from death penalty cases on the ground that the former involve a "fundamental right," while the latter do not. But this distinction, as applied to the Florida voting case, is fundamentally flawed. The right not to be selectively executed by the state on account of one's race or the race of one's victim is surely a fundamental right by any reasonable definition of that term. It is at least as fundamental as the right of a voter not to have another voter's ballot counted because it might be counted by a standard of intent different from that of yet a third voter. Moreover, this latter right has nothing to do with racial discrimination, which lies at the core of the equal-protection clause. To elevate a nondiscriminatory theoretical dilution of a vote to a status more fundamental than the right not to be executed based on race would be to turn the Fourteenth Amendment on its head. It cannot be the case that the equal-protection clause—which was designed to target racial discrimination against blacks—imposes a higher burden of proof on blacks seeking its protection against discrimination in life-or-death cases than on voters who claim that their vote may have been diluted by an unknown and tiny amount in a random, nondiscriminatory manner.

To demonstrate the hollowness of the distinction suggested by the majority opinion, consider the following general categories of equal-protection violations. The most compelling—and least controversial—would seem to be cases of purposeful racial discrimination involving a right that is undoubtedly fundamental. Thus, a statute that expressly limited voting rights to "members of the white race" would be a paradigm of unequal protection. But so would a statute that imposed the death penalty only on blacks convicted of murder, or only on anyone convicted of murdering a white.[35] At the other end of the spectrum—the least compelling and most questionable—would be cases involving neither race nor a fundamental right, such as a zoning law that limits expansion of a house to those who satisfy some general criterion such as "the interests of the community," as determined by a zoning board. In between these extremes would fall a wide range of variations and permutations. These include the following:

- Cases in which a state's action creates a significant and invidious racial disparity involving a fundamental right, but there is no proof that the action was purposeful. This would seem to include cases such as *McCleskey v. Kemp*, which challenge the imposition of capital punishment on the ground that blacks who kill whites are far more likely to be executed than whites who kill blacks.
- Cases in which the effect is to dilute the votes of racial minorities, but there is no proof that this was done purposefully.
- Racially neutral cases in which the votes of some people will be diluted in relation to others if a remedy is

not given, but in which the remedy will mean that the
votes of some people will be inflated and others not
counted at all.

There would seem to be little doubt that the last of these categories presents a far less significant and far more questionable
violation of equal protection than the first. Yet the majority
justices demand proof of purposeful discrimination in death
penalty cases, while applying special scrutiny to racially neutral
voting cases even in the absence of any proof of discriminatory
purpose or racially discriminatory effect. Even if it could be said
that the absolute denial of the right to vote is somehow more
fundamental than the denial of racial equality in life-and-death
decisions—a questionable proposition at best—the same cannot
plausibly be said about the right not to have someone else's
vote counted because some of those voters might have their
intentions discerned by imperfect standards. The five-justice majority in *Bush v. Gore* simply invented this application of the
right—made it up only to be used in this case and in this election. This makes no sense as a matter of constitutional law or
policy and violates the spirit of the equal-protection clause.

Moreover, the majority never even identified the person or
persons it claims were denied the equal protection of the law.
At the very least, the Court should be able to identify with some
degree of specificity the alleged victim of the equal-protection
violations. In other situations, Justice Scalia has demanded a
showing of "tangible injury and concrete harm" to specific people who claim they have been denied the equal protection of
the law.[36] The five majority justices, in a 1995 case, ruled as
follows:

[A]ppellees have failed to show that they have suffered the
injury our standing doctrine requires. Appellees point us to
no authority for the proposition that an equal-protection

challenge may go forward in federal court absent the showing of individualized harm, and we decline appellees' invitation to approve that proposition in this litigation.[37]

Yet the five justices willingly approved that very proposition in this case, without even acknowledging the precedent against it. Pursuant to that precedent, the Court should be able to answer the fundamental question of who has actually suffered some legally recognizable prejudice as the result of being denied the equal protection of the law. An abstract claim of inequality will not generally suffice to declare a statute unconstitutional.[38] For example, in capital punishment cases such as *McCleskey,* the law requires the condemned inmate to show that he has suffered purposeful prejudice from the claimed inequality. In voting-rights cases such as *Harper,* it is obvious who the victims were: those who had been denied the right to vote because they did not pay the poll tax. In other voting-rights cases such as *Reynolds,* millions of urban residents, many black, had been effectively disenfranchised by reapportionment strategies that deliberately made their votes less influential than the votes of rural white citizens. Even in affirmative-action cases, the claim is made that whites are disadvantaged by preferences given to blacks. In virtually every equal-protection case, it is easy to identify the victim. But who was the victim here? Who was denied the equal protection of the law? The majority never told us—and for good reason. There are only three possible candidates for the status of alleged victim in this case, and each is implausible.

The first consists of all those voters whose ballots were originally counted by machine and whose votes would be diluted by counting any additional votes by hand. But a valid Florida law requires a hand count under specified circumstances, and so those voters whose ballots were counted by machine can't complain about a dilution caused by a neutral law. Nor do they have standing to argue that there may be some inequality among the different categories of voters whose ballots were not originally counted by machine and are now to be counted by hand, since any such inequality between *others* does not prejudice *them*. To demonstrate that obvious conclusion, all one must do is hypothesize a situation in which the Florida law had created the kinds of specific and uniform rules required by the majority and that these rules required the counting of every single pregnant, dimpled, and scratched chad. Under such a uniform and broad rule, the votes of all those whose votes had originally been counted by the machines would have been diluted even more than they would have been under the actual Florida rule. Yet they would have had no equal-protection claim. *This* category of voters—those whose ballots were counted by machine—could not have been the victim of this claimed equal-protection violation.

The second possible category of claimed victims is a subcategory of those voters whose ballots were not counted by the original machine count, namely, those whose ballots unambiguously reflected an intent to vote for a particular presidential candidate (for example, chads punched through all the way, with one corner attached). They could claim that their votes would be diluted if the law permitted the counting of other ballots that were not originally counted by the machine and that reflected an ambiguous intent (for example, a dimpled chad only for president). But these unambiguous-intent voters could not have been the victims, since the majority decision ruled that *their* votes could not be counted either. That is not the way victims of equal-protection violations are treated. It would be absurd for a court to tell citizens whose votes might be in danger of some dilution from the counting of other votes that the remedy is not to count any of the votes, including theirs. Such a "remedy" substitutes disenfranchisement for dilution in the name of equal protection. It is obvious, therefore, that this cat-

egory of voters could not have been the victim of this claimed
equal-protection violation.

This leaves only candidate George W. Bush as the alleged
victim. But he was not even a Florida voter, and the majority
explicitly said that the question before the Court was whether
"the Florida Supreme Court" treated "members of *its* elector-
ate" arbitrarily (emphasis added).[39] Nor did Bush have any valid
legal claim to the votes of any specific category of voters. To
be sure, the uncounted votes in question were from heavily
Democratic counties selected for hand count by Al Gore. But
that was done pursuant to a neutral and valid state law, under
which Bush, too, could have cherry-picked the counties in
which he wanted hand counts. The law cannot presume that
the votes not counted by machine in any particular county belong to one candidate or the other. The right to have votes
counted belongs to *the voter,* not the candidate. If specific votes
for Bush had been selectively disqualified by biased counters,
then he might have had a valid claim of victimization under the
equal-protection clause. But the primary claim here was that
some votes that should not have been counted were being
counted. There was no claim of systematic discrimination
against Bush voters. Indeed, the claim was quite the opposite:
that there was no rhyme or reason why some votes were counted and others were not. It is difficult to see how Bush would
be a legally cognizable victim of any such claim of equal protection, especially since he had the right to pick his counties for
a hand count but deliberately waived that right. If there was
any inequality among the voters whose ballots were not originally counted by machine, it did not deny Bush the equal protection of the law, nor did it deny equal protection to Bush
voters as a class. At worst, it may have denied equal protection
randomly to some voters who voted for Bush and others who
voted for Gore.

This is the issue that, I am told, worried Bush lawyers when they considered bringing an equal-protection challenge. They realized that in other cases, Justice Scalia would be all over the lawyers, demanding to know who it was that was being denied the equal protection of the law. But in this case neither Scalia nor his colleagues appeared to be troubled by the absence of a victim.

It is apparent why the majority never identified the alleged victim of its claimed equal-protection violation: to do so would expose the fallacy in its reasoning, because there was no victim in this case other than the voters whose ballots were valid under Florida law but whose votes were never counted because of the Supreme Court's decision. Yes, there was an equal-protection violation in this case: the one produced by the U.S. Supreme Court's decision disenfranchising thousands of voters who cast valid ballots under Florida law, thus enhancing the value of the votes of others who also cast valid ballots.

"Limited to the Present Circumstances"

The majority per curiam opinion is likely to become one of the most analyzed, criticized, and defended opinions in the history of the Supreme Court. But it will be cited far less often in future judicial decisions because of one telltale line that revealed its true purpose: "Our consideration is limited to the present circumstances, for the problem of equal protection in election processes generally presents many complexities." Its meaning is obvious: In future election cases, don't try to hold the Court to what it said in *this* case, because it decided this case not on general principles applicable to all cases, but on a principle that has never before been recognized by any court and that will never again be recognized by this court. The purpose of the remarkable cautionary line—which is virtually an admission that this decision does not fit into a line of continuing precedents—was to cobble together a majority for Bush consisting of justices who almost never find equal-protection violations (except, perhaps, when white people are "discriminated" against by affirmative action) and who do not want a broad equal-protection decision waiting out there to be used as a precedent in other cases in which the result would be inconsistent with the political or ideological results they generally prefer. Like a great spot-relief pitcher in baseball, this equal-protection argument was trotted out to do its singular job of striking out Vice President Gore and was immediately sent to the showers, never again to reappear in the game.

It may be understandable why the majority would go out of its way to limit its equal-protection consideration to this case. The implications of its reasoning are so far-reaching that, taken to their logical conclusions, they would invalidate virtually every close election in our past and our future, since there is always considerable disparity among voting machines and standards employed to count and recount votes. But to limit a Supreme Court decision to a unique case is precisely the kind of decision that Justice Scalia and other judicial conservatives have repeatedly condemned. As he wrote in *United States v. Virginia*: "The Supreme Court of the United States does not sit to announce 'unique' dispositions. Its principal function is to establish *precedent*—that is, to set forth principles of law that every court in America must follow."[40]

Yet Scalia violated his long-held views and joined an opinion that announced no principle of general applicability in future cases. Indeed, if the unprecedented principle that the majority purported to announce—that "the formulation of uniform rules" is always "necessary" when "practicable"—were to be applied across the board, it would impose a radical equality entirely unacceptable to the right. It would revolutionize welfare law, access to legal services, death penalty law, and especially election law.

It's no wonder that so many commentators—at all points

along the political spectrum—found the decision lacking in legal support.[41] As one federal judge told Linda Greenhouse, the justices were "making it up as they go along," and the reason "why they made it up" in this case "just seemed so politically partisan."[42] And it's even less surprising that many judicial conservatives, while applauding the outcome, have been unwilling to support the equal-protection principle underlying its holding. Robert Bork, among the most conservative legal minds in America, acknowledged that the "per curiam opinion joined by five justices does have major problems" and that it "endorsed a new and possibly damaging rationale."[43] Professor Richard Epstein, another Bush supporter, characterized the majority's rationale as "this weird equal-protection theory" and called it "the broadest equal-protection test known to man."[44] He predicted that "this equal-protection dog [would bark] only once."[45] John DiIulio, writing in the conservative *Weekly Standard,* said that "the arguments that ended the battle and 'gave' Bush the Presidency are constitutionally disingenuous at best."[46] Conservative professor Michael W. McConnell, writing in the *Wall Street Journal,* bemoaned the fact that the Court's failure to remand the case for a proper recount deprived his candidate—George W. Bush—of the "clarity of victory that he must surely desire," and that this "means, unfortunately, that Mr. Bush will take office under conditions of continued uncertainty."[47] Terrance Sandalow, a conservative legal scholar and former dean of the University of Michigan Law school, characterized the decision as "incomprehensible" and "an unmistakably partisan decision without any foundation in law."[48] Several of Bush's own lawyers also found problems with the Court's equal-protection conclusion and remedy. As the *Washington Post* put it: "Conservatives . . . while privately pleased with the fruits of the Court's adventure . . . have not been eager to defend the opinion aggressively."[49] Even Richard Posner, one of the Court's staunchest defenders, characterized the equal-protection rationale as "wrongheaded," its reasoning as "quite thin and unconvincing" and the legal craftsmanship as a "big flop."[50] It is difficult to find many reputable scholars prepared to risk their credibility by defending the majority's equal-protection analysis.[51] Indeed, I challenge any law professor or Supreme Court litigator to defend the majority's equal-protection conclusion and remedy in a public debate.

The Article II Argument

If the Court's defenders are uncomfortable with the equal-protection argument, how do they justify the result? Many point to the Article II argument, put forth by a minority of three justices—that the Florida Supreme Court usurped the constitutional authority of the legislature. This argument has been embraced most widely by the right, especially among academics. Yet the Article II argument is, if anything, even weaker than the equal-protection argument that carried the day. The reason it is supported by judicial conservatives is that it poses no danger of becoming a broad precedent that could empower the lower courts to strike down a wide array of unequal rules. The Article II argument, by its nature and terms, is limited to presidential elections only and has no general applicability to other elections or to different areas of law, as does the equal-protection ruling.

The Article II argument in the final decision, written by Chief Justice Rehnquist and joined by Justices Scalia and Thomas, is little more than an elaboration of the perplexing and ahistorical suggestion put forward in the Court's original per curiam remand (see page 39). The three justices are correct in pointing out that this is a presidential election and that it implicates uniquely important national interests. But the Constitution allocates responsibility for choosing presidential electors to the states, not to the Supreme Court. To be sure, Article II specifies that "each state shall appoint [electors] in such manner as the legislature thereof may direct." The three justices interpret the last phrase of Article II to mean that "the text of the election law itself, and not just its interpretation by the courts of the state, takes on independent significance."

This repeats the mistake of ignoring our nation's long and unique history of judicial review of all legislative decisions. Even if the framers of our Constitution originally intended to vest exclusive power in state legislatures to determine the manner by which electors should be chosen—which is doubtful—the Supreme Court's own decision in *Marbury v. Madison* and its progeny recognized that *all* legislation must be consistent with the constitution that created the legislature, and that the courts are the ultimate guarantors of such consistency. *Marbury* is so important a decision that it has become, in essence, a part of the Constitution and cannot simply be ignored by the current justices. The words of the Constitution must be read in the context of that transforming case. For example, the U.S. Constitution vests authority in the Congress to enact laws, employing language even more restrictive of judicial intervention than the Article II language relied on by the three justices. Article I of the Constitution actually uses the word *all* in providing that "all legislative powers herein granted shall be vested in . . . Congress." Yet no one today would dream of suggesting that this allocation of power to the legislature eliminates the authority of the U.S. Supreme Court to interpret legislative enactments, to reconcile conflicting laws, and to strike down legislation that is inconsistent with the Constitution, because *Marbury* ruled that "it is emphatically the province and duty of the judicial department to say what the law is." This broad mandate does not exclude the election law of each state. The court offered no reason for denying the Florida Supreme Court the same power to interpret state legislation that it claims in regard to federal legislation.[52]

To be sure, the federal Constitution trumps state constitutions, as a result of the supremacy clause of the former. But it is the state constitutions that govern state legislation in the first instance. Surely a state's highest court has the authority to interpret its own legislation, especially when one law appears to conflict with another law and/or with the constitution itself. It has long been a traditional power of all state courts to interpret state statutes so as to bring them into conformity with state constitutions. That is precisely what the Florida Supreme Court said it was doing and did do, both in this case and in a long line of earlier cases ignored by the three justices. (See page 213, note 58.) As Justice Stevens said in dissent: "It did what courts do." Justice Scalia made a similar point only weeks before the election when he quipped: "The Constitution does not say the courts are supposed to interpret the Constitution. We do it by accident. Judges have to apply the law. We can't help it."[53]

Yet when the Florida Supreme Court did what courts do—apply the law—Scalia, along with Rehnquist and Thomas, found its action to be a violation of the U.S. Constitution. The three justices took it upon themselves to interpret the Florida election law, with its long-established clear-intent provision, as providing "no basis for reading the Florida statutes as requiring the counting of improperly marked ballots,"[54] even if these ballots contain a clear indication of the intent of the voter. In other words, if a voter properly punched his ballot but failed to inspect it to ensure that there were no hanging chads, the three justices would interpret Florida law to *forbid* the counting of that ballot. According to the three justices' interpretation, it would also be forbidden to count an improperly punched ballot on which the voter clearly printed the name of the candidate for whom he intended to vote, or one on which the voter used the wrong pencil.[55] This is simply false, since under Florida law—both legislative and judicial—all of these votes would have to be counted, because they show the clear intent of the voter even though improperly marked.

The implication of the three Supreme Court justices is that the Florida Supreme Court majority changed Florida law after Election Day 2000 specifically in order to bring about the election of Al Gore. That is, to put it bluntly, nonsense. It becomes worse than mere nonsense when one realizes that in suggesting this, the three justices ignored the line of cases—especially the wrong-pencil case—that proves the opposite conclusion, namely, that this was the law in Florida long before the 2000 presidential election and the Florida Supreme Court did not change it to bring about a particular election result.[56] In misreading Florida law in this fashion, the three justices effectively expunged from the statute the requirement that all votes must be counted if there is "clear indication of [voter] intent."[57]

Even if the three justices' interpretation of Florida law is a plausible reading of the Florida election law—and I believe it is not—it is surely not the *only* reasonable reading of this often confusing mishmash of legislation enacted over time by different legislative bodies.[58] To accuse the majority of the Florida Supreme Court, which has the constitutional authority to interpret its own state's laws, of deliberately distorting these laws because three U.S. Supreme Court justices happen to disagree with their reading is the height of judicial activism, and it fails to acknowledge the proper authority of state courts, pursuant to their own constitutions and precedents, to interpret and reconcile state legislation. As Justice Stevens pointed out, the relevant precedents of the U.S. Supreme Court have long interpreted Article II not as creating "state legislatures out of whole cloth, but rather tak[ing] them as they come—as creatures born of, and constrained by, their state constitutions." Citing an 1892 precedent,[59] Stevens reminded the majority that "'[w]hat is forbidden or required to be done by a State' in the Article II context 'is forbidden or required of the legislative power under state constitutions as they exist.'" And the Florida constitution grants its highest court the authority to review state legislation, as it did in this case.[60]

In support of their claimed authority to substitute their interpretation of state law for that of the state's highest court, the three justices miscite two civil rights cases from the late 1950s and early 1960s. In the first case, *NAACP v. Alabama ex. rel. Patterson,* the all-white Alabama Supreme Court—which represented the epitome of segregation and racism—tried to prevent the NAACP from bringing a civil rights case to the U.S. Supreme Court by willfully changing the rules for appeals *after* the petitioner had already filed its appeal in reliance on the existing rules.[61] In *Bouie v. City of Columbia,* 378 U.S. 347 (1964)—a case on which I worked as a Supreme Court law clerk—black sit-in demonstrators who had been given consent to enter private property were arrested after they refused to leave. But South Carolina law had always limited the crime of trespass to *entering* on private property without the consent of the owner. The Supreme Court ruled that for the courts to expand that law to include refusal to leave *after* the defendants relied on the original law would constitute the equivalent of ex post facto legislation, which is forbidden by the Constitution. In both of these cases, state courts acted in an unconstitutional manner by changing the previous law—both statutory and decisional—in order to deny blacks their civil rights. By contrast, in the 2000 election case, the Florida Supreme Court followed a long line of precedent *and* the language of the election law in order to vindicate the rights of voters.

Such selective use of inapt cases to achieve a desired political result is what drives lawyers and law students from realism to cynicism—and appropriately so. In this case, the three far-right justices misused precedent to concoct an argument they would have scoffed at had it been offered by Gore lawyers in a case in which a state supreme court had ruled in favor of Bush. Furthermore, for these three justices to use these civil rights cases—whose entire thrust was to demand fairness and equality for blacks—to disenfranchise voters, a disproportionate number of whom are black, is to thumb their noses at both the spirit and the letter of the law.

Justification by National Crisis

Some conservatives are now offering another after-the-fact justification for the Supreme Court's decision, which goes something like this: Okay, the majority justices were wrong on the law. Okay, they were inconsistent with their own precedents. But they didn't do it in order to get a *particular* president elected. They did it to get *a* president elected—that is, they intervened in order to prevent a messy and divisive fight in Congress.

The conservative federal judge and law professor Richard Posner acknowledges that this decision "cannot avoid the label 'activist' "—among the dirtiest words to a conservative—"since it expands federal judicial power without clear warrant in constitutional text or precedent." He does not believe that the Court's decision was "compelled by the Constitution" or "conclusive." Yet he supports it on the basis of "pragmatic, nonlegal considerations." Listen to Judge Posner's rhetorical question: "What exactly is the Supreme Court good for if it refuses to examine a likely constitutional error that, if uncorrected, will engender a national crisis?"[62]

In order to accept this "national crisis" justification, you must first believe that these justices would have intervened to prevent such a messy fight even if they knew that their intervention would have given the election to Gore. I don't believe this, and I doubt that many of the conservatives offering this justification believe deep in their hearts that diehard Republican justices such as Scalia, Rehnquist, Thomas, and O'Connor would have stepped in if the shoe were on the other foot. (See chapter 3.)

But even putting aside this motives test, the court's intervention to prevent the constitutionally authorized methods of resolving this dispute—messy as that resolution would have been—flies in the face of everything Justices Scalia, Thomas, and Rehnquist stand for. It was the Founding Fathers—the same ones who allegedly allocated to the state legislature all authority to select the manner by which electors are chosen—who allocated to Congress the power to resolve contested elections. Had the shoe been on the other foot, one can just imagine how Justice Scalia would have railed against the Supreme Court substituting itself for the constitutionally authorized body—namely, Congress—as the institution appropriate to resolve the issue. Messy political disputes are best confronted by institutions whose members are politically accountable to the voters—or at least that is what the Framers of our Constitution believed.

Even if it could be persuasively argued that the majority decision came to the right result for the wrong constitutional reason—that it prevented a political crisis by intervening even on questionable legal grounds—this argument, if accepted, would have dangerous implications for our democracy. The answer to Judge Posner's rhetorical question is that the Supreme Court is not true to its role in a democracy if it won't even tell the truth about why it is intervening and will not describe the nature of the "national crisis" from which it is protecting us. Under Posner's approach, the Supreme Court's members are "self-appointed national saviors"[63] with a roving commission to save us from ourselves even if we have selected other institutions to do the job. Moreover, the Court should be allowed to claim the power to withhold the truth from us, because we can't be trusted to understand what these justices are really doing on our behalf. It is entirely acceptable, under this view, to concoct and present a wrongheaded constitutional argument so long as the Court's real reason—which they have chosen to conceal—is a good one, at least from Posner's patronizing and elitist perspective. Judge Posner reminds me of the Jack Nicholson character in the movie *A Few Good Men,* telling the young lawyer, "You can't handle the truth!" Well, in a democracy, the people must be presumed to be able to handle the truth, and no judge is entitled to withhold it, even to prevent a crisis.[64]

The fact is, there was no impending national crisis on the horizon, unless the possible election of Gore or an overtly political resolution of the matter by Congress is deemed a greater crisis than the Supreme Court deciding a presidential election. The worst-case scenario would have been a messy and political resolution of a messy and political gridlock. Had the election been thrown into the legislature, politicians would have made deals and voted their political or personal interests, as the Framers of the Constitution—whose intent is always invoked by conservatives—obviously contemplated. Whoever was elected would have been chosen by elected officials with political accountability. Instead, there was a dignified, but undemocratic, resolution behind closed doors by unelected and politically unaccountable judges who are not supposed to be involved in making partisan decisions.

Crisis, of course, is in the eye of the beholder. As Charles Krauthammer, no friend of Gore's, wrote in criticizing the intervention of the Florida Supreme Court to order a recount: "Crisis is preferable to supine acquiescence."[65] He insisted that the Florida court should be "put in its place" in order "to rectify the constitutional imbalance created by the imperial judiciary. This is not a constitutional crisis. This is a constitutional opportunity."[66] Having the matter resolved in the manner specified in the Constitution—messy as that may be—hardly warrants Posner's hyperventilation in invoking the term "constitutional crisis" and surely does not justify an unconstitutional power grab by Republican justices determined to ensure the election of their man.

If the justices were really determined to prevent what they perceived to be a crisis, they had an obligation to be up front about what they were doing. When a decision made on non-legal, pragmatic grounds is camouflaged as a decision made on constitutional principle, it inevitably creates distrust in the Supreme Court as an institution. The justices must—at a minimum—acknowledge precisely what they are doing, so that the public may evaluate their decision by reference to the reasons given. There is no place in a democracy for paternalistic subterfuge or stealth opinions. As Justices O'Connor and Kennedy, who wrote most of the majority opinion in this case, cautioned only eight years earlier: "The Court must take care to speak and act in ways that allow people to accept its decisions *on the terms the Court claims for them,* as grounded truly in principle, not as compromises with social and political pressures having, as such, no bearing on the principled choices that the Court is obliged to make."[67] Or as Justice Thomas nicely put it: "Arguments should not sneak around in disguise."[68]

Nor is there any proper place, in my view, for academic justifications, especially from a sitting judge, of decisions that are presented as being based on a specific legal ground but which are secretly based on extralegal grounds. It is one thing for unelected judges to intrude themselves into the political process on unavoidable grounds of articulated constitutional principle—as Scalia put it, because "we can't help it." It is quite another thing for them to arrogate to themselves the power to head off perceived political crises—which, given their isolated perches, they may be in the worst position to observe accurately—on the basis of legal arguments that are nothing more than pretexts. This elitist approach—the judges know best—is reminiscent of the Grand Inquisitor's argument in *The Brothers Karamazov:* "We will decide all things, and they will joyfully believe our decisions, because it will deliver them from their great care and their present terrible torments of personal and free decision."[69] This is the antithesis of democracy. It is unacceptable in America. It is a desperate and unconvincing argument of last resort offered up by those who approve of the outcome but cannot defend the reasoning of the majority's indefensible decision on its own terms.

As I will demonstrate in the coming chapters, the decision in this case—and the reasoning on which it is based—is not simply wrong or "bad constitutional law." It is not a mistake (though honest mistakes by judges are common). Nor is it a reflection of the long-held judicial philosophies of the five justices who comprise the majority. In fact, the disturbing aspect of this decision—the element that makes it different from any decision previously rendered by the Supreme Court—is that the justices were willing not just to *ignore* their own long-held judicial philosophies but to *contradict* them in order to elect the presidential candidate they preferred. As the distinguished American historian Eric Foner put it, there are few "precedents for justices trampling on their own previous convictions" to reach a predetermined political result.[70] When this result is the partisan election of a presidential candidate, the justices have violated their constitutional duties.

In order to be fair, justice must be blind—not to the facts, the law, or even the policy implications of its decisions, but most certainly to the names and party affiliations of the litigants. As I will show, the majority justices in *Bush v. Gore* lifted the blindfold of justice and based their decision precisely on those factors that, persuant to the judicial oath, no judge is permitted to consider.

I, _____, do solemnly swear (or affirm) that I will administer justice without respect to persons . . .

—*Judicial oath taken by Supreme Court justices*

I don't want to believe it. I don't want to have to tell my students to believe it. It goes against everything I've been saying and teaching for decades. But there is no escaping the conclusion that if Bush had been the one seeking the recount, at least some of the majority justices would have voted the other way.

—*A senior law professor from a southern university who voted for Bush*

3: Would the Majority Have Stopped the Hand Count if Gore Had Been Ahead?

Several weeks after joining the decision that decided Election 2000, Chief Justice William Rehnquist declared that the election "tested our constitutional system in ways it had never been tested before."[1] He did not, of course, offer an opinion as to whether the Supreme Court—and its individual justices—had passed the test. In this and the following chapters, I will demonstrate that by any reasonable standard of evaluation, the majority justices failed this most important of tests—and they did it not because of incompetence, but rather because of malice aforethought.

I am convinced—along with many academics, editorial writers, litigators, and ordinary citizens—that if it had been Bush rather than Gore who needed the Florida recount in order to have any chance of winning, at least some of the five justices who voted to stop the recount would instead have voted to allow it to go forward—that is, they would have failed the shoe-on-the-other-foot test. To understand precisely how serious this charge is, imagine for a moment the public outcry if it could be proved conclusively that all, some, or even one of the majority justices would have voted to continue the count if the result of stopping it would have been to ensure the election of Al Gore. It is difficult to conceive of a scenario in which proof positive of such a grave impropriety might emerge; it is unlikely that any justice who voted on the basis of party affiliation would be foolish enough to commit to writing or confide in a law clerk or colleague his or her improper motive. But difficulty of proof does not mean that the wrong was not committed. In the view of many informed observers, it was, and in the next chapter I will seek to prove it.

Judicial Impropriety

Let us start with some general principles: There are several distinctly different categories of impropriety into which a judicial decision could, in theory, fall. At one extreme—the most benign—would be an honest mistake about the law or the facts. The usual remedies for this kind of mistake, which is common, include a petition for the court to rehear the case or an appeal to a higher court. They also include law review articles critical of the decision and the resulting diminution in the reputation of the offending judge. As Justice Scalia once wrote: "It is commonplace that the one effective check upon arbitrary judges is criticism by the bar and the academy."[2] At the other extreme— the most malignant—would be a decision corrupted by the payment of a bribe or the promise of some kind of material benefit. No case of this kind has been proven in the history of the U.S. Supreme Court,[3] though other courts have been plagued by out-and-out bribery of judges over the years. The case of one such judge, who sat on the U.S. Court of Appeals for the Second Circuit,[4] will be considered later in this chapter.

In between these two extremes of honest mistake and outright bribery lie a wide range of judicial improprieties, which include the following:

- Deliberate misstatement of the law or the facts
- Deciding a case (or motion) on the basis of laziness—for example, to avoid a lengthy trial or the need to read a long record
- Deciding a case for personal careerist reasons—promotion, retirement, postretirement opportunity
- Rendering judgment in a case in which the judge has a conflict of interest, such as a financial interest in the outcome
- Showing actual favoritism for (or bias against) a litigant or lawyer—or religion, gender, race, sexual preference, group, or political party

Short of accepting a bribe, which, of course, no one has accused any Supreme Court justice of doing, one of the clearest examples of abuse would be a situation in which a justice anticipates a material benefit if one of the litigants wins the case, and so the justice votes in favor of that litigant. No reasonable person could disagree with the proposition that the expectation of any significant material benefit is an improper thumb on the scales of justice, for at least four related reasons. First, it could consciously influence the vote of a corruptible justice. Second, it could unconsciously influence the vote of even the most fairminded justice. Third, it could cause an overly scrupulous justice to lean over backward against his or her own material interests. Fourth, even if it had no influence whatsoever on the justice, the appearance of impropriety could create distrust in the process.

For these reasons, virtually every code of judicial conduct in history—beginning with the Bible, which recognized that the expectation of material benefit "doth blind the eyes of the wise, and pervert the words of the righteous"[5]—has prohibited judges with a significant material interest in the outcome of a case from participating in its deliberations or decision. Following this principle, every contemporary American judicial code expressly prohibits a judge from "taking part" in any case "in which his personal self-interest" may be involved, and "self-interest" is broadly defined so as to avoid even the appearance of bias or the "impression that any person can improperly influence him or unduly enjoy his favor, or that he is afflicted by kinship, rank, position or influence by any party or other person."[6] As recently as 1969, a nominee for the Supreme Court was rejected, at least in part, because as a lower federal judge he sat on two cases in which he had an arguable, if peripheral, material interest in the outcome.[7]

There is, of course, a world of difference between accepting an actual bribe offered by a litigant and merely expecting a material benefit in the event that a particular litigant wins. Surely if a litigant were ever to offer a judge, a juror, or even a witness any sort of material benefit in exchange for his vote or testimony, there would be no question that this would constitute a corrupt offer, and its acceptance would complete a crime equivalent to bribery, even if no promise of cash was included and regardless of whether the offer in fact had any impact on the decision. The ethical violation occurs without regard to whether the anticipated benefit actually influences the ultimate decision.[8] This may seem different from a situation in which a judge expects to gain some material benefit of any type, immediate or delayed, should the litigant win his case; for one thing, the litigant himself may not even be aware of the hoped-for benefit, or if he is aware, he may simply have been the knowing beneficiary of it. But as an ethical matter, as it relates to the judge's state of mind, there is only a difference in degree between rendering judgment in a case in which a material benefit has been *promised* and doing so in a case in which a material benefit is realistically *expected*.

Hypothetical Cases Involving a Supreme Court Decision Regarding a Presidential Election

Now consider how some of these different degrees of impropriety might play out in a situation where the outcome of a presidential election may ride on a decision by the Supreme Court, and both of the candidates are litigants. Of course, this is exactly the sort of case that arrived before the Supreme Court in 2000, but here I will employ a heuristic device that is a staple of law school teaching—the gradually changing hypothetical case, which starts out with the clearest black-and-white example of abuse and then moves progressively toward more subtle tones of gray.

In the first version of the hypothetical, a memorandum is uncovered in which a justice sitting on a case that could decide the presidency of the United States informs his law clerk that he is anxious to retire from the Supreme Court for personal or family reasons, but that he will do so only if the election produces a president from his political party who will pick a successor who shares his judicial philosophy. The justice directs the law clerk to find some legal justification for deciding the election in his candidate's favor, so that he can retire.

How serious an offense would this be? Would it warrant the impeachment of the justice, who was appointed to serve only as long as he displayed good behavior? Would it require reopening the case and redeciding it without the participation of the offending justice? Would it call for some disciplinary sanction, short of removal, against the justice? Would it disqualify the justice from serving as a role model for law students and require good law schools no longer to honor such a person? Would it discourage decent law students from applying for clerkships with such an unethical justice? How would law professors teach about such a justice? And how would history judge him?

A second version is identical to the first, except that the justice hopes to be promoted to chief justice when the incumbent retires, as he is expected to do if a candidate of his party becomes president. The justice in this hypothetical knows that he could become chief justice only if the candidate of his party is elected. The difference is that in the first hypothetical the justice himself controls the personal benefit—it is he who decides whether and when to retire. In the second, the president determines whether to promote the justice to chief.

The third version of the progressively graying election hypothetical would postulate a justice with no personal or careerist motives, but with a strong desire to ensure the election of a particular presidential candidate. This desire might reflect the highest and most patriotic motives: a strong belief that the election of this candidate would be best for the country and the world, a desire to have a president who would nominate like-minded justices to the high court, or a simple preference for one party over another. The relevant point here is that the justice casts his vote so as to ensure the election of a particular presidential candidate, and that he would have voted differently had the candidates' positions been switched. The codes of judicial behavior prohibit a judge from promoting "the interests of one political party as against another."[9]

The fourth and most complex version of the hypothetical is reflected in the following mock memorandum from a fictional justice to his or her fictional law clerks:

To: Law Clerks

From: Justice ＿＿＿＿＿＿＿＿＿

Re: Recount case

As you know, the state supreme court has ordered the manual recount to go forward, based on the legislative standard of "the clear intent of the voter." I am deeply troubled by this development. This standard seems arbitrary to me and subject to differing interpretations by different counters. In my view, this suggests a serious potential equal-protection issue. This case is on the way up here, and I would like you to prepare a memorandum for me outlining the Supreme Court jurisprudence on equal protection and how it might apply to this case. I would also like you to summarize my own jurisprudence on equal protection, as developed in previous cases in which I participated as a justice.

My preliminary inclination is to vote to overrule the state Supreme Court and to stop the manual recount. There are several reasons why I think such a recount would be bad for the country. First, I see this election spiraling out of control, with the state legislature selecting one slate of electors and the courts selecting another. I would hate to see the election thrown into the hands of Congress, especially with the Senate divided 50–50 and a vice president potentially casting the deciding vote in favor of himself, while the House, which is controlled by the other party, casts its vote in favor of its candidate. I think we have a responsibility to avoid this mess if the law permits us to do so. I must admit, however, that I am not certain that I would feel exactly the same way if, by stopping the recount, I would be ensuring the election of the other candidate.

Second, I strongly believe that the election of my candidate will be far better for the country and the world. We have been laboring long and hard to come up with a majority of justices who support what I strongly believe is the proper role of the Supreme Court in our system of governance. We need more justices who support our views of the Constitution; the election of my candidate will ensure a solid majority, while the election of the other candidate will have the opposite effect.

Accordingly, I hope you will find that the law and my own opinions provide a basis for me to vote to stop the manual recount. I want to be sure that I can justify it legally. I know I can justify it by reference to values I hold dear, but my role as a justice does not authorize me simply to vote my politics. I need to be sure that the law provides support for the result I think is best on policy grounds. So if you can find me any case law to support stopping the recount, I will vote to do so. If there is absolutely no support in the law, I guess I will have no choice but to vote, reluctantly, to let it continue. I hope it won't come to that.

The law clerks advise the justice that there is no case law directly supporting the stopping of the recount, and what sparse election case law there is—especially in the lower courts—favors the opposite result. Moreover, the justice's own precedents strongly oppose stopping the recount. But, of course, by selectively choosing some precedents and ignoring others, an argument could be constructed for achieving the result the justice favors. On this basis, the judge joins the majority. He would not have done so had it meant the other candidate winning the election, but he also would not have cast his vote in favor of his candidate had there been absolutely no legal authority to support it.

Each of these hypothetical cases reflects some wrongdoing by the justice, since it is never proper to allow one's personal preference for a particular electoral outcome—regardless of the reason—to be given any weight in a deliberative process that in any way relates to that outcome. But the first and second hypothetical cases reflect more serious malfeasance than the third and the fourth, because they involve the expectation of personal material or career benefits. The third is worse than the fourth because it is explicitly based on partisan political considerations, despite its patriotic underpinning. The fourth involves mixed motives and a willingness to follow the law, though with a thumb, or at least a pinky, on the scale of choosing which law to follow.

The function of the law school hypothetical is to help clarify complex matters in a somewhat abstract setting—without arguing about the specific evidence—so that the principles may then be applied in real life. In Chapter 4, I will move from the hypothetical to the actual and see how close the actual evidence—as it is now known—comes to the hypothetical facts set out above. But before we turn to the case against individual justices, it is important to understand how difficult it is generally to prove that a judge was actually motivated by impermissible considerations in a given case—that he or she would have voted differently had the shoe been on a different foot.

The Difficulty of Proving an Improper Motive

In the absence of a smoking gun—a confession, a witness, or a paper trail—it is extremely difficult to prove that a judge was improperly motivated in rendering a decision favorable to a particular litigant. As with any human being, it is impossible to get into a judge's mind, heart, and soul. Even a judge who would benefit materially from the victory of a litigant could—at least in theory—render judgment in that litigant's favor without having been influenced, to any degree, by his expectation of benefit. It is precisely because improper motive is so difficult to prove that the legal system has enacted rules precluding judges from sitting on cases in which significant personal self-interest may be involved or in which their impartiality might reasonably be questioned for any other reason. A judge is guilty of violating these rules if he sits on any such case, regardless of whether it can be proved that he was actually motivated by any improper considerations. As the Supreme Court said in another context: "When the trial judge is discovered to have had some other basis for rendering a biased judgment, his actual motivations are hidden from review, and we must presume that the process was impaired."[10]

But it sometimes becomes necessary to prove an *actual* (rather than possible) improper motivation by a judge in a particular case. In a criminal, disbarment, or impeachment case, for example, a prosecutor might have to prove that a judge decided a case differently for one litigant than he would have for the other litigant. The case of Judge Martin T. Manton demonstrates the challenge we face in this case.

Judge Manton was among the most influential and respected federal judges in the early and mid-1930s. As chief judge of the U.S. Court of Appeals, he presided over thousands of federal cases from New York, Connecticut, and Vermont, and wrote more than six hundred opinions.[11] He received honorary degrees from several law schools, and his own alma mater, Columbia University, honored him as a distinguished alumnus. Because of the importance of his court—second only to the U.S. Supreme Court—Manton was "regarded as the tenth-ranking justice in the United States."[12] Indeed, President Herbert Hoover considered elevating Manton to the "Catholic seat" on the Supreme Court,[13] though the nomination was never made and Manton remained on the Court of Appeals. Manton was one of the most powerful judges in the country until he was publicly accused of corruption by District Attorney Thomas E. Dewey in 1939. Dewey accused him of having business dealings with businessmen who were litigants in his court and of voting in their favor in exchange for receiving loans. Shortly after the charges became public, Manton resigned from the bench, while asserting that his business interests did not bear "the slightest relation to my conduct as a judge or to any litigation in my court."[14] Following a trial in which Manton denied that any loans had influenced his decisions, he was convicted and sentenced to two years in prison.[15]

It is remarkable that none of his judicial colleagues ever openly suspected him of bribery, especially since appellate judges generally render their judgments as part of a panel of three judges. Two other judges joined most of Manton's opinions. On those few occasions where one dissented from Manton's decision, that judge presumably studied the record and Manton's opinion. Yet none ever accused him of perverting justice. Indeed, four extremely distinguished long-term colleagues of his—Judges Learned Hand, Augustus Hand, Harry Chase, and Thomas Swan—were all subpoenaed by the defense to testify at Manton's criminal trial. They were all asked the same question: whether, in any of the cases in which they sat with Manton, they had ever observed anything that led them to believe "he was acting otherwise than according to his oath of office and the dictates of his conscience."[16] Each answered that he had never seen or read anything that would suggest Manton had not decided each case on its merits. Subsequent reviews of his published opinions and unpublished internal memoranda—read even through the lens of proven corruption—disclosed no smoking guns in the opinions themselves or in the preliminary drafts or memoranda.[17]

The lesson of this case is that clever judges can always justify their decisions by grounding them in acceptable interpretations of existing law. Evidence of a judge's corrupt motives are rarely discoverable on the face of a published opinion. It will ordinarily have to be found in sources external to the opinion, as in the Manton case, where a paper trail of financial documents plus several cooperating witnesses provided strong—though far from conclusive—evidence that he had actually changed his decisions on the basis of his expectation of material benefit.

In some instances, a compelling circumstantial case can be made by comparing a suspect opinion to uncorrupted opinions in closely related areas. These baseline opinions demonstrate how the judge has generally decided comparable cases that do not involve self-interest. Using these cases as the constants, one can consider all the possible variables that might explain the inconsistent result, and if the only variable that could plausibly explain the different outcome is an improper motivation, this would give rise to a circumstantial inference of corruption. If this inference is corroborated by external proof—for example, uncontested evidence of a benefit anticipated in the event of the victory of one litigant—then the inference becomes stronger. If the conclusion is then confirmed by a commonsense look at the person's history and known biases, a convincing circumstantial case emerges. This combination of different kinds of proof is commonly used in criminal and civil cases. It is also the sort of triangulation often relied on by historians.[18] The standards of proof required for a criminal conviction, a civil judgment, and the verdict of history differ considerably, with the highest standard—proof beyond a reasonable doubt—being required in criminal cases, and considerably lower standards sufficing in other contexts. For example, in the context of a lower court judge's nomination to the Supreme Court or a Supreme Court justice's nomination for chief justice, even a well-founded suspicion of corruption might be enough for a senator to vote against confirmation. In *Bush v. Gore,* we are dealing with the verdict of history where the standards employed by respected historians vary somewhat but are generally higher than well-founded suspicion and lower than beyond a reasonable doubt. Sometimes the historian will simply lay out the available evidence and let the reader decide on the appropriate standard, depending on the use to which the conclusion will be put.[19]

Though an inference of guilt can sometimes be drawn from the face of an inconsistent and unpersuasive decision, an inference of innocence can never be drawn from the face of an opinion alone, regardless of how brilliant or consistent it may be. A clever judge, such as Martin Manton—and many of the scores of state judges who have been guilty of corruption over the years—can often find plausible arguments to justify a result that was, in fact, motivated by improper considerations. Most cases present plausible claims on both sides. Good lawyers are capable of constructing persuasive arguments on either side of a case. All an appellate judge has to do is to select arguments from the brief supporting the side whose victory would benefit him and then adapt them in a manner consistent with his prior opinions in related areas. That is precisely what Judge Manton did. After studying the internal court memoranda in a particular case in which a bribe had almost certainly been paid to Manton, Professor Gerald Gunther concluded that

> nothing on the face of Manton's memorandum suggested that he had been paid to reach his decision. True, Manton's memorandum was not as erudite as [his colleague] Hand's, but this was the norm; also, he had throughout his appellate career a reputation of being a "scissors and paste-pot" judge who produced many of his opinions simply by lifting useful passages, complete with precedents and legal authority, from the briefs of the prevailing side. [By] limiting his corrupt votes to reasonably close cases and arguably plausible positions, Manton made much of his dishonesty difficult to detect.[20]

Put another way, the plausibility and consistency of a judicial opinion on its face may be *necessary* to prove that it was motivated by appropriate considerations, but it can never be *sufficient* in cases where there is compelling evidence of improper motivation. That is why the arguments being offered by most of those seeking to defend the majority justices in *Bush v. Gore* are, at best, incomplete. These traditional legal arguments are limited to showing that an honest justice *could* have decided the case as the majority did, and could have done so entirely on the basis of plausible legal principles. Even if that limited claim is true in the Florida election case—and I believe that it is not—it would not prove that *these* justices *would* have decided this case as they did if the shoe had been on the other foot, since no one denies that there are also plausible legal principles that would justify the opposite result.

Academic Defenders of the Majority Justices

It is important to note that a number of prominent academics have come forward to defend the majority justices. Several have offered creative, intelligent, and cogent defenses of some of the arguments, especially the ones related to Article II. As is evident from what I have written, I disagree with the merits of these arguments. But I also have a different kind of disagreement with some of these defenders. I believe it is morally wrong for scholars to defend the majority justices, even if they think their arguments are theoretically defensible, unless they honestly believe that the justices themselves would have offered these arguments on behalf of Gore if the shoe had been on the other foot.

For brilliant academics, clever arguments are easy to come by. But to publicly defend an argument that was presented only as a rationalization for a decision based on partisan political grounds rather than nonpartisan legal grounds, is to become complicit in an intellectual fraud perpetrated by the Supreme Court majority on the nation, and to encourage its emulation in future cases. Dishonest justices should not be encouraged by smart academics to concoct arguments—plausible as they may be as an abstract matter—and then invoke them for partisan purposes, expecting that they will be defended by credible scholars. Academics who defend such arguments play right into the hands of partisan justices.

I cannot conceive of any responsible academic writing an article seeking to justify the decision of a judge who took a bribe. Even if the resulting decision and its reasoning were theoretically correct—by some abstract standard of correctness—no academic who abhors bribery would become complicit in the judge's immoral action by providing an after-the-fact academic justification for the result he was paid to reach. No scholar I know would have written a law review article supporting the conclusions reached by Judge Manton. Though there are obvious distinctions between taking a bribe and failing the shoe-on-the-other-foot test, both types of decisions are thoroughly corrupt. So let these five Supreme Court justices defend themselves—if they can—and let not the imprimatur of academia be placed on a decision that, even if correct in the abstract, would never have been subscribed to by these justices if the shoe had been on the other foot.

And so I pose the following challenge to my fellow academics: Do you honestly believe (I'm not asking whether you can prove) that these justices would have subscribed to these arguments if Gore had been ahead and Bush had been seeking the recount? If you can answer that question in the affirmative, then do so explicitly, by demonstrating how their opinions in this case can be reconciled with their opinions in prior cases as well as with their extrajudicial writings. If you cannot, then you should not lend your academic credibility to what they did in *Bush v. Gore,* even if you think the arguments they put forward may be academically defensible.

Ad Hominem Arguments and Analysis of Motive

It is understandable why so many academics and lawyers of goodwill would tend to limit their arguments—both in support of and in opposition to a Supreme Court decision—to the face of the opinion and its consistency, or lack thereof, with prior opinions. First, it is difficult to prove an improper motive. Second, to go beyond these traditional modes of criticism is to risk being accused of making an ad hominem attack on individual justices, and such personal attacks are regarded as unprofessional. As Professor Cass Sunstein cautioned with regard to this case: "No one should accuse any of the justices of bad faith or of trying to ensure that their man gets in."[21]

Well, that is precisely what I am accusing the majority justices of doing. Let me be as clear as I can: The criticism I am making of the majority justices includes a significant ad hominem component. I am not limiting my criticism merely to the intellectual or precedential weaknesses of their arguments. I am accusing them of partisan favoritism—bias—toward one litigant and against another. I am also accusing them of dishonesty, of trying to hide their bias behind plausible legal arguments that they never would have put forward had the shoe been on the other foot. These criticisms are directed at the justices *personally,* not only at their arguments, though it is the weakness of their arguments—and their inconsistency with prior views expressed by these very justices—that provides the probable cause for probing their motives.

In order to prove my serious ad hominem charges, I must, of course, analyze and criticize the face of the opinions and demonstrate their inconsistency with prior decisions, especially those by the same justices. But I will also go beyond the opinions and look to other evidence that bears directly on the motives of the individual justices.

This sort of motive analysis is largely outside the tradition of academic and professional criticism of the Supreme Court, as the admonition from Professor Sunstein suggests.[22] Academics characterize such personal criticism as "the fallacy of *argumentum ad hominem.*" And it *is* a fallacy to try to disprove the correctness of an argument on its merits by leveling a personal attack on the person who offered the argument, since an argument offered by the worst of human beings may nonetheless be correct. But it is equally fallacious to try to defend someone against well-grounded charges of *personal* dishonesty, bias, or corruption by demonstrating that the argument he made turns out to be correct on its merits. As we have seen, Judge Manton was no less corrupt because the arguments on which he based his judicial opinions were legally acceptable. Indeed, after his conviction, the Court of Appeals reconsidered at least one of the appeals in which Manton had cast the deciding vote and reaffirmed it on the merits, "after a fresh review of the old record and with full knowledge of Manton's bribery."[23] Notwithstanding that reaffirmation of the correctness of Manton's decision, Manton himself remained in prison, properly convicted of a crime on the basis exclusively of evidence directed against his actions as a person, rather than at his arguments.

An example of a proceeding at which ad hominem criticisms are entirely appropriate is a judicial confirmation hearing. Although different in some respects from an inquiry into whether a particular decision was based on improper considerations, it demonstrates that ad hominem inquiry is sometimes probative. The prior opinions of a judicial nominee who is being considered for promotion are obviously relevant, but so are his or her personal characteristics: Does he have a "judicial temperament"? Did he ever commit a crime of "moral turpitude"? Did she ever sit on a case in which she had a conflict of interest (without regard to the intellectual quality of the arguments she made in her decision)? Has he ever based a decision on favoritism toward one litigant or against another?

Recently, the U.S. Supreme Court considered a case in which an Illinois judge who had taken bribes to acquit certain murder defendants had imposed the death penalty on a murder defendant who had *not* bribed him.[24] This defendant sought a new trial on the ground that the corrupt judge "had an interest in a conviction here, to deflect suspicion that he was taking bribes in other cases." The narrow issue before the Supreme Court was whether the defendant had a right to try to prove—through discovery of evidence—that the bribe-taking judge had "actual judicial bias in the trial of his case." It would not be enough, the Court said, to prove that he was generally corrupt, implying that a judge who was "shown to be thoroughly steeped in corruption" could nevertheless render fair justice in another capital case in which he was not bribed. The defendant would have to prove "compensatory, camouflaging bias on [the judge's] part in petitioner's own case." In my view, the Court was wrong in this case precisely in ignoring the obvious implications of the ad hominem conclusion that a judge once corrupted by bribery can never again be trusted to render justice, especially in a life-and-death case. But the high court, recognizing the difficulty of meeting the burden it placed on the capital defendant, ruled that he should be provided the discovery tools—subpoenas, dispositions, and the like—needed to try to meet this burden.

The Supreme Court itself has sometimes engaged in motive analysis—a variation on ad hominem argumentation. In 1985, Justice Rehnquist wrote a unanimous decision for the Court striking down an Alabama statute that disenfranchised all persons convicted of crimes "involving moral turpitude."[25] The vague words "moral turpitude" were not further defined in the legislation, but the state supreme court said that they meant any act that is "immoral in itself, regardless of the fact whether it is punishable by law." This made the term even vaguer and more standardless. The law left the application of this term to the state's Board of Registrars. Interestingly, the Supreme Court did not find this standardless voting law on its face to violate the equal-protection clause, despite the inevitability that different registrars would apply different standards of morality and immorality. Indeed, Justice Rehnquist went out of his way to declare the law "on its face" to be "racially neutral" and refused to decide whether it "would be valid if enacted today without any impermissible motivation" (emphasis added). But there *was* an impermissible motivation: The Supreme Court concluded that the law had been originally motivated by a desire to disenfranchise blacks and to maintain white supremacy in Alabama. As evidence, the Court cited statements made by delegates to the all-white convention that had enacted the law years earlier. The Supreme Court struck down the law as a denial of equal protection because "its original enactment was motivated by a desire to discriminate against blacks on account of race."[26]

It would have been far easier for the Court to declare the statute unconstitutional without getting into the motivations of its enactors. The absence of standards and the vagueness of the phrase "moral turpitude" provided a possible alternative basis for finding an equal-protection violation, especially in a case involving both alleged racial discrimination and the right to vote.[27] But the Court chose instead to undertake a more difficult motive analysis, which required an evaluation of ambiguous legislative history. Perhaps the reason was that Justice Rehnquist, who wrote the opinion, could not—consistent with his prior opinions—find an equal-protection violation, no matter how standardless the criteria for disenfranchisement were, unless there was purposeful discrimination based on race. (More on this issue in Chapter 4, when Justice Rehnquist's views of equal protection prior to the Florida case are considered.) In any event, the Court embarked on an ad hominem motive analysis of the individuals who enacted the statute, and found them to lack a proper motive. This improper motive was not cured by the racially neutral statute they produced, any more than an improperly motivated decision in the Florida case would be cured by a logically neutral opinion.

Inquiry into the motives of judges, legislators, and others is thus useful and relevant in many contexts. I believe it is also useful and relevant in assessing the decision in *Bush v. Gore*.

Analyzing the Justices' Motives in *Bush v. Gore:* A Prelude

In Chapter 4, I will be delving into the motives of the five justices who voted to stop the Florida recount. I will be addressing the questions many Americans are asking: Did these justices deviate from precedent and from their own judicial principles to bring about the election of George W. Bush? Did any of them have a significant personal stake in the outcome of the election? Would they have voted the same way if the names of the litigants were switched? These are entirely appropriate questions that cry out for answers in a case of such great significance, especially since so many Americans reasonably suspect improper motives. I am not committing the fallacy of *argumentum ad hominem,* since these accusations are directed against the personal and political motivations of the individual justices; the quality and consistency (or lack thereof) of their arguments are merely evidence of their personal and political motivations (or lack thereof).[28]

Every institution in American life develops its own traditions for criticism, both internal and external. No one would raise an eyebrow if a newspaper challenged the motives of a congressman or a senator on the ground that he or she was partisan or biased toward a particular segment of the population. Nor would anyone be shocked if a legislator was accused of voting on the basis of an expectation of receiving a campaign contribution, an executive appointment, or some other benefit. Even personal payback—revenge—has sometimes been charged against senators and members of Congress. That kind of criticism of legislators is expected if warranted by the evidence. Moreover, the media is expected to investigate whether such criticism is or is not warranted by the facts. The same would be true of a president. But traditionally, such criticism is not expected of appointed judges, especially not of justices in the Supreme Court. With few exceptions, the media and the public have, in recent times, assumed the integrity, good faith, and bona fides of Supreme Court justices and their opinions. We feel free to criticize their logic, their use of precedent, and even their legal ideology. But it has not been part of the recent tradition to question their personal motives or their political partisanship. We need to believe in the good faith of our Supreme Court justices, since they have the final word on so many important issues, and since they are not removable by democratic means.

The justices have not always been exempted from personal criticism. In the early days of the Republic, attacks against federalist judges were extremely personal and pointed. Justice Samuel Chase—who was impeached—was called "partial, vindictive and cruel." President Thomas Jefferson used even stronger words in attacking Chief Justice John Marshall and his views: "In Marshall's hands, the law is nothing more than an ambiguous text, to be explained by his sophistry into any meaning which may serve his personal malice."[29] In more recent years, this kind of ad hominem criticism has been reserved for elected officials, especially in the legislative and executive branches.[30]

In making such criticisms of elected officials, we look at the public record, which may include prior voting patterns, statements of principle, public speeches, campaign contributions, and the like. When it comes to evaluating the decisions of Supreme Court justices, the public record is relatively sparse. It consists primarily of the justice's prior judicial decisions, the justice's record before he or she became a judge, and occasional statements of judicial philosophy that may appear in law review articles, published speeches, or confirmation hearings.[31] Rarely do we see Supreme Court decisions analyzed by reference to the partisan political affiliations of the justice. Indeed, there was something of a political scandal when Richard Nixon, then vice president, characterized Earl Warren as a great Republican chief justice.[32]

We have been brought up to believe that justices shed their party affiliation when they put on the robe, just as they are supposed to give no advantage to friends or former colleagues. It is widely known that many state court judges and some lower court federal judges play favorites among litigants and lawyers. Roy Cohn once famously quipped, "I don't care if my opponent knows the law, as long as I know the judge." In the old days, it was financial corruption—cash changed hands. Then it became the "favor bank," in which personal favors are quietly stored and exchanged.[33] I have seen it with my own eyes in the courts of Boston, New York, and elsewhere. But I had never heard of favoritism in modern U.S. Supreme Court history. I was brought up on the story of Tommy "The Cork" Corcoran, a Roosevelt advisor who had been helpful in the Supreme Court nomination for Justice Hugo Black, with whom he remained intimate. Years later, when Corcoran was in private practice, he went to see his old friend Hugo and began to discuss why he believed the Court should review a particular commercial case in which Corcoran had an interest. Black stopped him and warned his old friend that their relationship would terminate if Corcoran ever again so much as mentioned a pending case. It is this "Caesar's wife" tradition that has, for the most part, shielded the justices from personal attack over the years. *Bush v. Gore* has ended that tradition.

Bush v. Gore will be taught in law school and political science classes for years to come. For the most part, the analysis will be limited to the plausibility of the decision, its consistency with prior decisions of the Court as well as with those of the individual justices, and other conventional tools of legal scholarship. Although these tools are essential to understanding and criticizing this case, they are insufficient in this instance. Because so many Americans understandably believe that the decision in *Bush v. Gore* may well have been motivated by partisan political concerns—that is, a desire to see Bush rather than Gore as president—any full analysis of this case requires an assessment of the justices' motives. Different tools of analysis must be employed to supplement the traditional ones. There will be much controversy about the appropriateness of these tools in the context of Supreme Court cases, but in my estimation, they are essential whenever there is a well-grounded and widespread suspicion that the justices would have decided the case differently if the shoe had been on the other foot.

One such tool of analysis is to imagine if the one hundred most experienced observers of the high court—academics, Supreme Court litigators, journalists who cover the justices—had been presented, one year before the Florida case, with a hypothetical case based precisely on the facts of the Florida case, but without the names or party affiliations of the candidates. Imagine as well that these neutral experts had been given all the opinions ever written by the justices on the relevant areas of law (equal protection, voting rights, the criteria for granting a stay, the force of precedent) as well as their extrajudicial writings and speeches concerning the role of the Supreme Court. Imagine further that these experts were asked to predict how each justice would vote on the four determinative issues:

1. Would he or she agree to review the decisions of the Florida Supreme Court?
2. Would he or she vote to stay the hand count prior to hearing argument in the case?

3. Would he or she find the Florida law to be in violation of the equal-protection clause?

4. If the justice did find the law in violation of the equal-protection clause, would he or she order the hand count stopped rather than remanding the case back to Florida for a count with proper standards?[34]

Finally, imagine if the experts were asked to assess which justice was most likely to respond affirmatively to the first question, which most likely to respond affirmatively to the second question, and so on.[35]

I have now posed this thought problem to several dozen professors and Court watchers. Their responses have confirmed my view that few, if any, of the experts in my hypothetical test would have correctly predicted the outcome of the case or how the majority justices would vote on the four questions. (I believe that not a single expert would have predicted correctly, unless they imagined or guessed who the litigants would be.) Nor would the experts' inability to predict the justices' votes demonstrate any inadequacy on *their* part. The experts are "right," and the justices who voted yes on the four questions were "wrong." Law must be predictable if it is to be credible. "The known certainty of the law is the safety of all," said Lord Coke.[36] Oliver Wendell Holmes once described law as "the prophecies of what the courts will do in fact."[37] Predictability is the essence of judicial legitimacy and accountability. Judges are not supposed to make it up as they go along, especially when they know in advance that making it up in a certain way will elect a candidate they wish to see in office.

This is not to deny that some good decisions by some honest judges come as surprises to even the most knowledgeable observers, but these unpredictable decisions are extremely rare and generally occur in the context of quickly changing social conditions. The Supreme Court's most controversial decisions were entirely predictable, because they rested on a foundation of case law developed over a long period of time. *Brown v. Board of Education* followed decades of chipping away at *Plessy v. Ferguson*. *Miranda v. Arizona* was the culmination of several decisions imposing restrictions on the power of the police to elicit confessions in the absence of counsel. *Roe v. Wade* was entirely predictable after the Court recognized the right to privacy and reproductive freedom in the earlier birth control cases. Even the reapportionment decisions, which mandated significant changes in voting districts, did not come as a complete surprise following the civil rights cases. More relevant, for purposes of the argument made in this book, is that it was entirely predictable which justices were most likely (and which least likely) to vote for these changes, because their votes were largely consistent with their previously expressed legal views. The reason it was impossible for the hypothetical experts to predict which of the majority justices would vote which way on the four legal questions in the Florida case (presented above) without knowing the identities and party affiliations of the litigants is precisely because in that case, these justices voted not on the basis of the four legal questions, but rather on the basis of the identities and party affiliations of the litigants—facts that were not revealed in the hypothetical case. If those facts *had* been revealed, the accuracy of the predictions would have improved significantly.

I have also administered the shoe-on-the-other-foot test to dozens of large lecture audiences of law and professional people across the country, from Oregon to western North Carolina to central Florida and New York. I have specifically asked Bush supporters, of whom there were many, whether they actually believe deep in their hearts that the majority justices would have voted to stop the recount if the consequence had been a Gore presidency. Few hands have been raised, and many snickers have been heard. I have then asked Gore supporters how many believe the Florida Supreme Court justices who voted for the recount would have passed the shoe-on-the-other-foot test, and I received a similar response. When I have asked for a show of hands as to how many believe that all of the justices on both the U.S. Supreme Court and the Florida Supreme Court would pass the test, not a single hand has gone up.

It seems that the election case has, as Justice Stevens predicted it would, seriously damaged the faith of many Americans—on both sides of the political divide—in the neutrality and non-partisanship of our judiciary *as an institution,* though it still remains a daunting task to prove partisanship on the part of an individual judge in a specific case. Despite this difficulty, in the next chapter I will try to prove the serious and damning ad hominem charge that none of the majority justices would have voted to stop the hand count if Gore had been ahead in Florida and Bush needed the hand count to have any chance of winning.

4: The Inconsistency of the Majority Justices with Their Previously Expressed Views

In Chapter 2, I demonstrated the *general* inconsistency between the majority opinion in *Bush v. Gore* and the prior rulings of the Supreme Court. In this chapter, I will contrast the prior decisions and writings of the *particular* majority justices with the opinions they joined in this case. These dramatic discrepancies raise troubling questions. I will then move from this concrete evidence to a more speculative consideration of what may have motivated these inconsistencies. Let me begin with the justice who is widely regarded as the intellectual and moral leader of the majority, Antonin Scalia.

Justice Scalia

*The Supreme Court of the United States does not sit to
announce "unique" dispositions.*
—United States v. Virginia

Our consideration is limited to the present circumstances.
—Bush v. Gore

Throughout the Court's history, justices have approached their
role with varying levels of commitment to an overarching judicial
philosophy or jurisprudence. Some simply decide cases as they
are presented, with no reference to a particular legal theory.
Their goal, as Oliver Wendell Holmes once put it, is simply to
solve the problem before them. The criterion by which such judges seek to have their work evaluated is whether they have been
true to the law and fair to the litigants. They do justice on a case-
by-case and issue-by-issue basis. The judicial philosophies of
such "retail" judges can be discovered only over time, by looking
back at the totality of their work product and tying the divergent
cases together by strands of philosophical commonality. Some of
these justices appear to develop a consistent jurisprudence, while
others appear to rule on a more or less ad hoc basis.

At the other extreme, there are justices who come to their
job with a coherent and pervasive judicial philosophy that an-
imates their decisions and which they articulate in many of their
cases. These "wholesale" justices believe that the role of the
Supreme Court is to establish general precedents binding on all
other courts, and that it is the job of the lower courts to administer justice on a retail basis, applying these general precedents to particular cases. They do not think the Supreme Court
should be in the business of deciding individual cases that require unique dispositions based on the totality of the circumstances.

The embodiment of the second type of justice is Antonin Scalia, who has expressed his views—perhaps more extensively and intelligently than any justice in recent history—about the proper manner by which the Supreme Court should administer justice. As with any complex philosophy, it is difficult to summarize Scalia's jurisprudence briefly without losing nuance, but Scalia himself has provided a fair summary in his writings over the years. In a 1996 case, he wrote:

> The Supreme Court of the United States does not sit to announce "unique" dispositions. Its principal function is to establish precedent—that is, to set forth principles of law that every court in America must follow. As we said only this Term, we expect both ourselves and lower courts to adhere to the "rationale upon which the Court based the results of its earlier decisions." . . . That is the principal reason we publish our opinions.[1]

In a 1989 law review article, he explained how this approach to adjudication imposes "constraints" that are designed to hedge in the policy preferences of individual justices:

> [W]hen, in writing for the majority of the Court, I adopt a general rule, and say, "This is the basis of our decision." I not only constrain lower courts, I constrain myself as well. *If the next case should have such different facts that my political or policy preferences regarding the outcomes are quite the opposite, I will be unable to indulge those preferences;* I have committed myself to the governing principle. In the real world of appellate judging, it displays more judicial restraint to adopt such a course than to announce that, "on balance," we think the law was violated here—leaving ourselves free to say in the next case that, "on balance," it was not. It is a commonplace that the one effective check upon arbitrary

judges is criticism by the bar and the academy. But it is no more possible to demonstrate the inconsistency of two opinions based upon a "totality of the circumstances" test than it is to demonstrate the inconsistency of two jury verdicts. Only by announcing rules do we hedge ourselves in. (Emphasis added)[2]

In other writings, he has argued persuasively that the doctrine of *stare decisis*—fidelity to precedent—is central to the role of the justice for several interrelated reasons. First, by requiring the justice to build on the past—to make every decision a part of an ongoing process of articulating and applying the law— the doctrine of *stare decisis* precludes the justice from exercising arbitrary discretion and indulging his own political preferences. Second, by making the justice look to the future—to the precedential effect this decision will have on subsequent cases—it commits the justice to formulating general principles that will govern his decisions in cases whose political implications cannot now be known. Third, by requiring the decision to be based on objective principles of general applicability, rather than the necessarily subjective "totality of the circumstances," the doctrine of fidelity to precedent makes it harder for the judge to implement any personal preferences he may harbor. Fourth, *stare decisis* also promotes predictability, which is essential to any fair legal system. As Scalia wrote in 1989:

[There is an] obvious advantage of establishing as soon as possible a clear, general principle of decision: predictability. Even in simpler times uncertainty has been regarded as incompatible with the Rule of Law. Rudimentary justice requires that those subject to the law must have the means of knowing what it prescribes. It is said that one of emperor Nero's nasty practices was to post his edicts high on the columns so that they would be harder to read and easier to

transgress. As laws have become more numerous, and as people have become increasingly ready to punish their adversar-
ies in the courts, we can less and less afford protracted uncertainty regarding what the law may mean. Predictability,
or as Llewellyn put it, "reckonability," is a needful characteristic of any law worthy of the name.[3]

Predictability also requires that the legitimate expectations of the
public not be disappointed by changing the law without good
reason. Scalia explained why in a 1995 concurring opinion:

> The doctrine of *stare decisis* protects the legitimate expecta-
> tions of those who live under the law, and, as Alexander
> Hamilton observed, is one of the means by which exercise of
> "an arbitrary discretion in the courts" is restrained. . . . Who
> ignores it must give reasons, and reasons that go beyond mere
> demonstration that the overruled opinion was wrong (oth-
> erwise the doctrine would be no doctrine at all).[4]

In addition to these constraints on a justice—respect for precedent, announcing general principles, and eschewing unique
dispositions—Scalia is well known for his commitment to the
text of the Constitution and his reliance on "unbroken national traditions" in interpreting such provisions as the equal-
protection clause of the Fourteenth Amendment. He summarized these views in *United States v. Virginia* (1996):

> [I]n my view the function of this Court is to *preserve* our
> society's values regarding (among other things) equal protec-
> tion, not to *revise* them; to prevent backsliding from the de-
> gree of restriction the Constitution imposed upon democratic
> government, not to prescribe, on our own authority, pro-
> gressively higher degrees. For that reason it is my view that,
> whatever abstract tests we may choose to devise, they cannot

supersede—and indeed ought to be crafted *so as to reflect*—
those constant and unbroken national traditions that embody
the people's understanding of ambiguous constitutional texts.
More specifically, it is my view that "when a practice not
expressly prohibited by the text of the Bill of Rights bears
the endorsement of a long tradition of open, widespread, and
unchallenged use that dates back to the beginning of the Republic, we have no proper basis for striking it down."[5]

These are among the principles that Antonin Scalia not only
insists he lives by as a justice, but demands of all other justices.
It was these principles that brought him to the attention of those
responsible for his appointment, first to the Court of Appeals
for the District of Columbia Circuit and then to the United
States Supreme Court. These are the principles he continues to
espouse in lectures and decisions even following *Bush v. Gore.*

In joining the majority opinion in *Bush v. Gore,* Antonin
Scalia violated every single one of these salutary principles to
enable him to vote his political preferences. Not only did he
violate these rules, but he did so specifically in order to avoid
their intended prophylactic effect.

Consider Scalia's admonition against the Supreme Court's
announcing "unique" dispositions rather than performing its
"principal function" of establishing precedent—that is, setting
forth principles of law that every court in America must follow,
based on the "rationale . . . of its earlier decisions." It would be
difficult to imagine an opinion more inconsistent with these
principles than the majority opinion in *Bush v. Gore.* The majority went out of its way to emphasize that its disposition in
this case was unique, based on the totality of the circumstances
and not on principles of general applicability to future cases:
"Our consideration is limited to the present circumstances, for
the problem of equal protection in election processes generally
presents many complexities."

First of all, this claim is utterly unconvincing as a matter of fact. Election cases present no greater complexities than many other types of cases, such as those involving the death penalty, affirmative action, or the rights of the indigent. Indeed, the majority in *Bush v. Gore* focused on the *non*complexity of the "thing" at issue in this case—a simple ballot with "marks or holes or scratches" on it. Moreover, even if election cases presented a unique set of complexities—not subject to general principles of broad applicability—that very uniqueness would be a good reason why Scalia would normally refrain from having the Supreme Court decide the case, since unique dispositions leave the justices who joined them free to say precisely what Scalia believes justices should not feel free to say: namely, that "on balance, we think the law was violated here," but in the next case, the "totality of the circumstances" may seem different and we will therefore be free to decide it differently without being accused of "inconsistency." Yet that is precisely what the majority justices left themselves room to do in the next case after deciding this one on their political preferences.

Moreover, *Bush v. Gore* does not build on the past or fit into any clear line of precedent. Indeed, as I have shown in Chapter 2, it is dramatically at odds with prior equal-protection precedents. And the majority gave no reasons for ignoring these precedents—precedents it will almost certainly continue to follow in future cases. These precedents in no way constrained the justices from indulging their "political or policy preferences" in this one important case.

Nor did the decision in *Bush v. Gore* satisfy Scalia's criteria of "predictability" and "reckonability." If it is true, as I have argued, that the one hundred most experienced Court watchers could not have predicted this decision (without knowing the names or party affiliations of the litigants), then the decision did not possess this "needful characteristic of any law worthy of the name."

Finally, and most troubling, are the merits of the equal-protection decision itself and the inconsistency between the result reached and Scalia's own criteria for finding a violation of the equal-protection clause. Scalia has repeatedly said that his job is not to "revise" the equal-protection clause, nor to "prescribe" on his own authority "progressively higher degrees" of equality. The equal-protection clause, in his view, cannot "supersede . . . those constant and unbroken national traditions that embody the people's understanding of ambiguous constitutional texts." He has argued, specifically, that when a practice "not expressly prohibited by the text of the Bill of Rights bears the endorsement of a long tradition of open, widespread, and unchallenged use that dates back to the beginning of the Republic, we have no proper basis for striking it down."

The Florida standard for hand-counting votes—the clear intent of the voter—fits precisely into Scalia's criteria for a law or practice that should not be struck down: It is not expressly prohibited by the text of the Constitution, it bears the endorsement of many states over a long period of time, and it has never previously been challenged. Yet Scalia voted to strike it down, despite his previous strong view that there is no proper basis for striking down such a standard. Nor has Scalia ever before demanded perfection for a state legislative standard to withstand constitutional scrutiny: "[T]he value of perfection in judicial decisions should not be overrated."[6] "This is a world in which nothing is flawless," he has said, citing "G. K. Chesterton's observation that a thing worth doing is worth doing badly"[7]—except, it seems, if that thing is hand-counting votes that may give victory to Scalia's political opponents. In another case, Scalia presciently warned that if the Supreme Court tries to "inject itself into every field of human activity where irrationality and oppression may theoretically occur," it "will destroy itself."[8]

Nor was Chief Justice Rehnquist's concurring opinion based

on Article II of the Constitution, in which Scalia joined, consistent with Scalia's previously expressed philosophy. It, too, was limited to the unique facts of this case involving a presidential election. It announced no general principles and was inconsistent with the deference usually accorded state courts in the interpretation of their own statutes. Moreover, it failed to acknowledge the existence of long-established Florida law—particularly the wrong-pencil case described in Chapter 2—that undermined its implication that the Florida Supreme Court had changed the law after the election to ensure a Gore victory. Most fundamentally, it omitted any reference to the most important—and highly relevant—precedent in Supreme Court history, *Marbury v. Madison,* a case that is entirely inconsistent with the central assertion in the Rehnquist opinion: that under Article II the text of a statute must be given "independent significance" beyond "its interpretation by the courts of the state." This concept—that any state statute can be self-defining and somehow exist in a realm independent of the long-accepted mechanism for interpreting it—is so radically at odds with, and alien to, the American history of judicial review since *Marbury v. Madison* that it is difficult to reconcile it with Scalia's judicial philosophy of accepting constitutional practices that enjoy a long tradition of unchallenged use.

Additionally, the three justices, in substituting their interpretation of what the Florida legislature meant for the interpretation of the Florida Supreme Court over the years, did precisely what Antonin Scalia said it was improper for a judge to do:

The practical threat is that, under the guise or even self-delusion of pursuing unexpressed legislative intents, common-law judges will, in fact, pursue their own objectives and desires, extending their own lawmaking prerogatives from the common law to the statutory field.[9]

Scalia might reply that this is also what the Florida Supreme Court did when it interpreted the Florida legislation. There are, however, several important differences—differences that Scalia would ordinarily acknowledge. First, the Florida interpretation predates this case and was part of a long process of interpreting Florida's election law that spanned three-quarters of a century. The Florida Supreme Court could not be accused, as the Supreme Court now stands accused, of simply making it up for the purposes of this case and this result. Second, if the Florida legislature was in disagreement with this long-standing interpretation, it had a remedy: It could have clarified or changed the law. Third, if the people of Florida were dissatisfied with what their state supreme court had done, they, too, had a remedy: They could employ the political processes of Florida to change the makeup of its supreme court. No such remedies are available when it is the United States Supreme Court that interprets Florida law. Finally, it is not the job of the nation's highest court to impose its theory of statutory interpretation on state court judges.

Scalia's previous writings are also inconsistent with the notion, put forward by several of the majority's defenders,[10] that the decision was intended to save the nation from the "political crisis" that would have occurred if the election had been thrown into the House of Representatives, as the Constitution mandates in the event of a deadlock. In a previous case, Scalia condemned "the ad hoc approach to constitutional adjudication . . . that will make the majority of the Court happy" and said that he preferred "to rely upon the judgment of the wise men who constructed our system, and of the people who approved it, and of two centuries of history that have shown it to be sound."[11] But this sort of ad hoc approach is exactly what he took in *Bush v. Gore.*

Justice Scalia's dissent in yet another case could serve as an object lesson about the Florida election case:

[B]y foreclosing all democratic outlet for the deep passions this issue arouses, by banishing the issue from the political forum that gives all participants, even the losers, the satisfaction of a fair hearing and an honest fight, by continuing the imposition of a rigid national rule instead of allowing for regional differences, the Court merely prolongs and intensifies the anguish.

We should get out of this area, where we have no right to be, and where we do neither ourselves nor the country any good by remaining.[12]

But in *Bush v. Gore*, Scalia willingly jumped feet first into this highly political area, imposing the sort of rigid rule he had previously excoriated and forcing the banishment of the issue from the political forum.

Perhaps the most challenging test of long-espoused philosophies arises when they come into conflict with strongly held immediate preferences. The Florida election case, with its high stakes, presented such a test to Antonin Scalia. His personal and political views strongly favored a Bush victory, while his judicial philosophy and his previously stated approach to the role of courts under our Constitution plainly favored nonintervention by the Supreme Court. Throughout his professional life, Scalia has boasted about his fidelity to principle and the subordination of his personal views to the Constitution. The overarching policy underlying Scalia's philosophy has been to constrain justices from imposing their own values on the nation, especially when these personal or political values are strongly held. At his confirmation hearing, Scalia said he worried about whether his decisions reflected "the most fundamental, deeply felt beliefs of our society, which is what a constitution means, [or whether], I am reflecting the most deeply felt beliefs of Scalia, which is not what I want to impose on the society."[13] Had he passed the test posed by this case, history might well have remembered him as the man of principle he claims to be. It would have constituted his judicial profile in courage. But he failed the test, and failed it badly. His vote was entirely inconsistent with the restraining rules he has claimed to live by. He ignored these rules in the Florida election case specifically in order to escape their restraints. He even lacked the courage to try to justify what he was doing by writing a separate opinion on the merits[14]—which he often does when he feels that his actions require explanation.[15] Judged by his own standards, Scalia is guilty of precisely what he has accused others of doing: being part of a "self-righteous Supreme Court, acting on its members' personal views of what would make a more perfect union [who] impose [their] own favored . . . dispositions."[16] His life work must be judged by what he has done, not by what he has said is the right thing to do. What he did in this case cannot be justified by any acceptable standard of judicial behavior. He peeked beneath the blindfold of justice and decided the case not on neutral principles or precedents designed to govern future cases, but rather on the basis of whom he wanted to see win this election. In doing so he violated his judicial oath to do justice "without respect to persons. . . ."

Justice O'Connor

[T]o turn these matters over to the federal judiciary is to inject the courts into the most heated partisan issues. . . . I do not believe . . . that the Framers of the Constitution intended the judicial power to encompass the making of such fundamental choices about how this Nation is to be governed.
—Davis v. Bandemer, 478 U.S. 109 (1986),
O'Connor concurring

In Chapter 2, we saw how inconsistent the majority opinion is with the prior equal-protection rulings of the Court in general.

It is also inconsistent with the approach to equal protection specifically taken by Justice O'Connor in her prior decisions. Until she joined the majority's equal-protection decision in *Bush v. Gore,* O'Connor had insisted that racial discrimination lies at the core of equal protection and that the Court should be reticent about telling states how to define equality in contexts where there is no discrimination based on suspect classifications, such as race or gender. Even in paradigmatic cases of alleged racial discrimination, she has found no violation of the equal-protection clause in the absence of a discriminatory purpose. According to her consistent pattern of decisions in such cases, a discriminatory *effect,* even if proved conclusively, is simply not enough. Based on that bedrock principle, she cast the deciding vote in the 1987 case of *McCleskey v. Kemp*—the Georgia case that ultimately sent dozens of black defendants to execution despite compelling statistical evidence that black defendants convicted of killing white victims were far more likely to be sentenced to death than white defendants who killed black victims.[17] It is sufficient to point out here that in the thirteen years between that decision and the Florida election case, O'Connor had never departed from the principle that formed the core of that ruling: that absent a discriminatory purpose—a purpose not present in *Bush v. Gore*—it does not violate equal protection to execute blacks under a system of capital punishment that produces a discriminatory effect.[18]

Yet despite the fact that discrimination against blacks lies at the historical root of the equal-protection clause and the fact that there was not even an allegation of racial discrimination in the Florida election case, O'Connor abandoned her long-held principles and precedents and voted to invent a new equal-protection right—for use in this case and this election only—in order to ensure the victory of the candidate whose election she supported. She also ignored her own decision in a 1995 case holding that no equal-protection challenge can succeed without a "showing of individualized harm" by a specific victim or class of victims.[19] In *Bush v. Gore,* there was no such showing, and there was no such victim or class. O'Connor's votes to grant a stay and then to end the hand count without a remand were also inconsistent with her prior decisions regarding such matters.[20]

Finally, as the quotation at the beginning of this section suggests, O'Connor's long-expressed judicial philosophy—from her confirmation process until the Florida election case—stood strongly against Supreme Court intervention into political questions, especially when these questions have been decided by state courts. Until this case, she—a former state court judge— had been a champion of the powers of state courts to interpret their own laws, and she had applauded the reticence of federal courts, including the Supreme Court, to become involved with such partisan issues.[21] It was this long-held philosophy that worried Bush lawyers when the equal-protection challenge was first proposed. As Ben Ginsberg, chief counsel for the Republicans, recalled, "[T]here was some concern about O'Connor as a former state legislator, that she might believe the Supreme Court should not intervene."[22] It turned out they had little to worry about, because O'Connor would not let her judicial philosophy get in the way of the political result she wanted in this case.

These departures from precedent are particularly damning for Justice O'Connor, because she has written so consistently and eloquently about the force of precedent.[23] Of all the members of the Supreme Court who participated in the Florida election case, few have been more vocal in their support of consistency and congruence with earlier cases. She has insisted that "any departure from the doctrine of *stare decisis* demands special justification."[24] This is especially true of "long-established precedent that has become integrated into the fabric of the law." Overruling such precedent may have dire consequences for "the ideal of the rule of law."[25]

Although she almost certainly would not have joined the original decisions in such cases as *Roe v. Wade* and *Miranda v. Arizona*, O'Connor has voted to reaffirm these controversial decisions. She jointly authored the Court's majority opinion in *Planned Parenthood v. Casey* (1992), which emphasized the "obligation to follow precedent" unless specified conditions—for example, that a priori prior rule "has proven to be intolerable" or "unworkable"—are clearly met. She joined the Court's opinion in *Dickerson v. U.S.*, a case decided only six months before *Bush v. Gore*, which said:

> Whether or not we would agree with *Miranda*'s reasoning and its resulting rule, were we addressing the issue in the first instance, the principles of *stare decisis* weigh heavily against overruling it now.[26]

O'Connor ignored these salutary principles in the Florida election case within six months of agreeing with them in the *Dickerson* case, joining an opinion that simply ignored precedent and created a novel equal-protection argument that explicitly disavows any claim to establishing a precedent for future cases. Although there is a difference between expressly overruling prior precedent and silently ignoring it, the difference cuts against one of the primary principles underlying fidelity to precedent—namely, constraining individual justices from substituting their personal preferences for the institutional and historical rulings of the Court. Expressly overruling precedent requires the articulation of reasons, whereas simply ignoring it in one political case can be done with far less accountability. O'Connor ignored the dangers to the Supreme Court, and to the nation, from a Court that abandons consistency with principle and precedent—a danger about which she wrote so eloquently eight years earlier in *Planned Parenthood v. Casey*:

The country's loss of confidence in the Judiciary would be underscored by an equally certain and equally reasonable condemnation for another failing in overruling unnecessarily and under pressure. Some cost will be paid by anyone who approves or implements a constitutional decision where it is unpopular, or who refuses to work to undermine the decision or to force its reversal. The price may be criticism or ostracism, or it may be violence. An extra price will be paid by those who themselves disapprove of the decision's results when viewed outside of constitutional terms, but who nevertheless struggle to accept it, because they respect the rule of law. To all those who will be so tested by following [*sic*], the Court implicitly undertakes to remain steadfast, lest in the end a price be paid for nothing. The promise of constancy, once given, binds its maker for as long as the power to stand by the decision survives and the understanding of the issue has not changed so fundamentally as to render the commitment obsolete. From the obligation of this promise, the Court cannot and should not assume any exemption when duty requires it to decide a case in conformance with the Constitution. A willing breach of it would be nothing less than *a breach of faith,* and no Court that broke its faith with the people could sensibly expect credit for principle in the decision by which it did that. (Emphasis added)

She then warned about the difficulty of restoring lost trust:

It is true that diminished legitimacy may be restored, but only slowly. Unlike the political branches, a Court thus weakened could not seek to regain its position with a new mandate from the voters, and even if the Court could somehow go to the polls, the loss of its principled character could not be retrieved by the casting of so many votes. Like the character of an individual, the legitimacy of the Court must be earned over time.[27]

The dissenting justices in *Bush v. Gore* couldn't have said it better.

Justice Kennedy

Non-uniformity cannot be equated with constitutional infirmity.
—Pacific Mutual Life Ins. Co. v. Haslip, 499 U.S. 1, 41 (1991),
Kennedy concurring

The formulation of uniform rules to determine intent [is constitutionally] necessary.
—Bush v. Gore, 121 S. Ct. 525, 530 (2000)

In the days leading up to the decision, many legal experts viewed Anthony Kennedy as the justice most likely to break with the extreme right wing of the Court in *Bush v. Gore*. Kennedy, who was selected by President Reagan after the failed nomination of Robert Bork, is usually classified as a moderate-conservative justice. Although he generally sides with the Rehnquist-Scalia-Thomas group—especially in criminal cases—he sometimes, either alone or with O'Connor, joins with Breyer, Ginsburg, Souter, and Stevens,[28] especially in following established law rather than breaking new ground. He was seen, prior to this case, as far less ideological and—like O'Connor—more committed to following precedent than his fellow Reagan appointees: "He strikes those who know him as a quiet pragmatic [political and legal conservative], open to persuasion."[29] Unlike some other justices, he is regarded by experienced Supreme Court litigators as someone who will occasionally change his mind on the basis of a good argument. A lawyer who often argues before the Supreme

Court told me: "Kennedy actually uses his ears during oral argument, as contrasted with Scalia, who uses only his mouth." At the time his nomination was under consideration by the Senate Judiciary Committee, his supporters pointed to the fact that the five hundred or so opinions he had written during his twelve years on the Court of Appeals for the Ninth Circuit "are cautiously and narrowly crafted, sticking close to precedent and avoiding sweeping statements on social issues."[30] Kennedy himself assured the senators of his commitment to the principles of judicial restraint: "The court must adhere to the text of the Constitution and the controlling statutes as they have been announced, not as the courts wish to see them applied."[31] And until this case, Kennedy had generally followed these principles.[32]

As already argued, neither the text of the Constitution nor the case law supported Supreme Court intervention in the Florida presidential election, and Florida was employing a standard little different from that long used in other states without challenge. Usually this combination would ensure that Kennedy would follow the course of judicial restraint, which he has long espoused. Gore's lawyers were cautiously optimistic, therefore, that despite Kennedy's Republican background, he would follow his principles and not join an unprecedented decision ending the hand count on equal-protection grounds. Especially encouraging was the fact that Kennedy, in his years on the Court, had always insisted that "nonuniformity" in the application of broad, flexible standards—such as the clear intent of the voter— did not give rise to an equal-protection violation.

Until the Florida election case, Justice Kennedy's views on equal protection had been similar to those long articulated by Justice O'Connor. He voted to affirm numerous death-penalty cases against claims that capital punishment is administered in a racially discriminatory manner. He, too, has insisted that an equal-protection claimant must show purposeful discrimination based on race (or another invidious classification such as gender or national origin), as well as actual victimization. Moreover, Kennedy's approach has been marked by its flexibility and acceptance of wide discretion in the administration of general standards, such as voter intent. One case in particular illustrates his prior attitude toward nonuniformity in general. In voting to uphold punitive damage awards in tort cases, he cited the flexibility permitted even in capital sentencing:

> Some inconsistency of jury results can be expected for at least two reasons. First, the jury is empanelled to act as a decisionmaker in a single case, not as a more permanent body. As a necessary consequence of their case-by-case existence, juries may tend to reach disparate outcomes based on the same instructions. Second, the generality of the instructions may contribute to a certain lack of predictability. The law encompasses standards phrased at varying levels of generality. *As with other adjudicators,* the jury may be instructed to follow a rule of certain and specific content in order to yield uniformity at the expense of considerations of fairness in the particular case; or, as in this case, *the standard can be more abstract and general* to give the adjudicator flexibility in resolving the dispute at hand.
>
> These features of the jury system for assessing punitive damages discourage uniform results, but nonuniformity cannot be equated with constitutional infirmity.[33]

In that decision, Kennedy did not single out the jury as a unique institution. Instead, he generalized about all fact-finding bodies, specifically comparing the jury to "other adjudicators." Among these other adjudicators, arguably, are voting officials. Yet without making any reference to his previous decisions and his unwillingness to condemn nonuniformity, Kennedy ruled in *Bush v. Gore* that nonuniformity alone made the Florida hand count unconstitutional.[34]

Kennedy went on in the punitive damages case to caution about the limited role of federal courts in dictating to the states how much discretion they should give to adjudicators:

> In my view, the principles mentioned above and the usual protections given by the laws of the particular State must suffice until judges or legislators authorized to do so initiate system-wide change. We do not have the authority, as do judges in some of the States, to alter the rules of the common law respecting the proper standard for awarding punitive damages and the respective roles of the jury and the court in making that determination. Were we sitting as state-court judges, the size and recurring unpredictability of punitive damages awards might be a convincing argument to reconsider those rules or to urge a reexamination by the legislative authority. We are confined in this case, however, to interpreting the Constitution, and from this perspective I agree that we must reject the arguments advanced by petitioner.

Although election cases are different from tort cases and capital punishment cases, and although vote counters are not exactly the same as jurors, the principles of equal protection applicable to different kinds of cases should bear some similarity to each other. There must, after all, be some general principle underlying the equal-protection clause. That general principle, according to Kennedy, is that "nonuniformity cannot be equated with constitutional infirmity," and if that principle governs in cases involving punitive damages and the death penalty, it should also govern in vote-counting cases. It is true that in the former cases, a jury is evaluating people and complex actions, whereas in the voting case, an election official is examining a ballot. But as I have shown in Chapter 2, this is a difference of degree and not of kind, and in all of these cases, narrower and more uniform standards would be feasible. Yet Kennedy has never insisted on uni-

formity in other contexts. Only in the voting context—and perhaps not even in all voting cases—does he now demand "specific
rules designed to ensure uniform treatment."

Justice Kennedy abandoned his long-held principles when he
wrote the per curiam opinion in the Florida election. Like the
other majority justices, he also ignored his own precedents in
stay cases: He had voted to deny stays and allow defendants to
be executed even in cases where the Supreme Court had already
granted review. In ignoring these past decisions and principles,
he also ignored the importance he had always attributed to past
precedents of the Court. Recall that he, too, was one of the
authors of the Court's joint opinion in *Planned Parenthood v.
Casey,* which spoke so eloquently about the need to follow past
precedents even when one may not agree with them.[35] He also
joined the Court's opinion in *Dickerson,* in which an extremely
unpopular prior decision—*Miranda v. Arizona*—was reaffirmed despite the disagreement that he and several other justices had with it. In the Florida election case, Justice Kennedy
ignored precedents he *did* agree with—and will again agree with
in the future. It is clear to me, and to many others, that he
would not have ignored these precedents had the shoe been on
the other foot.

Chief Justice Rehnquist

Don't bother so much with the reasoning.
It will only trip you up.
—Chief Justice Rehnquist giving advice to another justice
struggling with the reasoning in an opinion, cited in
Edward Lazarus, *Closed Chambers*

According to Linda Greenhouse, who reports on the Supreme
Court for the *New York Times,* it was Chief Justice Rehnquist
who quarterbacked the high court's intervention into the Flor-

ida recount case: "Although his role was less visible [than Scalia's], Chief Justice Rehnquist took an active part from the beginning in shaping the Court's response to the events in Florida."[36] This should not surprise anyone familiar with Rehnquist's long history of unprincipled, partisan judicial activism and his freewheeling approach to the Constitution as a means of serving his political and ideological and personal agendas. I don't know anybody who had any real doubt that Rehnquist would vote to decide the case in favor of Bush. He has always been known as a result-oriented judge who never let judicial philosophy stand in the way of his politics. He also has a disturbing history in relation to the equal-protection clause of the Fourteenth Amendment, which I will discuss shortly.

Justice Rehnquist, though joining with Justice Scalia and Thomas in their separate opinion based on Article II, also joined the per curiam equal-protection opinion. Yet Justice Rehnquist's previously expressed grudging views on equal protection appear to be even more at odds with the rationale in the per curiam opinion than those of the other justices. Perhaps his willingness to join an opinion with which he fundamentally disagreed in order to achieve a result he very much wanted was an example of the advice he once gave another justice: "Don't bother so much with the reasoning." For Rehnquist, it has always been the result that counts.

Rehnquist has insisted that the equal-protection clause was designed to deal with racial discrimination, both insidious and benign. This limitation to racial discrimination is more than ironic in light of Rehnquist's approval of state-supported racial segregation earlier in his career.[37] When race was used primarily to *discriminate* against blacks, Rehnquist saw no equal-protection problem caused by racial discrimination. But now that race is used primarily to *benefit* blacks, in the affirmative-action context, suddenly Rehnquist has become a convert to a color-blind view of equal protection. While any classification based on race or ethnicity, whether its purpose is to accomplish segregation or affirmative action, is suspect, that is not the case with regard to nonracial (or closely related) classifications.[38] In an opinion dissenting from a ruling that discrimination against aliens requires special scrutiny,* Rehnquist wrote the following:

> The principal purpose of those who drafted and adopted the 14th Amendment was to prohibit the States from invidiously discriminating by reason of race . . . and, because of this plainly manifested intent, classifications based on race have rightly been held "suspect" under the Amendment. But there is no language used in the Amendment, nor any historical evidence as to the intent of the Framers, which would suggest to the slightest degree that it was intended to render alienage a "suspect" classification, that it was designed in any way to protect "discrete and insular minorities" other than racial minorities. . . . Our society, consisting of over 200 million individuals of multitudinous origins, customs, tongues, beliefs, and cultures is, to say the least, diverse. It would hardly take extraordinary ingenuity for a lawyer to find "insular and discrete" minorities at every turn in the road. Yet, unless the Court can precisely define and constitutionally justify both the terms and analysis it uses, these decisions today stand for the proposition that the Court can choose a "minority" it "feels" deserves "solicitude" and thereafter prohibit the States from classifying that "minority" differently from the "majority." I cannot find, and the Court does not cite, any constitutional authority for such a "ward of the Court" approach to equal protection.[39]

---

*Black's Law Dictionary defines strict scrutiny as the test that "requires state to establish that it has compelling interest justifying [a federal or state law that is found to adversely affect a fundamental right and] . . . that distinctions created by law are necessary to further some governmental purpose."

Nor has Rehnquist generally advocated strict scrutiny in other equal-protection contexts, especially in cases in which it is impossible to identify the group—whether "insular," "discrete," or anything else—that was denied the equal protection of the law.[40]

Prior to the Florida case, all Rehnquist seemed to have required, in equal-protection challenges not involving race-related discrimination, was that the state have a rational basis for the classification it has chosen. Moreover, he has recognized that the state cannot possibly account for every contingency with specificity and that it need strive only "for a level of generality that is administratively practicable." He has acknowledged that some inequality may have to be tolerated because of the impossibility of attaining perfect equality in the real world,[41] and he has been extremely critical of the kind of judicial intervention in which he himself joined in *Bush v. Gore.* In an earlier case,[42] he had criticized other justices for having

> produced a syndrome wherein this Court seems to regard the Equal Protection Clause as a cat-o'-nine-tails to be kept in the judicial closet as a threat to legislatures which may, in the view of the judiciary, get out of hand and pass "arbitrary," "illogical," or "unreasonable" laws. Except in the area of the law in which the Framers obviously meant it to apply—classifications based on race or on national origin, the first cousin of race—the Court's decisions can fairly be described as an endless tinkering with legislative judgments, a series of conclusions unsupported by any central guiding principle.

He went on to caution that

> in providing the Court with the duty of enforcing such generalities as the Equal Protection Clause, the Framers of the

Civil War Amendments placed it in the position of Adam in the Garden of Eden. As members of a tripartite institution of government which is responsible to no constituency, and which is held back only by its own sense of self-restraint . . . we are constantly subjected to the human temptation to hold that any law containing a number of imperfections denies equal protection simply because those who drafted it could have made it a fairer or a better law.

In *Bush v. Gore,* Rehnquist easily succumbed to the temptation to use the equal-protection clause to declare unconstitutional an arguably "imperfect" law that had nothing to do with the central concerns of the Fourteenth Amendment, has long been in use in several states, and did not discriminate against anyone.

Rehnquist's long-standing approach to equal protection would seem entirely consistent with upholding the Florida law, which, by mandating the clear intent of the voter as the governing standard, strove for a level of generality that is administratively practicable and, indeed, practiced in many other states.[43] Yet Rehnquist joined the opinion striking down the Florida law and stopping the recount. He did not let "reasoning" trip him up. He knew where he wanted to end up—with Bush as president—and to accomplish that result, he joined an equal-protection decision that was totally at odds with his previously expressed views.

Nor was his concurring opinion ending the recount on Article II grounds consistent with his previously expressed views about the role of the Supreme Court in regard to matters generally left to the states. Since his earliest years on the high court, Rehnquist has expressed concern over the propensity of "the national government"—including the Supreme Court—to "devour the essentials of state sovereignty," which in his view are protected by the Tenth Amendment.[44] Few matters are more essential to state sovereignty than the power of the state supreme court to interpret its own laws without being second-guessed by federal judges. More recently, Rehnquist has restated a position that, he says, is among the "first principles" of federalism: that the federal government has limited powers in relationship to the states. Quoting James Madison, he has insisted that the powers "delegated . . . to the federal government are few and defined."[45] Before *Bush v. Gore,* these powers were never understood to include telling a state supreme court that it could not interpret a state election statute consistent with how it has been interpreted for more than three-quarters of a century.

Chief Justice Rehnquist would not ordinarily subscribe to the pragmatic argument that despite the absence of explicit constitutional authority, it is the job of the Supreme Court to intervene in order to avoid a political crisis. He has written eloquently about how the Framers of our Constitution realized that "no charter of government could possibly anticipate every future contingency, and they, therefore, left considerable room for 'play in the joints.'"[46] Yet in this case, he left no room for the election to be resolved by the political processes mandated by the Constitution.

It is simply inconceivable to me, and I suspect to many other students of Rehnquist's prior decisions, that he would have voted to stop this hand count—on any constitutional ground—had the beneficiary of that ruling been Al Gore.

Justice Thomas

In my view, [if judges] are not impartial,
they are no longer judges.
—Justice Thomas in a speech before the Federalist Society
National Convention, November 12, 1999

The heart of Thomas's strategy for striking back at his liberal
critics is, of course, to utilize the Supreme Court itself.
—Jeffrey Toobin, "The Burden of Clarence Thomas,"
The New Yorker, September 27, 1993

Prior to the Florida recount case, Justice Thomas's views on equal protection were extremely narrow and grudging. In a 1996 dissenting opinion, he wrote:

> [T]he Equal Protection Clause shields only against purposeful discrimination: A disparate impact, even upon members of a racial minority, the classification of which we have been most suspect, does not violate equal protection. The Clause is not a panacea for perceived social or economic inequity; it seeks to "guarantee equal laws, not equal results." . . . [W]e have regularly required more of an equal protection claimant than a showing that state action has a harsher effect on him or her than on others. . . . Our frequent pronouncements that the Fourteenth Amendment is not violated by disparate impact have spanned challenges to statutes alleged to affect disproportionately members of one race . . . members of one sex . . . and poor persons seeking to exercise protected rights.[47]

Both in his opinions and in his public statements, Thomas has railed against using the courts to achieve the kind of perfect symmetry or equality demanded by the majority in the Florida election case. In an earlier case, he made the following point:

> Whether embodied in the Fourteenth Amendment or inferred from the Fifth, *equal protection is not a license for courts to judge the wisdom, fairness, or logic of legislative choices.*

He quoted the following passage from *Vance v. Bradley* with approval:

> The Constitution presumes that, absent some reason to infer antipathy, even improvident decisions will eventually be rectified by the democratic process and that judicial intervention is generally unwarranted no matter how unwisely we may think a political branch has acted.[48]

Thomas has also complained about courts substituting their personal or political predilections for the rules, messy as they may be, set out in the Constitution. In a previous voting rights case, he argued:

> The choice [of how legislatures engage in redistricting] is inherently a political one, and depends upon the selection of a theory for defining the fully "effective" vote. . . . In short, what a court is actually asked to do in a vote dilution case is "to choose among competing bases of representation—ultimately, really, among competing theories of political philosophy." . . . Such matters of political theory are beyond the ordinary sphere of federal judges. . . . The matters the Court has set out to resolve in vote dilution cases are questions of political philosophy, not questions of law. As such, they are not readily subjected to any judicially manageable standards that can guide courts in attempting to select between competing theories.[49]

In other words, the Supreme Court should not be in the business of choosing among different ways that a state may decide to count votes. Yet in *Bush v. Gore,* too, there were "competing theories" regarding vote counting. Florida, along with several other states, had opted for a voter-intent theory, which erred on the side of overinclusion of questionable votes rather than

underinclusion. Yet Thomas joined an opinion denying Florida
the power to select "among competing theories of political philosophy."

Thomas also joined Chief Justice Rehnquist's concurring
opinion stopping the hand count on Article II grounds, having
previously joined numerous opinions extolling the powers of the
states in relation to the federal government. He joined the opinion in a 1992 decision that referred to a truth "so basic" it is
"like the air around us":

> States are not mere political subdivisions of the United States.
> State governments are neither regional offices nor adminis-
> trative agencies of the Federal Government. The positions
> occupied by state officials appear nowhere on the Federal
> Government's most detailed organizational chart. The Con-
> stitution instead "leaves to the several States a residuary and
> inviolate sovereignty" . . . reserved explicitly to the States by
> the Tenth Amendment.[50]

This, of course, must include the state's highest court if it has
been empowered by state law to interpret state statutes. But in
Bush v. Gore Thomas ignored these principles of federalism
when he joined the concurring opinion, which, for purposes of
a presidential election, treated the Supreme Court of Florida as
if it were a lower federal court that had erred in interpreting a
federal statute.[51]

In a 1995 case in which the Supreme Court struck down an
Arkansas term limitation amendment for members of the U.S.
House and Senate,[52] Justice Thomas wrote a scathing dissent
(joined by Chief Justice Rehnquist and Justices Scalia and
O'Connor) in which he extolled the virtues of state sovereignty
and the power of states, in the context of electing *federal* officials, to determine their own standards. Thomas focused on the
words of the Tenth Amendment, which leave all reserved pow-

ers to "the states respectively, or to the people." He interpreted
this as leaving the states entirely free to take any position they
choose "on the division of power between the state govern-
ments and the people of the States. It is up to the people of
each State to determine which 'reserved' powers their state government may exercise." Quite simply, in regard to elections,
Thomas is saying that it is up to the people of each state, including Florida, to decide how to allocate authority among the
voters, the state legislature, the courts, and any other state institutions. The federal government has no power to interfere
with any such allocation unless it violates the U.S. Constitution.
Pursuant to this power, the Florida legislature allocated to its
courts, including its Supreme Court, the power to interpret its
statutes, including its election statutes. Article II doesn't take
that power away in elections for presidential electors. As *Mc-
Pherson v. Blacker,* the 1892 case cited by Chief Justice Rehnquist in his concurrence, ruled, "[w]hat is forbidden or required
to be done by a state" in the context of Article II "is forbidden
or required of the legislative power under state constitutions *as
they exist.*"[53] Indeed, Justice Thomas explicitly referred, in his
opinion in *U.S. Term Limits v. Thornton,* to "even the selection
of the President—surely the most national of national figures"
as being accomplished by electors "chosen by the various
States." But in *Bush v. Gore,* Thomas joined an opinion that
would forbid the state of Florida to allocate to its own supreme
court the power to interpret and apply its own election laws in
a manner consistent with what it has been doing for generations.

These glaring and dramatic inconsistencies between the views
previously expressed by the majority justices and their decision
in *Bush v. Gore* are not merely the incidental or inevitable results of many cases with different law clerks over long judicial
careers. Rather, they go to the core of everything these justices

have stood for over many years—and will continue to stand for over the years to come. The centrality of these discrepancies raises a compelling inference of willfulness, deliberateness, and calculation in the making of the decision in the Florida case. This inference, in turn, raises the question of why. Why would these justices risk their reputations and that of the Court by rendering a decision that appears so partisan to so many?

Why?

One of the most venerable principles of law is that the prosecution need not establish a motive in order to prove guilt. Yet jurors inevitably speculate about motive, and the absence of one can be seen as evidence of innocence, just as the presence of one can add to the evidence of guilt. Accordingly, most prosecutors seek to introduce as much evidence of motive as is available and admissible, so that the jury may include it in its overall assessment of the case. Necessarily, any such evidence will be somewhat subjective, imprecise, and speculative, since no outsider can ever know with certainty which factors might have motivated certain actions, and even the actor himself may lack insights into his true motives, which are often mixed and not always conscious. Rationalization is a powerful force allowing people to believe that they were motivated by factors somewhat more elevated and acceptable than the ones that may actually have influenced their conduct.

Despite the difficulty of assessing motives, I know—as a practicing lawyer with many years of experience in trying to predict how judges will decide cases—how important this sort of informed speculation can be in making decisions about the nature of arguments to be presented, the likelihood of success, and the need to consider settling a case out of court. Lawyers must cut through the rationalizations, the abstractions, and the self-deception in order to give their clients commonsense advice about why judges decide cases the way they do. In order to make the kind of "prophecies"—predictions about what the courts will do—that Holmes saw as central to the law, lawyers not only have detailed knowledge about judges' prior decisions, but also have a perceptive understanding of what actually motivates judges in their decisions. Reading their past opinions is obviously necessary, but it is not sufficient. A good lawyer must go beyond the opinions and beneath the rhetoric to get at the essence of the judge. The courthouse scuttlebutt, the barroom gossip, the experiences of insiders, the insights of former law clerks—these are what the client pays to get, over and above what any first-year associate can find in the library. That is why local lawyers are an important part of any complete legal team.

A great lawyer needs an instinct for the jugular, a sense of what is really going on in the mind, heart, and soul of the judge. Nearly all the successful practicing lawyers I know have employed biographical information about justices to speculate about their motivations, and this is what the lawyers on both sides of this case did, in regard not only to the justices of the Supreme Court, but to the lower court judges as well.

Since I am both a practicing lawyer and an academic (with an extensive network of sources regarding the Supreme Court justices), I feel it part of my responsibility to my readers to share with them all of the tools I commonly employ in my work—to serve as a kind of "local counsel." These tools include both case analysis and the kind of biographical information and assessment of motives that I will now briefly present. I believe that even without any specific evidence of possible motives, I have made a compelling case in support of my accusation that none of the five majority justices would pass the shoe-on-the-other-foot test, and I leave it to each reader to decide how much weight, if any, to assign to this additional material.

Let me begin by acknowledging that an individual may have

more than one motive for a single act. A domestic killing may be motivated by love, hate, jealousy, fear, and financial benefit. A decision to abandon a long-held judicial philosophy in order to ensure the election of a particular candidate may be motivated by patriotism, ideology, partisanship, ambition, and the expectation of material benefit.

I have little doubt that each of the five majority justices was motivated, at least in part, by patriotism: They honestly believed that the election of George W. Bush would be best for the country, the world, and the Supreme Court. They no doubt believe strongly in the appointment of federal judges and justices who share their party background and jurisprudence, and they may even have felt that the actions of the Florida Supreme Court provided them with a moral (if not legal) justification for their actions.

Supreme Court justices are, of course, entitled to have strong political views and to act on them—on Election Day, when they cast their votes as ordinary citizens. They are not entitled, however, to act as partisan patriots when they are deciding a case as Supreme Court justices. When acting in that capacity, they have taken an oath to be politically blind to the identity, party affiliation, and ideology of the litigant-candidates whose case is before them. Their job as justices is not to decide who would make the best president, but to determine which litigant has the law on his side. This cannot be easy for any human being, even a judge, to do. Indeed, that is one of the many good reasons why judges should be, and generally have been, reluctant to decide election cases. Election cases are political by nature, and courts try to stay out of the political thicket. Elections are often rough-and-tumble affairs, not easily amenable to resolution by principles familiar to judges. And when judges decide hotly disputed elections, they "foreclose . . . all democratic outlets for the deep passions" engendered by these elections, as Justice Scalia once put it.[54]

In addition to these institutional reasons, judges may also have personal considerations that counsel caution about deciding elections, especially elections in which they, as citizens, have previously voted for one of the litigants. In such cases, they have declared their stake in the outcome. By voting for a particular candidate who is now a litigant in his court, the judge has indicated that he favors that candidate. Arguably, there are times when the stake is minor or nonexistent, as it might be in a local election for a relatively insignificant office. When the election is for president of the United States, however, it is likely that the judge, as a voter, feels somewhat strongly about what is best for the country, even if neither candidate is his absolute favorite. This is particularly true of Supreme Court justices, whose future colleagues will be nominated by the winner of the election, and for whom the composition of the Court determines their own status as majority or dissenting justices.[55]

There will, of course, be occasions on which judges have no choice but to decide election cases. In such cases, they are expected to put aside their political preferences, but this cannot be easy, even when a judge has no greater stake in the outcome of the election than any ordinary citizen. This is always uneasy terrain for a judge to traverse, since in the typical case, he has no interest in the outcome, beyond the duty to decide it correctly on its legal merits.

Oliver Wendell Holmes once described a good judge as one who has "no thought but that of which he is bound" and who has learned "to solve a problem according to the rules by transcending his own convictions and to leave room for much that he would hold dear to be done away with"—a difficult challenge for any human being even in a case in which he has no personal stake.[56] Judges are expected to confront that challenge in the election cases that occasionally come before them. But when a particular judge stands to benefit or lose something ma-

terial—something palpable, personal, or strongly ideological—
in addition to what every other citizen has at stake in a presidential election, it may be too much to ask that judge to decide
the case as if it were an ordinary litigation involving strangers,
with no possible impact on the judge's life. That is why the
rules of judicial conduct expressly forbid a judge to sit in any
case in which he or she has a personal interest. It doesn't matter
whether the judge is actually motivated—in whole or in part—
by the prospect of personal gain or loss. The possibility alone
creates an appearance of impropriety and casts suspicion on the
integrity of the judicial process.

I believe that some judges are capable of voting for one candidate on Election Day and then ruling against that candidate
in a postelection legal controversy. Indeed, many observers expected that Justice Kennedy and/or Justice O'Connor might do
just that. I myself harbored the belief that Justice Scalia might
decide the case on the basis of his strong views that the Court
should not become involved in a case such as this one. I know
of no experienced lawyer who realistically thought that Chief
Justice Rehnquist or Justice Thomas would decide the case in
Gore's favor.

In addition to the general patriotic-partisan motive that all
of the majority justices shared,[57] I believe that some of them had
additional possible motives to help ensure the election of
George W. Bush. In several instances these motives were so
obvious and public that several commentators called for certain
justices to recuse themselves from the case.[58] I do not know—
and I'm not even certain all of the justices themselves know—
whether these additional motives played any role (and if so,
how much of one) in their decision. Social scientists talk about
"overdetermination," meaning that a given act can be caused
by several factors, any one of which alone might have been
strong enough to have fully caused the act, and that may well
have been what happened in *Bush v. Gore*.

Justice O'Connor

The patriotic-partisan motive alone might well have caused Sandra Day O'Connor to decide the case in favor of Bush, even if she had not also had a unique personal motive to help guarantee a Bush victory. A closer look at the O'Connor situation may help us to understand both the difficulty and the importance of trying to assess motive in this kind of a situation. It may also help us understand why we need prophylactic rules of judicial disqualification in close cases involving the possible combination of proper and improper motives.

It has been widely reported that O'Connor was hoping for a Bush victory so that she could retire from the Supreme Court with the assurance that her replacement would be named by a Republican president. According to reports, O'Connor—who is seventy years old and a breast cancer survivor—was anxious to join her ailing husband in Arizona but planned to delay her retirement in the event of a Gore victory. A story in *Newsweek* reported that while watching the media coverage on election night with friends, she responded to news projections that Gore had won Florida by exclaiming, "This is terrible!" The *Newsweek* report continued:

> She explained to another partygoer that Gore's reported victory in Florida meant that the election was "over," since Gore had already carried two other swing states, Michigan and Illinois.
>
> Moments later, with an air of obvious disgust, she rose to get a plate of food, leaving it to her husband to explain her somewhat uncharacteristic outburst. John O'Connor said his wife was upset because they wanted to retire to Arizona, and a Gore win meant they'd have to wait another four years. O'Connor, the former Republican majority leader of the Ar-

izona State Senate and a 1981 Ronald Reagan appointee, did
not want a Democrat to name her successor. Two witnesses
described this extraordinary scene to *Newsweek*. Responding
through a spokesman at the high court, O'Connor had no
comment.[59]

Personal retirement plans constitute self-interest under the codes
of judicial conduct, and so if these reports are true, then
O'Connor probably should not have participated in any of the
presidential election cases. Whether or not she was actually influenced by this personal motivation, the possibility that she
might have been—or that reasonable observers could honestly
believe she was—is enough to raise a serious question about the
appearance of justice. One former Supreme Court law clerk,
noting O'Connor's "newly petulant attitude during oral arguments" in this case, commented that the high court's 5–4 vote
"has raised the specter that some of the conservative justices,
yearning for retirement, suffered from a serious conflict of interest when deciding the case."[60] The only other justice to whom
he could have been referring is Chief Justice Rehnquist, who
suffers from severe back problems; it has been widely reported
that he wishes to retire from the high court, but only if his
replacement will be named by a Republican president.[61] Unlike
O'Connor, he apparently did not talk as openly about his retirement plans or about how "terrible" a Gore victory would
have been. But the Bush administration is aware of Rehnquist's
wish to retire, and it is already gearing up to find a suitable
replacement.

Some of the lawyers with whom I have discussed the matter
have suggested that in O'Connor's case, her *personal* motive
may not have been the deciding factor, since she already had a
strong *political* inclination toward favoring a Bush victory, and
what she meant by "terrible" was terrible for the country, not

terrible for her and her retirement plans, despite her husband's statement to the contrary. She is, after all, a lifelong Republican who has served in various leadership roles in that party. She was "extremely active in the Arizona Republican Party and in Barry Goldwater's 1964 presidential campaign" and was co-chair of Richard Nixon's Arizona reelection campaign;[62] she served as the Republican leader of the state senate and was considered as a Republican candidate for governor. "She was a very political animal," said one observer at the time of her nomination. "She started out as a moderate Republican and then . . . moved toward the right."[63] After paying her dues to the Republican Party, she was brought to the attention of President Ronald Reagan by her law school classmate William Rehnquist and by Senator Barry Goldwater, though she had served as an Arizona intermediate appellate court judge for less than two years at the time.[64] She was interviewed by then–Justice Department lawyer Kenneth Starr, who reported back that she was a law-and-order judge who was likely to defer to other branches of government.[65] She was quickly nominated and confirmed as the first woman to serve on the Supreme Court.

She was not, of course, the first politically active elected official to serve on the high court, but traditionally politicians have left their partisanship behind when joining the Court. Not so with O'Connor. While serving as a justice, she has been criticized by judicial ethics experts on at least two occasions for using her position as a justice to support partisan Republican causes.[66] Such criticism is rare in the Court's history.

The first incident that raised ethical questions occurred in 1987, when O'Connor agreed to conduct a "private briefing" on the workings of the Supreme Court for Republicans who had contributed at least $10,000 to a political action group called GoPac, which was seeking to gain Republican control of Congress. She bowed out of this partisan fund-raising event only after ethics experts publicly criticized her actions as violating the

American Bar Association's Code of Judicial Conduct—but not until after her name had been used successfully in the fundraising solicitation. Two years later O'Connor responded to a request from an Arizona Republican asking her to write a letter in support of a proposed Republican Party resolution declaring the United States to be "a Christian Nation . . . based on the absolute law of the Bible, not a democracy." She did so, and her reply—written on Court stationery—was circulated as part of the campaign to help the Arizona Republican Party.[67] When her letter was publicly disclosed, Justice O'Connor issued a statement regretting that the "letter she had written to an acquaintance . . . was used in a political debate." The Court press office said that she had "had no idea" the letter would be used politically. The available evidence points to the opposite conclusion. The request itself made it unmistakably clear that she was being asked to write her letter specifically for use in the campaign by conservative Republicans to take votes away from Democrats in Arizona:

> Republicans are making some interesting advances in this heavily controlled Democratic area. Some of us are proposing a resolution which acknowledges that the Supreme Court ruled in 1892 that this is a Christian Nation. It would be beneficial and interesting to have a letter from you.[68]

Justice O'Connor has thus twice publicly endorsed partisan Republican causes. Her regrets—which were incomplete and misleading—came only after public criticism. Nothing in her background suggests that she would have risked criticism for comparable Democratic causes. In light of the close association she has maintained with Republican causes and officials, it came as no surprise when, in 1988, an aide to George H. Bush, then a presidential candidate, characterized O'Connor as a Bush "dream pick" for vice president if he received the Republican presidential nomination.[69]

Although O'Connor has not repeated her openly partisan mistakes in recent years, her obvious dismay at Gore's apparent victory on election night shows that her allegiance to her old party is still strong. The conservative Republican columnist Robert Novak, in a recent article praising Justice O'Connor's role as a "flexible politician" on the high court, quoted a "well-connected conservative lawyer" as saying that after nearly twenty years on the Court, she is "what she always has been and always will be: the Republican floor leader of the Arizona Senate."[70] If we accept this picture of O'Connor as a still-loyal Republican politician who has already acknowledged that she wants her replacement to be picked by a Republican president, we can certainly speculate that she might have voted for the Republican candidate for these reasons alone. According to this scenario, her vote was motivated not by personal, material considerations—namely, her wish to retire—but instead by party loyalty. Or, to put the best partisan face on it, she was motivated by a desire to see the best man elected as president.

She was also reportedly "furious" at the Florida Supreme Court for what she believed was its partisan intervention in favor of Gore. It is impossible to know whether this fury was institutional or personal: Would she have been as angry had a state court similarly intervened in favor of Bush?

There is, of course, no way to separate completely the personal from the partisan in this situation, because it is O'Connor's *choice* not to retire unless her replacement would be named by a Republican president. Were it not for this partisan choice, she could have satisfied her personal desire to retire at any time, regardless of who won the election.

Of course, even if the personal could be separated from the partisan, the suggestion that the deciding factor in her decision was her partisan support for the Republican candidate rather than her personal desire to retire does not put O'Connor in a much better light. Her judicial vote was improper if it was influenced by *either* personal or partisan political considerations. Her vote would be proper only if she would have voted exactly the same way if stopping the recount would have ensured a "terrible" Gore victory, rather than a personally and politically beneficial Bush victory. In order to prove this highly unlikely— and incomplete[71]—defense, one would have to demonstrate a pattern of judicial voting, in other relevant cases not involving personal or partisan outcomes, consistent with her vote in this case. Such a pattern is, to say the least, not evident.

If Election 2000 had been decided by a legislature of which O'Connor was a member, she certainly would have been questioned about her apparent conflict of interest. But because she is a justice of the Supreme Court—an institution deemed above partisanship—there is a tendency to resolve doubts in favor of her integrity. In this case, however, there do not appear to be real doubts to resolve. The available evidence, in my view, strongly suggests that Justice O'Connor, at the very least, had the appearance of a conflict of interest following her revealing statement on the night of the election. How much of a role, if any, her retirement motive played in causing her to fail the shoe-on-the-other-foot test is impossible to calibrate. That she did fail this test seems clear from the totality of evidence.

While O'Connor was in the process of being confirmed to the high court, she told the senators that she would like to be remembered with the following epitaph: "Here lies a good judge who upheld the Constitution."[72] She has recently acknowledged to a mutual friend that her vote in the election case may have hurt her reputation and endangered her place in history. She is right.

The crowning irony is that O'Connor may not now be able to retire from the Court without confirming the worst suspicions about her motives. A recent story in the *New York Times* has reported that "associates of Justice O'Connor have signaled that she wants it known that she will not retire after this term" (which ends in July, 2001).[73] I have also been told that O'Connor wants more time to rebuild her tarnished legacy and does not wish to be remembered by her vote in *Bush v. Gore*.

Justice Kennedy

Mixed motives may also have been at play with regard to Anthony Kennedy's decision to join the majority. I have been told by a source close to the Court that Anthony Kennedy has a quiet but determined ambition that could be satisfied only if Bush became president: He wants to become the next chief justice of the United States when William Rehnquist steps down, as he is expected to do now that a Republican president is in office.

Kennedy realized that because of his own background in Republican politics—he had ties to Ronald Reagan during Reagan's governorship and to Reagan's executive secretary, Edwin Meese, and had worked as a lobbyist—he would stand little chance of being promoted to chief justice by a Democratic president. He has confided his ambition to trusted friends and former law clerks, who have shared this information with my source. One former clerk has pointed out that in recent years, as the prospect of a vacancy has drawn closer, Kennedy has changed his vote in several cases to enhance his standing as a strong candidate to fill that vacancy.[74]

This speculation has also been reported by Robert Novak, who has excellent sources within the conservative movement: "Kennedy's recent swing to the right led court-watchers to conclude that he was readying himself for a chief justice vacancy in a Republican administration."[75] Novak had previously pinpointed one decision by Kennedy that "raised suspicions in legal circles that he is launching a campaign to be the next chief justice if a Republican is elected president."[76]

It has now been reliably reported—and I have been able to confirm independently—that Justice Kennedy was the primary author of the Court's final per curiam opinion.[77] I have also been told that Justice Kennedy wishes to have his authorship known to the Bush administration. In his campaign for the chief justiceship, he has emphasized that because of his generally moderate views, he is the only inside candidate who is confirmable by the Senate, but—as evidenced by his vote in *Bush v. Gore*—he is also a moderate who can be counted on when push comes to shove.

We can't know for certain whether my source is correct about Kennedy's ambition and, if so, whether it played any role in his vote in the Florida recount case. What we do know is that his vote and the arguments he presented in the opinion to support it were inconsistent with his previously expressed substantive views on equal protection, with his long-held attitudes toward the force of precedent, with his previous votes on stay applications, and with his frequently stated position on the limited role of courts in cases involving large issues of politics and policy. So at the very least, there is evidence of a motive other than the desire to follow his previous decisions and rule fairly.

There is no public information that would have justified Kennedy's recusal in this case, but if he in fact chose personal ambition or party loyalty over principle, then he has, in my view, morally disqualified himself from becoming chief justice or earning a place of honor in the history of the Supreme Court. A justice who once bends the rules to favor a particular litigant can never again be trusted not to break them if the stakes are sufficiently high. A justice who allows himself to become blinded by personal ambition should not be rewarded by having his ambition satisfied.

Justice Thomas

Clarence Thomas is a reliable member of the Court's right wing[78] and is also, according to people who know him well, consumed by the need to strike back at those Democrats who put him through the "high-tech lynching" of the Anita Hill hearings.[79] Thomas divides the world into friends and enemies. "Good versus evil" is how his wife, Virginia Thomas, described the "spiritual warfare" of his confirmation hearings, which left Thomas with a long enemies list consisting primarily of Democratic senators who voted against his confirmation—among them Al Gore and Joseph Lieberman.

At the time, Gore said his negative vote was based on Thomas's "judicial philosophy" and his testimony—which Gore did not believe—that he had never discussed *Roe v. Wade,* implying that he had no fixed views on the abortion issue. Lieberman, who originally supported Thomas's nomination, changed his mind after hearing Anita Hill's testimony, which, he concluded, was "believable." Gore also found Hill to be "believable and credible,"[80] which carried the implicit assertion that Thomas was lying. On the other hand, George W. Bush's father nominated Thomas to the Supreme Court, declaring him to be "the best man for the job," and stood behind him in the face of Democratic attacks. During the campaign, George W. Bush characterized Thomas, along with Antonin Scalia, as his two favorite justices. Gore criticized Bush for singling out these two justices, saying that "when the names of Scalia and Thomas are used as benchmarks for who would be appointed, those are code words."[81] One can only imagine how Thomas must have reacted to being characterized as a code word.[82]

Following his close confirmation, Thomas began to withdraw, both publicly and privately. He almost never spoke during Supreme Court arguments, though he had been an active questioner during his days on the Court of Appeals. According to one observer, Thomas "not only remained unvaryingly silent but looked uninterested, often not even bothering to remove the rubber band from his stack of briefs.[83] He stopped watching the news on television or reading mainstream newspapers or magazines. He limited his information sources to "reliably conservative publications" and to Rush Limbaugh—"[f]or entertainment, he says he likes to listen to tapes of Rush Limbaugh poking fun at feminists, environmentalists and all manner of liberal crusaders."[84] The groups he publicly says he likes to hear fun made of are, of course, often litigants in cases before him. He almost always rules against them.[85]

Thomas speaks primarily to right-wing groups, and he, too, was criticized for agreeing to give a dinner speech to the Claremont Institute, a group that was actively seeking President Clinton's impeachment, that was scheduled for just three days before the impeachment vote.[86] According to the *Los Angeles Times,* Thomas, "alone among the justices, . . . has spoken regularly before groups that espouse strongly conservative views,"[87] despite the Judicial Code of Conduct, which prohibits a judge from "being a speaker or guest of honor at an organization's fundraising events" or "making speeches for a political organization."[88] Thomas has spoken to and been honored by several partisan organizations that supported his nomination.[89] At one such event, he expressed his "sense of gratitude and sense of loyalty."[90] Thomas not only provided an "exclusive and challenging message deep from his heart" to the Concerned Women for America, but sat on cases in which they had filed briefs—and voted in favor of their positions.[91] His loyalty to those who supported him is as powerful—and as influential on his decisions—as his hatred for those who opposed him.

At the time of the Supreme Court's decision in the Florida recount case, Virginia Thomas was working for the Heritage Foundation, a conservative group with close ties to the Bush campaign, gathering resumes for the Bush transition team.[92]

Many observers, including a federal judge, believe that Justice Thomas should have recused himself from the case because of his wife's connections to the Republican Party and her substantial interest in a Bush victory.[93]

An even more compelling argument for his recusal would have been his abiding hatred for Gore and Lieberman (coupled with his deep sense of loyalty to the Bush family). According to Court watchers, even Thomas's "jurisprudence on the Court seemed guided to an unusual degree by raw anger."[94] Jeffrey Toobin quoted a longtime friend of the Thomases about the effect of the confirmation hearings on his role as a justice: "The real tragedy of this event is that his behavior on the court has been affected. He's still damaged. He's still reeling. He was hurt more deeply than anyone could comprehend." His anger continues to "churn within" him. According to a close friend, "[h]e never wants the world to forget the price he paid to get" on the Court. He refuses to "let bygones be bygones" lest that be seen as "capitulation" to his enemies. His rage on the subject of his confirmation "is evergreen."[95] Thomas has acknowledged that he was a very angry man even before the hearings.[96] After that transforming event, he became consumed with anger, hatred, and revenge. "His votes on the Supreme Court—and his public life as a justice—have reflected, with great precision, the grievance that simmers inside him."[97] His chambers "exuded a sense of score settling," and his wife has said that he "doesn't owe any of the groups who opposed him anything[98]—suggesting that he does owe something to those who supported him. As Jeffrey Toobin has put it: "The heart of Thomas's strategy for striking back at his liberal critics is, of course, to utilize the Supreme Court itself."[99] Both sides regarded him as a sure vote for Bush, despite the fact that his previous decisions seemed to have favored the Gore positions on their merits.

Justice Scalia

Antonin Scalia is certainly the most ideological and opinionated justice on the Court today.[100] Although some critics sought his recusal because two of his sons worked for law firms that represented the Bush side, I find it difficult to believe he was actually motivated by such personal factors.[101] According to people who know him, Scalia's primary motive is to pack the high court, as well as the lower courts, with judges who share his ideology. He has a loyal and dedicated following among former clerks, members of the conservative Federalist Society, and other like-minded right-wing Republicans. As his former colleague at the University of Chicago, Judge Richard Posner, recently put it:

> The real conflict of interest is that justices are not indifferent to their colleagues and successors, and the president appoints them. That's an inherent serious conflict, because even if the justices play it straight and each says to himself or herself, I'm not going to think about the effect of this decision on my legacy as a Supreme Court justice, you can't exclude the possibility of an unconscious influence. If these justices had not been so interested in this case for themselves, they might not have picked up on some of the mistakes by the Florida Supreme Court. What a judge notices as "something bad enough to require action" is likely to be influenced by unconscious factors. You are just alert to things the way a drug-sniffing police dog is alert to cocaine.[102]

Scalia himself does not fit neatly into any familiar political or ideological category. He is not a classic conservative, as that term has traditionally been defined in this country. American conservatism has always had more of a libertarian streak than

Scalia seems to embrace.[103] His conservatisms, according to a professor who is an expert in these matters, are "of the Old World European sort, rooted in the authority of the Church and the military. It is more reminiscent of French, Italian and Spanish clerical conservatism than of American conservatism with its libertarian bent." According to a *Washington Post* story, Antonin Scalia was sent to "an elite church-run military prep school in Manhattan," where one of his classmates remembered him at age seventeen as "an archconservative Catholic [who] could have been a member of the curia."[104] When he was nominated to the Supreme Court in 1986, the American Civil Liberties Union presciently summarized his views in the following terms:

> In virtually every opinion that he has written addressing civil liberties issues, Judge Scalia has decided against the individual. He has restricted the protection of the First Amendment, made it more difficult for plaintiffs in discrimination cases to proceed and succeed, always upheld the state's position against that of the accused, almost always restricted the public's access to government information and has insulated executive action from judicial review.[105]

One of Scalia's staunchest supporters was far less prescient—at least about the justice's vote in the Florida election case. Norman Podhoretz, editor of *Commentary,* wrote in 1986 that "Scalia has decided against judicial intrusion into the business of the political branches."[106] If he had been truly prescient, he would have added: ". . . except when necessary to get his candidate elected."

Scalia's vote in *Bush v. Gore* has shown that the most accurate guide to predicting his judicial decisions is to follow his political and personal preferences rather than his lofty rhetoric about judicial restraint, originalism, and other abstract aspects of his so-called constraining judicial philosophy, which turns out to be little more than a cover for his politics and his desire to pack the Court with like-minded justices.[107] Because I like Justice Scalia as a person, I was most disappointed with his precipitous abandonment of principle in the name of partisanship.

Chief Justice Rehnquist

I was neither surprised nor disappointed by the actions of Chief Justice Rehnquist. No one I know seriously considered the possibility that Rehnquist had an open mind in this case—and not only because of his wish to retire and have his successor named by a Republican. He has always been a partisan justice. He was appointed for that reason. The tapes made in the Oval Office during Nixon's administration recorded White House chief of staff H. R. Haldeman telling President Nixon that Rehnquist "wouldn't have a snowball's chance of getting on that court" if the Senate hadn't been exhausted from the battle over the failed nominations of Clement Haynsworth and G. Harrold Carswell. On the tapes, Henry Kissinger asks whether Rehnquist is "pretty far right," and Haldeman replies, "Oh, Christ, he's way to the right of Patrick Buchanan."[108]

Despite Rehnquist's prior decisions limiting equal-protection claims to racial grounds and his strong support for state sovereignty under the Tenth Amendment, he too was considered a sure vote for Bush. His motive may have been mixed and somewhat more difficult to decipher than some of the other justices', but his vote was a sure thing for the Republican candidate. Lawyers on both sides did not bother to speculate about why Rehnquist would vote in favor of Bush, because they were absolutely certain he would do so.

*   *   *

The relevant information that might shed light on the mixed motivations of some of the majority justices varies from hard, undisputed, direct evidence to circumstantial inference and even, in some instances, to what would have to be characterized as courtroom scuttlebutt. Some of this information would be admissible in a court of law; some would not. Some of the facts raise questions about whether the justice should have participated in the case; some do not. Much of it was used by the lawyers in this case in an effort to help them decide which justices were sure votes and which were possibly open to persuasion. I'll leave it to the reader to decide whether a commonsense case has been made as to why some of these justices might have been motivated to place partisanship over principle.

In the case of Sandra Day O'Connor, the evidence of a palpable material benefit seems clear and has not been disputed. In the case of Anthony Kennedy, the evidence is far less certain. Though I have great faith in the source of my information about his ambition to become chief justice and about the actions he has taken to further that ambition, I must acknowledge that it is difficult to assess this kind of information. As to Clarence Thomas, the information about his anger at those who opposed his nomination and his loyalty to those who supported it is confirmed by numerous sources, yet by its nature it is subjective. In regard to William Rehnquist, it is impossible to identify a single motive beyond his general partisanship. Antonin Scalia, because he is the most brilliant of the majority justices, is also the most complex; his motivations, too, are difficult to pinpoint. Yet the conflict between his long-expressed ideology and his vote in this case is more dramatic and more disturbing than that of any other justice.

The question of why is ultimately unanswerable. Yet evidence of motive, when combined with evidence of otherwise unexplained inconsistency, in so important a case raises a compelling

inference of impropriety. Though I am personally convinced beyond all reasonable doubt that none of the majority justices
would have voted to stop the hand count if the shoe had been
on the other foot, I cannot claim to know with any degree of
certainty the precise reason or reasons why these four men and
one woman would risk their hard-earned personal reputations
and the accumulated integrity of the Court by abandoning their
previously expressed judicial philosophies in so transparent and
partisan a manner. Historians and others will long speculate
about this question, as they have every right to do, and perhaps
someday we will learn more than we presently know.[109] For
now, we know enough to pass judgment on these justices based
on the hard record of inconsistency between what they said a
justice *should do* when legal principles conflict with personal
preference and what they *did do* when such a conflict actually
occurred in *Bush v. Gore*. As a result of their decision, the
power and influence of the majority justices may be enhanced
in the short run. They will be rewarded in the many subtle ways
an administration can reward its favorites. They will have some
say in future appointments to the high court. Their law clerks
and allies will fill the Republican bureaucracy, spreading their
gospel of conservatism. These are the spoils of political victory,
and the majority justices are seen by many as responsible for
the Bush victory.

In the course of writing this book, I have spoken to dozens
of highly successful lawyers—lawyers who win because they
understand judges. Virtually every one of them, Democrat or
Republican, agrees with me that the majority justices in the
Florida election case fail the shoe-on-the-other-foot test. As one
usually cautious lawyer who practices extensively before the
high court told me, "It insults our intelligence to suggest otherwise." Many agree with the characterization "cheating."
Some disagree, arguing that what the justices did here is on a
continuum with what many judges routinely do in criminal cas-

es in which they believe the defendant did it but also that the police violated the defendant's rights: They find ways to reach the result they favor (conviction of the factually guilty) even though the law demands a result they disfavor (release of the bad guy). Others believe that nearly all the judges in this highly politicized case—the Supreme Court dissenters, the Florida Supreme Court majority, and the lower court judges—would fail the shoe-on-the-other-foot test, and they contend that it is wrong to single out the majority justices for criticism. This is one heck of a commentary on the current status of our judiciary.

On May 9, 2001, President Bush, in introducing his initial nominees to the United States Courts of Appeal, said that he hoped these judicial nominees, if confirmed, would comply with the judicial oath, which reads, in part, as follows:

> "I, ————, do solemnly swear (or affirm) that I will administer justice *without respect to persons . . .*" (emphasis added).

The irony is that if the majority justices in *Bush v. Gore* had not violated that oath by deciding the case *with respect* to the persons and political parties involved, George W. Bush might not have been the president.[110]

5: The Importance of *Bush v. Gore* to All Americans

Bush v. Gore is certainly not the first bad Supreme Court ruling. Over the years, the justices have rendered many evil, immoral, even dangerous decisions, most of which have been overturned by later courts and condemned by the verdict of history. Heading the list, of course, is *Dred Scott v. Sandford,* which essentially declared African-Americans to be property, without rights. Included on this list of infamy is *Plessy v. Ferguson,* which announced the principle of "separate but equal." *Korematsu v. United States,* which permitted Americans to be put in detention camps during World War II entirely because of their race, also deserves a place of dishonor, as does the decision in 1872's *Bradwell v. State* declaring women unsuited to the practice of law. But each of these decisions was rendered by justices who almost certainly believed that they were following the dictates of the Constitution. For the most part, the justices who wrote or joined the majority opinions for these terrible decisions were acting consistently with their own judicial philosophies—wrongheaded as they may have been. *Bush v. Gore* was different because the majority justices violated their own previously declared judicial principles—principles they still believe in and will apply in other cases.

In this respect, the decision in the Florida election case may be ranked as the single most corrupt decision in Supreme Court history, because it is the only one that I know of where the majority justices decided as they did because of the personal identity and political affiliation of the litigants. This was cheating, and a violation of the judicial oath. The other dreadful Supreme Court decisions, dangerous as they were, do not deserve to be placed into this special category of judicial misconduct, though their impact on history may have been more serious and enduring.

It is the uniquely corrupt nature of the decision in *Bush v. Gore* that explains the extraordinary vituperativeness of the language employed by so many usually cautious critics of the high court. In the nearly half a century I have been following the Supreme Court, I have never seen or heard such strong negative language used about the justices by responsible critics. Jeffrey Rosen, a legal writer and law professor typically respectful of the high court, mounted a scathing attack on the majority within days of the decision. He had previously criticized the Florida Supreme Court for going too far in changing the rules after the election. But his criticism of the U.S. Supreme Court was far more bitter. Calling them "four vain men and one vain woman," he accused the five of voting their "self-initiated political preferences" rather than applying the rule of law. Focusing particularly on Justices Kennedy and O'Connor—from whom he obviously expected more—he said the opinion "unmasks them more nakedly than a TV camera ever could." In an unusual personal attack, he called them "preening" as well as "addled and uncertain." He characterized the opinion as politically driven drivel with no law to support it because it was "tailor-made for this occasion." The majority justices, Rosen said, "played us all for dupes" and "sent themselves to hell in the process." His article was entitled "The Supreme Court Commits Suicide."[1]

Vincent Bugliosi, the generally moderate former prosecutor known for securing the conviction of the Charles Manson gang, used even stronger language, accusing the Supreme Court's "brazen, shameless majority" of "being a knowing surrogate for the Republican Party instead of being an impartial arbiter of the law."[2] He characterized these justices as "criminals in the truest sense of the word" and described their opinion as "fraudulent." My Harvard Law School colleague Randall Kennedy called the Supreme Court's intervention "a scandal" and its decision outrageous. He accused the Court of acting "in bad faith and with partisan prejudice" and concluded that the high court is now "unworthy of deference."[3] Scott Turow said the decision "was the most overtly politicized action by a court that I have seen in 22 years of practicing law" and labeled it "an act of judicial lawlessness."[4] Professor Bruce Ackerman of Yale Law School accused the majority of "vulgar partisanship."[5]

Professor Cass Sunstein, who had praised the Supreme Court's initial unanimous decision, called its final one "illegitimate, undemocratic and unprincipled."[6] Even Anthony Lewis, who had written one of the most hagiographic accounts of the justices in modern history, *Gideon's Trumpet,* declared the decision to be "a dismal failure" and quoted favorably from a thoughtful British columnist who said the ruling "put an indelible stain on the Court's half-illusory reputation as honest guardian of the Constitution." He also quoted a law professor as asking rhetorically, "How can I convince my students now that the integrity of legal reasoning matters?"[7]

Some of the words used to characterize the justices are so strong that they could, in times past, have constituted unethical conduct under the canons of professional responsibility, or even contempt of court. Indeed, Randall Kennedy titled his article "Contempt of Court," as if to throw down the gauntlet. And these were the words spoken in public, for attribution. I can attest that in private conversation, even stronger terms were used. Lawyers, in general, are not a courageous group given to public criticism of judges and justices. They are more like Mae West, who, in one of her films, was accused by the judge of showing contempt for the court—to which she replied, sotto voce, "I'm trying my best to conceal my contempt." But in one respect, the kind of language used to criticize the majority justices was to be expected. It is the language of political, rather than judicial, discourse, and this was a political, rather than judicial, decision about an issue that not only divided a nation but divided the courts.*

Why Criticism and Accountability Are Important

Beyond its high ranking on the list of corrupt decisions and its unprecedented criticism by academics, why should Americans really care about the Supreme Court's decision in *Bush v. Gore*? Nothing anyone now discovers or says will turn back the clock, allow the hand recount in Florida to continue, and enable us to find out who really won this election. Nor is it at all likely that the Supreme Court will ever again be in a position to determine a presidential election. The majority justices themselves implied that the case will have little or no impact on future equal-protection claims. As of this writing, all seems back to normal at the high court, almost as if what transpired in the late fall of 2000 was simply another divisive case in which some dis-

---

*Of the sixteen supreme court justices who ruled in this case—seven in Florida and nine in Washington—eight ruled for Bush and eight for Gore.

senting justices employed strong language but are now prepared to forgive and forget. So why all the fuss? Why the extraordinary outpouring of academic and journalistic criticism, not only of the decision, but also of the justices themselves? Is this yet another example of academics and pundits being out of touch with the concerns of the average American? I don't believe that this is necessarily the case, but I do think many Americans are looking at *Bush v. Gore* in too narrow a fashion.

Many Americans remain outraged at the decision of the Supreme Court in *Bush v. Gore*—but some for the wrong reason. They believe the Supreme Court gave the election to the wrong candidate. Many of these Gore partisans would have eagerly accepted a Supreme Court decision that intervened on behalf of *their* candidate. Such criticism is as unprincipled as its mirror image: partisan support of the decision because it favored Bush. True, the combination of events that seemed to go against Gore—from the butterfly ballot and the allegations of racial discrimination to the Republican "riot" in Miami—are understandably galling to Gore supporters. But these issues were not before the high court in *Bush v. Gore*. Moreover, it remains uncertain—and probably will always remain subject to some dispute—whether the Supreme Court's intervention actually had any impact on the outcome of the election.

It should not matter who, if anyone, was the beneficiary of the Court's unjustified intervention, but it apparently does to a great many Americans. Judge Richard Posner has observed that *Bush v. Gore* will be judged "on the success of Bush's presidency. If he turns out to be a terrible flop, some of the ignominy will adhere to the Supreme Court. If he's a successful President, and if, as appears to be the case, people outside of academic circles have lost interest in the decision, then it won't be infamous other than in professional circles."[8] This kind of result-oriented evaluation should be irrelevant to any nonpartisan criticism of the Supreme Court's decision. What matters is whether

the five justices who stopped the hand count violated their judicial oath. If they concocted arguments to which they never
would have subscribed had the recount been necessary to give
Bush any chance of winning the election, then they most certainly did cheat, regardless of how the election would have
turned out without their intervention. I think I have provided
strong evidence in support of this conclusion in the preceding
chapters. If I am correct about *that,* then little else matters. It
does not even matter that some scholars can now, after the fact,
come up with plausible rationalizations in support of the equal-
protection or Article II arguments put forward by the majority
justices. If these justices themselves would not have accepted
these arguments had the shoe been on the other foot, then the
fact that they might be acceptable to others does not mitigate
the justices' corruption.

If a majority of the Supreme Court acted corruptly, then all
Americans, regardless of whom they voted for in the election
or what they think about its eventual outcome, should be outraged and concerned. They should be outraged because an institution many of them trusted to be above politics has violated
that trust. They should be concerned because the institution that
generally serves as the last barrier to tyranny has become complicit in corruption. When the courts become corrupted, the
road to tyranny becomes more accessible. A nation with an
independent and respected judiciary is less subject to the will of
a dictator or the whims of a transient majority impatient with
the rights of minorities. A nation whose highest court cannot
be trusted in challenging situations is a nation whose liberty is
at greater risk.

All Americans should look beyond the short-term effects of
this decision and their own political preferences and toward the
long-term impact of the majority's corrupt action on our system
of checks and balances. Today's targets of the Court's corruption were Gore and those who voted for him, but tomorrow's

targets may well include some who applauded the Bush victory. A morally weakened Supreme Court poses a danger to all Americans who care deeply about the Constitution and the liberties it protects. The danger may not manifest itself in the immediate future, but a morally strong Supreme Court serves as an insurance policy against unpredictable yet inevitable threats to liberty over time. Just because these threats do not appear imminent does not mitigate the ultimate dangers resulting from the loss of moral capital sustained by the high court.

This was not the first time the Court resolved an issue determining the fate of a president, but it is the first time it has done so in a decision that was neither unanimous nor principled. In the Nixon tapes case and in the Clinton–Paula Jones case, the justices unanimously[9] articulated a principle that all Americans could accept, even if they did not approve of its application to the particular president involved. In both of those cases, the Supreme Court ruled that no American, not even the president, is above the law. But, ironically, these same justices have virtually placed *themselves* above the law, not only by rendering this lawless decision, but by refusing to be bound by the same rules of judicial conduct that govern all other judges.

There is today no effective mechanism for questioning the integrity of Supreme Court justices. When a commission delicately recommended several years ago that "the Supreme Court may wish to consider the adoption of policies and procedures for the filing and disposition of complaints alleging misconduct against justices of the Supreme Court,"[10] there was a resounding silence from the justices. To be sure, if any justice committed a federal crime, he or she could be indicted or impeached, but short of the radical surgery of criminal prosecution or congressional impeachment, there is no effective medicine that the body politic could administer to a sick Supreme Court. Indeed, we even lack the tools necessary to make the diagnosis, not only because of legal limitations, but also because of unwritten laws and traditions that govern the manner by which we may challenge the integrity of the justices. Every other judge in the United States is subject to some peer review or outside review. For example, all lower court federal judges—on the district or appellate court—are subject to investigation and sanctions administered by the Judicial Conference. The Supreme Court is exempted from this procedure.[11]

The Florida election decision has rekindled the debate over the Supreme Court's exemption from the Code of Judicial Conduct and the mechanism for judicial peer review. It has also opened a new debate over the high court's traditional, but largely extralegal, immunity from the kind of public scrutiny and accountability to which other branches of government are regularly subjected. Such immunity is no longer acceptable at a time of widespread suspicion of the motives of the five justices who, contrary to their own previously expressed judicial views, rendered a decision that millions of Americans understandably believe was motivated by the desire to see George W. Bush elected president. The public has the right to know whether the thumb of partisan bias may improperly have been placed on the scales of justice. There is no compelling reason why journalists and scholars should not demand, for example, that Justice O'Connor respond to probing questions about her widely reported election-night sentiments regarding the impact of a Gore victory on her retirement plans.[12] Nor are there good reasons why journalists and scholars should not raise questions with each of the majority justices about inconsistencies between the views they expressed in the recent election case and views they expressed in earlier election and other equal-protection cases. The justices may decline to answer difficult or embarrassing, but relevant and legitimate, questions about the performance of their duties—just as a senator, representative, or president may decline. The point is that we, the public, should no longer be satisfied with the traditional judicial boilerplate, "Justices do not answer questions or explain their decisions." Why not? If their decisions decide presidential elections and are so woefully inadequate in their logic and consistency as to raise widespread plausible suspicions of partisan bias, there is every reason to insist that the justices defend their actions. Some justices have tried to do so—but entirely on their own terms and without displaying any willingness to respond to probing questions and follow-ups.[13]

Our system of checks and balances does not begin and end with the judiciary checking and balancing the legislative and executive branches through their self-proclaimed power of judicial review. The legislature, too, must be able to check a Supreme Court that may have abused its constitutional powers. The exercise of this important function is not limited to Senate confirmation of all federal judges. It should also include the enactment of legislation compelling the televising of all oral arguments. There is no excuse for leaving it up to the Supreme Court to decide the manner and level of public scrutiny of its decision-making processes. This is an issue to be decided democratically, rather than by an elite institution.

Moreover, Congress should enact conflict-of-interest rules binding on the justices. Today, the justices make up their own rules and they are often inadequate, self-serving, and inconsistent. For example, Justice Antonin Scalia has two sons who work in law firms that represented the Republicans in the recent election case. The high court's rules permit this so long as the firm deducts from the justice's children's compensation the proportion of income directly attributable to appearances before the Supreme Court. This formulation is naive in the extreme, since firms that win before the high court reap enormous indirect financial benefit in the form of new clients. Congressional hearings should be conducted to hear evidence about this and other potential conflicts, and Congress should enact rules that serve the public interest.

Congress should also enact mechanisms for enforcing the conflict-of-interest rules and other rules of judicial conduct, and imposing sanctions on justices who violate them. The Supreme Court, which has subjected presidents and legislators to the rule of law, should not be allowed to place itself above the law applicable to all other judges. It is no longer entitled (if it ever was) to this special status. Now that it has jumped into the partisan political fray, it must be treated like the other political branches—with respectful but probing scrutiny. We are a nation of cynics, especially when it comes to politics. Now this cynicism has been extended to the Supreme Court and to the process by which we elect our president.

Judicial misconduct should have consequences in a democracy. If the majority are permitted the spoils of their illegitimate victory—a victory achieved by cheating—they will have corrupted the Supreme Court beyond repair. It will have lost its legitimacy as a moral institution above partisan politics. It will no longer serve as an effective check and balance against the political branches, because it will have become just another political branch. The ultimate check in any democracy is, of course, the citizenry. If the consequence of the Supreme Court's gross misconduct in the Florida election case is greater scrutiny by an informed and concerned citizenry, then something positive may yet emerge from this supreme injustice. But if we simply rally around the Supreme Court and act as if its partisan decision was business as usual, then we risk the danger of recurrence.[14]

Courts must, of course, retain their independence and their duty to check and balance the other branches of government and to vindicate the constitutional rights of individuals. Their decisions will often be unpopular, both to a majority of the citizens and to many elected officials. Courts should not be attacked for rendering unpopular decisions, and if attacked, they should be defended even by those who disagree with the decisions. But partisan decisions, based on extralegal factors, are different. Any decision that cannot pass the shoe-on-the-other-foot test is corrupt and unworthy of a court. It must be exposed and attacked, both for the good of the court and for the good of the nation. As Justices O'Connor and Kennedy (along with Souter) warned in their decision in another case:

> If the Court's legitimacy should be undermined, then, so would the country be in its very ability to see itself through its constitutional ideals. The Court's concern with legitimacy is not for the sake of the Court, but for the sake of the Nation to which it is responsible.[15]

It is not the critics who undermine the legitimacy of a corrupt Court. It is those members of that Court who engaged in the corruption. It is not the dissenters who have fouled their own nest, as some critics have charged.[16] It is the majority that has done the fouling. The dissenters, like the critics, have fulfilled their democratic commitment to tell the citizens the truth about what happened inside the people's marble temple of justice.

I have focused on the majority justices because they are the ones who determined the outcome of the election. The decision of the majority justices was final—to paraphrase Justice Robert Jackson's pithy comment—not because it was right, but because Americans obey Supreme Court decisions whether or not we agree with them. That is the meaning of the rule of law. In my view, the justices were not only wrong, they cheated, and by doing so they have diminished their moral authority. No honest person can any longer trust them to do justice, as distinguished from politics. This is a tragedy not only for those individual justices and for the Court on which they sit, but for all Americans who have come to rely on the Supreme Court to use its moral authority to implement often unpopular constitutional rights. We will obey their orders, because we are a nation of laws, but many of us will no longer respect the source of these orders. Their power now lies in their physical ability to enforce their decrees by the threat of contempt, not by the moral force of their reasoning or their role as neutral judges. In this regard, the Supreme Court will become more like the legislative and executive branches of our government. We comply with statutes enacted by our legislatures and with executive orders signed by our presidents and governors whether or not we agree with these laws or respect the individuals who enacted or signed them. We are, in general, a law-abiding people, despite our deep distrust of the politicians who write our laws. Now this distrust has spread to the Supreme Court. Although the objective evidence of cheating is very strong, it may be difficult for the general public and some less experienced academics to believe that justices of the Supreme Court are capable of such corruption, especially since there are no crass allegations of cash for votes, as there have been in the courts of Chicago and other cities. The cheating here is elite and subtle, and the general public is not accustomed to this sort of "cheat elite"[17] among our most respected and elevated judges. But in a democracy there can be no exemption from probing scrutiny at any level of government. Perhaps the need is even greater with regard to unelected judges who are appointed for life and are accountable to no one. As Clarence Thomas once acknowledged:

> Open debate of judicial decision-making only strengthens the legitimacy of the judiciary. If our decisions can withstand public scrutiny and reasoned discussion, then the people will only accept them all the more. What is a matter of concern are proposals by some bar associations that would impose penalties upon lawyers who level "unfair" or "inaccurate" criticism against judges of their opinions. Judges are adults; we do not need cyberpatrol or surfwatch to protect our sensibilities. The First Amendment guarantees free speech exactly

so that citizens can discuss matters of important public policy. Salving the psychological wounds of judges simply is not
worth restricting anyone's ability to say what they please.[18]

I believe that the criticisms I have leveled are fair, accurate, and
supported by the available evidence. I also believe that they are
good, not bad, for the Supreme Court as an institution, and
perhaps for some of the individual justices against whom they
are directed. Thirty years ago, Professor John Ely and I wrote
an article in the *Yale Law Journal* challenging the candor of
two fairly new justices—Chief Justice Warren Burger and Associate Justice Harry Blackmun. We documented repeated instances in which these justices misstated the factual records in
two cases they decided.[19] Chief Justice Burger, I later learned,
was furious at the article. Justice Blackmun, on the other hand,
went out of his way to thank us for exposing a serious problem
within the Supreme Court—a problem that he committed himself not to repeat. Criticism is a necessary first step if anything
positive can possibly emerge from this inexcusable decision. The
next step is to derive the appropriate lessons from this supreme
injustice.

Some Lessons to be Learned from *Bush v. Gore*

The decision in *Bush v. Gore* marks the end of an important
period in American history: the era in which advocates of civil
rights and civil liberties placed their trust in the courts, most
particularly the Supreme Court, to expand various constitutional protections so as to include the right of a woman to choose
abortion, the right of minorities to racial equality, the rights
and remedies of criminal defendants, the rights of political and
religious dissenters, and other, often unpopular, rights. Though
the beginning of this era is often demarcated by the nomination
of Earl Warren to the chief justiceship in 1953, its gradual evo-

lution actually began decades earlier with the nomination of Louis Brandeis as an associate justice in 1916. The Warren Court, especially between 1954 and 1969, marked the culmination of judicial support for these rights and hence the apex of liberal trust in the judicial branch. Nor did this era suddenly end with the replacement of Earl Warren by Warren Burger. Historic epochs rarely begin or end on particular days or even in specific years, despite the penchant among history-book writers to date every period with a precise beginning and end. Indeed, the Supreme Court's most controversial "liberal" decision—*Roe v. Wade*—did not occur until years after Chief Justice Warren's retirement. The subsequent process of conservative retrenchment took several years and several appointments—especially those of Justices Rehnquist, Scalia, and Thomas—to create a solid right-wing majority on the high court. Two of the post–Warren Court justices—O'Connor and Kennedy—were reluctant to overrule prior decisions with which they may have disagreed. And so, until *Bush v. Gore,* many liberals still continued, with some reservation and concern, to place their trust in the Supreme Court.

Bush v. Gore has ended that trust. It is one of those rare events in history that truly marks the close of an era with a specific action and date. The reasons this particular decision is so significant are manifold.

First, the decision marks the high point in conservative judicial activism. Granting a stay and then rendering a decision that permanently stopped the counting and ended the election has been widely perceived as so inconsistent with the alleged conservative approach to judging—judicial restraint, applying existing law rather than making up new law, not entering the political thicket—that it signals a new conservative boldness, which is unlikely to abate (except, perhaps, in the immediate short run).[20]

Second, the decision is seen as so partisan and result-oriented that any sense of trust in the "moderate middle"—O'Connor and Kennedy—has been diminished to the point of vanishing.

Third, the effect—if not one of the motives—of the majority decision has been to allow the conservative majority, in effect, to name its own successors on the high court, as well as the replacements for any of the minority justices and the hundreds of lower federal court judges who may retire or die during the Bush administration.[21]

Legal realists—and all good lawyers must be realists—have long understood that the arguments put forward by courts to justify their decisions are often simply after-the-fact rationalizations of results reached for reasons they are unwilling to acknowledge publicly—reasons such as ideological, religious or economic preferences. Lawyers are taught to argue both sides of every issue. Any good lawyer is capable of rationalizing virtually any conclusion he wishes to reach by plausible arguments. The majority justices' wholesale abandonment of their long-stated judicial philosophy in the interests of their partisan preferences should remind us that the concept of "judicial philosophy" is, for the most part, a malleable cover for personal, political, and ideological predisposition. It is widely misunderstood by the public and misused by presidents who appoint judges, senators who confirm them, and judges who seek judicial appointments and promotions.

In a recent interview with the *New York Times,* President Bush's White House counsel, Alberto R. Gonzales, described the criteria his office was employing in recommending federal judges:

> The truth of the matter is that a judge's personal views of an issue is irrelevant or should be irrelevant if a judge does her job right. We ask questions about their philosophy. We ask how they construe statutes, how do they resolve disputes and what do they believe is the appropriate role of the judge.

Gonzales said that he and Bush agree that "the role of judges should be fairly limited."

This was not their view, of course, when the Bush campaign insisted that a federal judge intervene to stay the hand recount in Florida. It was not their view when they demanded that the U.S. Supreme Court stay and then permanently stop the recount.

Most conservatives believe in a limited role for courts—so-called judicial restraint—only when the other branches of government are controlled by fellow conservatives. The same is true, in mirror image, of most liberals. Indeed, the very concept of judicial restraint was first developed as a guiding legal principle[22] by a liberal Supreme Court justice, Louis Brandeis, whose activist conservative colleagues were striking down liberal legislation enacted by liberal legislatures.[23]

Many of today's conservative judges—and the politicians who appoint and confirm them—couldn't care less about abstract judicial philosophies. I doubt that President Bush even understands what a judicial philosophy (as contrasted with a political philosophy) really is. He is interested in nominating judges and justices who will vote his way and who will perpetuate his political ideology after he is no longer president.[24]

Some judges, of course, do actually apply the law in a neutral manner, without regard to their personal preferences. Others deceive themselves into believing that the arguments they are offering are neutral—that is, not explicitly calculated to produce a desired outcome. As an experienced judge once told me, "The judicial capacity to kid oneself is limitless, because judges want to—need to—persuade themselves that they are doing the right thing."

But this observation, whether or not it is valid in the run of cases involving specific ideological, religious, or economic preferences, has no validity when applied to a case such as this one, where no minimally self-aware judge could mislead himself or herself about what the majority was doing. And certainly no one should mince words about the seriousness of such judicial misconduct.[25]

All of this does not necessarily mean that liberals will no longer bring cases to the Supreme Court. They have nowhere else to go with certain kinds of issues, especially those that truly belong in the high court, such as cases involving the constitutional rights of unpopular minorities, which are unlikely to be vindicated by the popular branches of government. Why, after all, does a democratic society need an unelected judiciary with the power of judicial review? Certainly not to serve as yet another branch of government responsive to the immediate needs of transient majorities. Popular branches of government—elected every two, four, or six years—are sufficiently sensitive to the needs of the majority, the politically powerful, the economically influential, and the socially popular. The quintessential role of the Supreme Court in a democracy is to vindicate the constitutional rights of minorities, of dissidents, of the unrepresented, of the disenfranchised, of the unpopular. Yet the current Supreme Court majority has turned this important role on its head. It has generally vindicated the interests of the powerful at the expense of the rights of the powerless. It has struck down statutes designed to protect the disabled, children, women, racial minorities, members of minority religions, and others who do not have full access to the political processes.[26] At the same time, it has championed the interests of corporations and others with full and complete access to the political processes. Most state courts have also turned conservative over the past several decades. Indeed, it is fair to say that for the first time in modern American history, virtually all the branches of government are effectively controlled by Republicans and conservatives. The presidency belongs to the Republicans, and the Senate, the House, and the Supreme Court all have Republican majorities.[27] Most state governors and legislators are conservative. In the lower federal courts—district courts and courts of appeals—the Democrats still cling to a thin and rapidly narrowing overall majority, which President Bush has made it his priority to elim-inate. With almost a hundred vacancies on the lower federal courts and the prospect of numerous retirements over the next few years, Bush should have no problem quickly shifting the balance of power. In part this is because President Clinton did not make a concerted effort to appoint liberal ideologues to the bench (perhaps because he himself is not a liberal ideologue), the Senate was controlled by Republicans during much of his presidency, and his priorities in making judicial appointments were related more to appointing women and minorities then people with a strong ideological bent.[28]

Whatever the reason for this Republican domination of con-temporary American politics, including judicial politics, the re-ality is that advocates of civil rights and liberties have few op-tions these days other than the courts, especially when the rights of unpopular and marginalized minorities are at stake. At a more fundamental level, our system of checks and balances is some-what out of balance because there is no branch of government that can effectively check the Republican-controlled govern-ment. Despite losing the popular vote for the presidency and be-ing in the minority in most states, the Republicans have managed to gain control over virtually all the branches of our multifaceted governmental system. The fact that they may have gained control over the presidency *because* they already had control over the Su-preme Court is what is disturbing to so many people who care deeply about our system of checks and balances.

In this regard, there is something perversely positive that can come out of the Supreme Court's intervention into the 2000 presidential election, precisely because it is such an obviously partisan and unprincipled decision. Liberals may finally come to realize that their undue reliance on the judiciary was always somewhat risky and unhealthy to the body politic. Placing so

much of the fate of the Republic in the inexperienced and un-
steady hands of nine justices appointed for life reflects a deep
distrust in democracy and an unwarranted trust in an elite institution far removed from the people. That trust was violated
in the case of *Bush v. Gore,* but the seeds of this violation were
planted many years earlier by some of the same liberals who
have complained most vociferously—and, in my view, correctly—about the high court's "power grab" in this case.

The Wages of *Roe v. Wade*

In my estimation, the seeds were planted by the campaign to
constitutionalize a woman's right to choose abortion, which
culminated in the Court's controversial decision in *Roe v.
Wade.* The abortion issue is quintessentially political. It involves
a clash of ideologies, even worldviews. Unlike the issue of state-
enforced racial segregation, in the controversy over abortion
there is no absolute right and wrong, either morally or constitutionally. Virtually everyone today acknowledges that segregation was both immoral and unconstitutional. All it took was
a strong push by a unanimous Supreme Court to set in motion
a process that was ongoing in most other democracies throughout the world but which had gotten stuck in the United States
because the "channels of democracy"—to use John Hart Ely's
elegant phrase—had been blocked by malapportioned legislatures and other perversions of the democratic process. Over a
period of years, the Supreme Court placed its moral imprimatur
on desegregation and eventually unblocked these channels of
democracy. It worked—not perfectly, but perfection is rarely
possible in a heterogeneous and divided democracy.

Abortion is different. The Supreme Court's decision, now
more than a quarter century old, changed few minds on this
issue, because those who believe that abortion—or certain kinds
of abortion—is tantamount to murder are not like those who

believed that segregation was right. The former believe that they occupy the moral high ground. And they do *if* their underlying premise—that a fetus is a human being—is correct. No rational argument, whether made by philosophers or Supreme Court justices, will ever disprove the truth of that a priori premise. Nor will experience alter it, unlike views concerning segregation, which have been markedly changed by experience.[29]

Moreover, the nation was—and remains—closely divided about the morality of abortion, both in the abstract and under various circumstances. Advocates of a woman's right to choose abortion could have organized politically to win that right (at least for most women under most circumstances) in the elected branches of government. According to the American Civil Liberties Union:

> Between 1967 and 1971, under mounting pressure from the women's rights movement, 17 states decriminalized abortion. Public opinion also shifted during this period. In 1968, only 15 percent of Americans favored legal abortions; by 1972, 64 percent did. When the Court announced its landmark 1973 ruling legalizing abortion in *Roe v. Wade,* it was marching in step with public opinion.[30]

But it is not the proper role of the Supreme Court to march in step with public opinion. That is the role of the elected branches of government. Instead of devoting all their resources to continuing the legislative and public opinion battle, the pro-choice movement devoted much of its resources to the litigation option, whose goal it was to get the Supreme Court to constitutionalize a woman's right to choose abortion. It worked as planned, thus sparing the pro-choice movement the difficult political task of organizing and fund-raising on a state-by-state basis. The justices did the work for them by simply striking down most abortion laws in one fell swoop.[31]

The short-term consequences of constitutionalizing the abortion issue were powerful and positive for the pro-choice movement. The long-term consequences were disastrous. *Roe v. Wade* provided the religious right and the conservative wing of the Republican Party one of the best organizing tools and rallying cries imaginable. The right-to-life movement was energized by this decision and became one of the most potent political forces both nationally and in a large number of states. At the same time, the pro-choice movement became lethargic, celebrating its great judicial victory and neglecting the hard work of organizing and fund-raising—at least in the beginning.*

Roe v. Wade helped secure the presidency for Ronald Reagan by giving him a "free" issue. It was free because he—and other right-to-life Republicans—could strongly oppose all abortion without alienating moderate Republican women and men who favored a woman's right to choose but felt secure in the knowledge that the Supreme Court would continue to protect that right, regardless of what Reagan and others said or did. Abortion thus became the most important issue for right-wing religious zealots and a marginal issue for moderate Republicans who favored a woman's right to choose but who also supported the Republicans' economic and other programs. This helped to destroy the moderate wing of the Republican Party (the so-called Rockefeller Republicans) and drove former moderates such as the elder George Bush to the right. (He started as a pro-choice Republican and ended up as a right-to-life Republican whose hands were tied by the Supreme Court.)

Though *Roe v. Wade* is still the law, that decision—and the

---

*As the ACLU has put it: "[T]he backlash was swift and fierce. Anti-choice forces quickly mobilized, dedicating themselves to reversing *Roe*. In 1974, the ACLU established its Reproductive Freedom Project to advance a broad spectrum of reproductive rights" (*ACLU Position Paper: The Right to Choose* [fall 2000]). Litigation continued to be the weapon of choice in this battle.

ensuing power of the right-to-life lobby—almost certainly pressured Republican presidents to nominate activist right-wing justices such as Antonin Scalia and Clarence Thomas.[32]

Professor John Hart Ely criticized *Roe v. Wade* shortly after it was rendered, largely on constitutional and doctrinal grounds, but implicit in his criticism was a concern that it could resurrect the activist courts of the past, which intruded into the democratic process by striking down laws of which they disapproved, without an adequate basis in the Constitution. He characterized *Roe v. Wade* as the "wages of crying wolf."[33] In some respects, the majority decision in *Bush v. Gore* can aptly be characterized as "the wages of *Roe v. Wade*."

The lessons of *Roe v. Wade* and *Bush v. Gore* are not easy to distill, but at bottom they represent opposite sides of the same currency of judicial activism in areas more appropriately left to the political processes. Courts ought not to jump into controversies that are political in nature and are capable of being resolved—even if not smoothly or expeditiously—by the popular branches of government. Judges have no special competence, qualifications, or mandate to decide between equally compelling moral claims (as in the abortion controversy) or equally compelling political claims (counting ballots by hand or stopping the recount because the standard is ambiguous). Absent clear governing constitutional principles (which are not present in either case), these are precisely the sorts of issues that should be left to the rough-and-tumble of politics rather than the *ipse dixit* of five justices. As Senator John Sherman, a principle supporter of the Electoral Count Act of 1886–87 (which was enacted following the Tilden–Hayes election) presciently warned:

> It would be a very grave fault indeed and a very serious objection to refer a political question in which the people of the country were aroused, about which their feelings were

excited, to this great tribunal, which after all has to sit upon the life and property of all the people of the United States. It would tend to bring that court into public odium of one or the other of the two great parties.

There are, of course, considerable differences between *Roe v. Wade* and *Bush v. Gore.* No matter how critical one may be of *Roe,* no one can accuse the justices who voted for it of being politically partisan. Its author was a Republican, appointed by President Nixon. At the time of the decision, the abortion issue was not as much of a partisan—Democrat versus Republican—issue as it has since become. The division over the constitutionality of abortion laws was more ideologically and religiously doctrinal than politically partisan. If I am right that it ultimately helped elect conservative Republicans, then it certainly was different from *Bush v. Gore.* Moreover, no one can reasonably accuse the justices who voted for *Roe* of cheating. *Roe* was the entirely predictable culmination of a long process of articulating and expanding the rights of privacy and reproductive freedom. Reasonable people could argue that the majority in *Roe* went too far, too fast, and in too sweeping a manner. But if the same one hundred law professors who could not have predicted the vote in *Bush v. Gore,* absent the names and party affiliations of the candidates, had been asked to predict the outcome of *Roe v. Wade,* several months before it came to the court, most would have gotten it right, because it was fairly predictable. They certainly would have been able to predict which justices were likely to line up on which side of that issue, because they voted in a manner consistent with their long-expressed judicial philosophies.

These differences, and the deep commitment many of us have to a woman's right to choose abortion, have made some liberals reluctant to acknowledge any relationship between *Roe v. Wade* and *Bush v. Gore.* But there is no longer any reluctance to acknowledge their lack of trust that the high court will be fair and impartial when it comes to political and other agenda-driven issues. Until *Bush v. Gore*, the attitude has been, "What do we have to lose?" The worst that happens if we try to secure relief in the Supreme Court and lose is that we are back where we started from. *Bush v. Gore* demonstrated the harm in empowering the courts to become actively involved in solving the nation's political problems—a harm liberals ignored as long as the solutions were ones they favored. Much depends, of course, on what is meant by "solve." Those who favor a particular judicial outcome—for example, the recognition of a woman's right to choose abortion—declare the problem to have been "solved." But these same people do not regard the judicial termination of the Florida hand recount as having "solved" that problem, but rather as having caused a problem. I'm certain that right-to-life zealots similarly believe that *Roe v. Wade* caused, rather than solved, the abortion problem. Solution or aggravation is truly in the eye of the beholder.

Many liberals had been brought up to believe that whatever happened to the other branches of government, the Supreme Court belonged to "us." It was "ours." Nobody could take that away. We could count on the justices, perhaps not in every case, but certainly over the long run. They would set matters straight when it came down to it.

It was for this reason that so many liberals of my generation became lawyers and so much faith was placed in litigation. The corollary is that even fewer became politicians, political organizers, and political fund-raisers. We eschewed the rough-and-tumble of dirty politics in favor of the neat and elite high road of the judiciary.

This trend had already begun to shift even before *Bush v. Gore*.[34] Over the past decade, liberal lawyers were becoming less likely to pursue careers in litigating civil rights and civil liberties cases before the high court, and conservative lawyers—many of whom have joined the highly influential Federalist Society—were now specializing in federal and Supreme Court litigation. But until *Bush v. Gore,* the liberals had some hope that the moderates plus the soft right could be counted on not to overrule the liberal residues of the past and occasionally to cobble together a majority to expand old rights or articulate new ones.

They were stunned, however, when the two members of the soft right joined the three members of the hard right in the most activist, unprecedented, and unprincipled decision in recent Supreme Court history. Moreover, this decision was rendered in the most visible and controversial case ever, thus sending a powerful message that the justices would not be deterred by public opprobrium, academic criticism, or even charges of partisan politics. Finally, the liberals were shocked into the realization that they had lost the Court. Not only was it no longer "theirs," but it was now squarely in the hands of their political and ideological enemies. The Supreme Court was now a full-fledged activist, right-wing, Republican court. Now that we recognize this reality, we can act accordingly—and perhaps even try to remedy the problem.

Changing How We Pick Our Justices

Another significant lesson for the American public to learn from *Bush v. Gore* is that it really does matter who is appointed to the Supreme Court. This decision proves that it is not better *doctrine* we need; it is better *justices. Bush v. Gore* does not represent a failure of legal doctrine; it represents a failure of judicial personnel. The majority justices wrote and spoke eloquently and repeatedly about the need to be constrained by precedent in order to preclude individual justices from smuggling their personal, ideological, or political preferences into the judicial decisions they wrote for the Court. That doctrine is plainly correct. The majority justices were right in what they have *said* about precedent and restraint over the years. They were wrong in what they *did*. When partisanship and personal advantage came into conflict with doctrine and principle, they chose the path of hypocrisy and opportunism. This case demonstrates that legal doctrine alone can never constrain a politically loyal partisan in robes who is determined to find a way around the constraint of precedent. It takes greatness to resist the temptation of partisan and personal advantage, and the majority justices simply lacked that quality.

With the benefit of hindsight, we should not have been surprised that these five justices were prepared to subordinate doctrine—their own and the Court's—to partisan politics. Their biographies should have put us on notice. These were not, for the most part, great lawyers, with long histories of distinction, who were appointed to the high court because they were the most qualified prospects. In fact, two of them, Thomas and O'Connor, got less than the highest ratings from the American Bar Association.[35] Rather, they were appointed precisely because their biographies showed them to be right-wing ideologues and Republican partisans. Unlike many past justices throughout our history, none of these justices would have warranted any mention in our history books but for the fortuity of having been appointed to our highest court. These were not men and women who had reached the pinnacle of their profession before they ascended the bench, as had Oliver Wendell Holmes, Louis Brandeis, Benjamin Cardozo, Lewis Powell, Thurgood Marshall, Arthur Goldberg, John Harlan, and Harlan Fiske Stone, to mention but a few. Nor had they achieved distinction in politics, as had William Howard Taft, Earl Warren, Hugo Black, or Charles Evans Hughes. Rehnquist and Thomas were middle-level government lawyers;[36] O'Connor was a middle-level state court judge. Kennedy was a competent but relatively unknown federal judge who had previously been an

ordinary lawyer and politically connected lobbyist. Even Antonin Scalia, who was a highly regarded law professor before
his appointment to the Court of Appeals for the District of
Columbia Circuit, was known more for his ideological extremes
than for his scholarship. Few would have ranked him among
the most distinguished theoreticians of constitutional law; but
everyone would have ranked him as among the most ideological
of right-wing theorists. Had he been a moderate Republican—
like, for example, the distinguished constitutional theorist John
Hart Ely—Scalia never even would have been considered for
appointment to either the Court of Appeals or the Supreme
Court. It was his extremism, not his academic distinction, that
brought him to the attention of the Reagan administration and
ultimately got him his job on the high court.[37] (Scalia's extremism also contributed to the determination of the Democrats to
defeat the nomination of an even more extreme Reagan nominee, Robert Bork. The resulting confirmation battle may also
have led presidents to be more cautious about nominating even
distinguished lawyers who were burdened with long and controversial paper trails.)

It should come as no surprise, therefore, that the majority of
this Court—a majority selected by Presidents Nixon, Reagan,
and Bush precisely because of their partisan reliability—should
have come through for the Republicans. "You dance with him
who brung you" is an old political maxim, and the Republicans
not only brung the majority justices, they brung them with specific expectations. These expectations were not satisfied in every
case, but when it came to crunch time, the Republican policy
of judicial appointments paid off.[38]

These justices will be remembered not for the well-crafted
nonpartisan decisions they may have rendered over the years,
nor for the judicial philosophies they long espoused, but rather
for their partisanship in the most important case they decided

and by their failure to adhere to their philosophies when these came into conflict with strongly held partisan and personal preferences in the most challenging case of their careers.

Bush v. Gore demonstrated that ideological extremism is incompatible with greatness in a justice, because greatness requires an ability and a willingness to transcend partisan politics and result-oriented decision-making. The Supreme Court cannot be a great institution without great men and women serving on it. The robe and the gavel do not—with rare exceptions—turn middle-level politicians, average lawyers, and ideologically extreme professors into justices of the highest caliber. For a person to excel as a justice, he or she must have exhibited excellence transcending partisanship before becoming a judge. But the method by which we now select our justices virtually ensures that they will be somewhat partisan. It also now makes it nearly certain that they will be reliable. "No more Souters," which is the current mantra of the Republican right, is a euphemism for "Be absolutely certain we can count on his or her vote."

As this book goes to press, the *New York Times* is reporting on its front page that both conservatives and liberals are "busily preparing for the possibility of a Supreme Court vacancy."[39] Three justices are over seventy, and two have long been rumored as being anxious to retire when a Republican president is in office. It has been nearly seven years since the last high court vacancy, and, as one Courtwatcher put it, "a retirement is overdue."[40]

Conservative activists are pushing the names of several extreme right-wingers who oppose abortion, favor the death penalty, support prayer in public schools, oppose affirmative action, and generally adhere to the conservative political agenda.[41] They have a receptive audience at the White House, which seems resolved "to reshape the nation's courts," especially the Supreme Court.[42] Indeed, the Bush administration has already taken the bold move of "eliminating the American Bar Asso-

ciation's historic role of screening prospective nominees."[43]
"The message seems to be a right-wing takeover," observed an
expert who has tracked judicial nominations since the 1960s.[44]

Liberal activists seem to be more specifically focused on the
abortion issue. A mailing by The National Abortion and Reproductive Rights Action League warned that "a woman's right
to choose now faces its greatest threat since the Supreme Court
decided *Roe v. Wade* in 1973,"[45] and Kate Michelman, the president of the National Abortion and Reproductive Rights Action
League, was explicit about her single-minded, agenda-driven
criterion for nomination to the Supreme Court: If President
Bush does not select an opponent of *Roe v. Wade,* she said, "I
will hold a press conference and say this is marvelous."[46] But
the abortion issue may be resolved, or at least mitigated, by
science within a few years,* and it would be a shame to pack
the Court with justices who were nominated because of their
views on this single issue. The point is broader, however: If a
nomination to the Supreme Court is to be made on the basis of
the nominee's views on a particular issue, then why should a
president not select someone who agrees with him on that

---

*The early-stage abortion issue is likely to be resolved in favor of a woman's
right to choose by the easy availability of the "morning-after" pill (which is a
contraceptive, as it prevents conception or implantation) and other pharmaceu-
tical remedies (the vast majority of Americans will not regard very early-term,
pharmaceutically induced pregnancy termination as real abortion; rather, it seems
more on a continuum with birth control, which nearly all Americans favor). In
regard to very late-term abortion, science is likely to give a victory to the right-
to-life movement by making it easier to save the lives of viable fetuses without
endangering the lives of pregnant women (Americans will not accept the killing
of viable late-term fetuses unless their destruction is necessary to save the life or
protect the physical health of the woman.) So science will narrow the abortion
debate by resolving these extreme situations while leaving the issues of middle-
term abortion, parental consent, government funding, fetal research, and others
for the people and the courts to decide. Even though the remaining issues are
contentious, the abortion debate is likely to move from center stage over the next
several years.

issue?[47] Regardless of the issue under contention, it seems as if neither side cares much about the quality of the justices—their greatness—as long as the nominees pass their particular political litmus test. This is a prescription for even further politicization of the high court.

The time has come to change the criteria for Supreme Court nominees and to depoliticize the process of appointing justices. If justices are simply lawyers appointed for their political reliability, then why should the public accept their decisions? For a court to have legitimacy, it must carry the moral authority of the ages and of a historical continuity with the past. It must display a commitment to precedent that constrains the incumbents even when they are strongly tempted to follow their own preferences. The public must be rightly convinced that the decision is a product not of the justices alone but of history, precedent, and law.

Responsible Democrats and moderate Republicans in the Senate are now in a position to bring about needed changes in the criteria used in selecting Supreme Court nominees. But these changes must have widespread support among the public in order to overcome the advantages to the incumbent administration of staying with the present system. Most important, there must be an institutional commitment to make certain that any selection criteria demanded of Republican presidents will also be demanded of Democratic presidents.

The Constitution vests the power to appoint justices jointly in the president and the Senate. The Senate not only confirms—that is, "consents" to—the president's choice, but also has the constitutional duty to advise the president about who should be nominated. This suggests a role before as well as after the nomination is made. Moreover, the Senate's role should be far greater in the selection of justices and judges than in the appointment of the president's Cabinet members and other members of the administration. Justices of the Supreme Court, once appointed, do not work for the president. They are not part of the executive branch or the administration. Indeed, an important part of their job is to check and balance the executive branch as well as the legislative branch. Accordingly, the responsibility to make these important lifetime appointments—which will transcend any administration and legislative session—must be shared by the president and the Senate. This would seem especially to be the case when the nation is deeply divided politically, as evidenced by the president having lost the popular vote and won the electoral college (with the possible help of the Supreme Court and the unquestioned assistance of the butterfly ballot) by a few hundred votes, and by the Senate being divided down the middle. There could be no more auspicious time to change the accepted criteria for appointment to the Supreme Court.

The first step must be to distance the process from partisan politics and to demand that greatness be the major criterion for appointment to the high court, as it is in many other countries, and as it has often been in the history of this nation. The Senate and the president could begin by jointly appointing a nonpartisan commission to gather the names of the two dozen or so most distinguished lawyers and judges in the nation, assessed by peer review under the broadest criterion of greatness, without regard to party affiliation, race, gender, ideology, or other such factors. After a thorough investigation, this list would probably be pared down to about ten candidates. The president would be expected—though he could not be compelled—to pick a nominee from that pared-down list, unless he could produce good reasons why another person, not included on the commission's list, qualifies as a potentially great justice. Any name selected from the commission's list would carry a strong presumption of confirmability by the Senate.

Obviously, this process provides no absolute guarantee either of greatness or of nonpartisanship. But it moves the process toward a tradition under which these salutary criteria are the publicly articulated and expected ones. Today, even that is not the case.

If the president insists on nominating justices based on partisan considerations rather than greatness, the Senate should refuse to confirm them. As an early commentator on the Constitution interpreted the role of the Senate in the appointment of justices: "A party nomination may be justly met by party opposition."[48] Democratic senators should feel entirely comfortable voting against any Republican loyalists who will put the interests of their party—and its candidates—before the law. Nor should moderate Republicans, who place loyalty to the Constitution above zealotry in the service of their party, vote to confirm any nominee for the high court who has not exhibited extraordinary distinction transcending party platform.

If the president and the Senate refuse to take up this effort to depoliticize the process by which justices are nominated, then I believe the bar and the academy should step in. They should appoint a commission to produce a nonpartisan list of the most qualified potential nominees based on criteria agreed upon in advance. This would put pressure on the president and the Senate to look to similar criteria, because the public will insist on the highest possible quality if it is presented as an alternative to partisanship.

In my estimation, the public is ready to insist on greatness as the criterion for service on the Supreme Court, so long as it is assured that this criterion will be employed honestly by both parties. Most Americans were outraged when Senator Roman L. Hruska (R-Neb.) supported Richard Nixon's nomination of Judge G. Harrold Carswell to the high court in 1970 by arguing that "[t]here are a lot of mediocre judges and people and lawyers, and they are entitled to a little representation [on the Supreme Court], aren't they? We can't have all Brandeises, Frankfurters, and Cardozos." Americans rightfully expect more than mediocrity. All of our justices can be as notable as the ones Hruska named so dismissively and the many others—like Holmes, Marshall, Harlan, Jackson, and Stone—who are included on virtually everyone's list of greats. But we can accomplish this high goal only if we pressure our elected officials to approach the process with criteria different from those now employed.

Greatness is not single-dimensional. It is not limited to creative academics or eminent practitioners or respected public officials. It may be difficult to define, but it is not difficult to see in a truly remarkable person. Lack of greatness, too, is not difficult to identify. One conclusion that would seem beyond dispute is that no truly great Supreme Court justice would ever fail the shoe-on-the-other-foot test. Nor would their actions even give rise to the suspicion that they decided a case on a partisan basis. Greatness transcends partisanship. Its reward is not the spoils of an immediate political victory, but rather the verdict of history over time that the particular justice has been true to the Constitution.

The verdict of history will be extremely critical of the justices who hijacked Election 2000 from the people. Their places in history have been irrevocably established by their corrupt decision in this most important of cases, which tested them as no previous case had done. The self-inflicted wound by the majority in *Bush v. Gore* will fester so long as any of these justices remain on the Court. As a federal judge "with many close Republican ties" told Linda Greenhouse of the *New York Times,* these judges must now "rehabilitate" themselves—a term commonly used in connection with convicted criminals and disgraced politicians.[49] I doubt they will be able to do so, since no process of rehabilitation can begin without an acknowledgment of wrongdoing, and it is unlikely we will see such an acknowledgment from any of the majority justices. The current Supreme Court majority will remain on probation, at least in the eyes of constitutional scholars, until the current majority is re-placed by new justices with clean hands.

In a larger sense, the memory of the wound will endure even beyond the tenure of any current justice. It has left a permanent scar on the credibility of the Supreme Court. People will—and should—trust it less, because it proved untrustworthy when tempted by partisanship and personal advantage.

The only way to ensure a rightfully skeptical citizenry that its trust in the justices will never again be violated is to appoint only men and women of the highest possible integrity and dis-tinction to serve in this unique role in the American system of governance. *Bush v. Gore* has demonstrated that a Supreme Court can be no greater than the justices who serve on it, and that doctrine alone—regardless of how often it is repeated—is no guarantee of justice in the hands of easily tempted partisans eager for immediate political or personal gratification.

It will not be easy to make greatness the accepted criterion for appointment to the Supreme Court, but it is possible to establish a tradition under which it is the standard against which all candidates are judged. We should take up the chal-lenge and act now. The Supreme Injustice perpetrated by the five majority justices in *Bush v. Gore* makes this an opportune moment to demand greatness as the alternative to partisanship.

Notes

Note to Reader

The book's appendices are posted on the internet at
www.oup-usa.org/sc/0195148274/

1. Federal election law:
   Safe-harbor provision
   U.S. Constitution, Article II
   U.S. Constitution, Amendment Twelve
2. *Bush v. Palm Beach County Canvassing Board*
   Supreme Court of the United States, December 4, 2000
3. *Gore v. Harris*
   Florida Supreme Court, December 8, 2000
4. The Stay
   Supreme Court of the United States, December 9, 2000
5. *Bush v. Gore*
   Supreme Court of the United States, December 12, 2000

Introduction

1. The Tilden–Hayes election was decided by a single justice, but he was serving as a member of a bipartisan electoral commission, which had been established by Congress to decide the disputed presidential election of 1876. See William Bennett Munro, *The Government of the United States* (Macmillan, 1946), 151–52; C. Vann Woodward, *Reunion and Reaction: The Compromise of 1877 and the End of Reconstruction* (Doubleday, 1956), 161–62; Sidney I. Pomerantz, "Election of 1876," in Arthur M. Schlesinger Jr., ed., *History of American Presidential Elections, 1789–1968* (Chelsea House, 1971); and www.elections.harpweek.com/4Overview/overview-1876-2.htm.
2. John DiIulio Jr., "Equal Protection Run Amok," in E. J. Dionne Jr. and William Kristol, eds., *Bush v. Gore: The Court Cases and the Commentary* (Brookings Institution, 2001), 323.
3. Cass Sunstein, "What We Will Remember in 2050," in Dionne and Kristol, eds., *Bush v. Gore,* 340
4. Ibid.
5. See Randall Kennedy, "Contempt of Court," 337; Michael S. Greve, "The *Real* Division in the Court," 324; and Scott Turow, "A Brand New Game" (quoting Sandalow), 304, all in Dionne and Kristol, eds., *Bush v. Gore.*

6.   On Jan. 13, 2001, an advertisement signed by 554 law professors was published in the *New York Times*. It asserted that "when a bare majority of the U.S. Supreme Court halted the recount . . . the five justices were acting as political proponents for candidate Bush, not as judges."

7.   Under the Constitution, the people can actually be denied the right to vote for electors, but every state grants them that right. See page 17.

8.   "An 1887 law states that if there are two slates of electors, the one certified by the governor should be counted. But the meaning of the statute is not clear." David E. Rosenbaum, "An Electoral Road Map: Where the Battle for Florida Might Head Next," *New York Times,* Dec. 9, 2000.

9.   Quoted in "Unsafe Harbor," (editorial in the *New Republic*), in Dionne and Kristol, eds., *Bush v. Gore,* 318.

10.   *Deadlock: The Inside Story of America's Closest Election,* by the Political Staff of the Washington Post (Public Affairs, 2001), 171.

11.   See, e.g., *Coleman v. Thompson,* 501 U.S. 722 (1991), opinion by O'Connor in which Rehnquist, White, Scalia, Kennedy, and Souter joined, holding that federal habeas courts generally may not review a state court's denial of a state prisoner's federal constitutional claim if the court's decision rests on a state procedural default that is independent of the federal question and adequate to support the prisoner's continued custody; *Castille v. Peoples,* 489 U.S. 346 (1989), opinion by Scalia for a unanimous Court, holding that a state prisoner's federal habeas petition should be dismissed if the prisoner has not exhausted available state remedies as to any of his federal claims; and *Wainwright v. Sykes,* 433 U.S. 72 (1977), opinion by Rehnquist, holding that a convicted man's failure to make timely objection to the admission of his inculpatory statements in the state court proceeding barred federal habeas corpus review of his *Miranda* claim.

12.   See, e.g., Robert Bork, introductory remarks, American Enterprise Institute Annual Dinner and Francis Boyer Lecture, Feb. 13, 2001 ("The per curiam opinion joined by five Justices does have major problems"); Harvey Mansfield, "What We'll Remember in 2050," *The Chronicle of Higher Education,* Jan. 1–15, 2001 ("It was unfortunate that the majority of the court had to go to the equal-protection clause"); Benjamin Wittes, "Maybe the Court Got It Right," *Washington Post,* Feb. 21, 2001 ("Posner agrees with critics of the U.S. Supreme Court that its reliance on the doctrine of equal protection in reversing the Florida Court was wrongheaded"); Michael W. McConnell, "A Muddled Ruling," *Wall Street Journal,* Dec. 12, 2000; and Richard A. Epstein, "In Such Manner as the Legislature Thereof May Direct," in Cass Sunstein and Richard Epstein, eds., *The Vote: Bush, Gore, and the Supreme Court* (forthcoming, available from www.thevotebook. com) ("Any equal protection challenge to the Florida recount procedure quickly runs into insurmountable difficulties").

13.   Linda Greenhouse, "Another Kind of Bitter Split," in Dionne and Kristol, eds., *Bush v. Gore,* 297–98.

14.   Commentary, 1979 *Wash. U. L. Q.* 147.

15. Some conservative commentators have condemned the dissenters for "fouling their own nest." In doing so, they have failed to understand the inaptness of this scatological metaphor. The dissenters are merely calling attention to the fouling done by their majority brothers and sisters.

16. "Analysis of Florida Ballots Proves Favorable to Bush," *New York Times*, April 4, 2001, A18.

Chapter 1

1. *Bagaz* is the acronym used to refer to the power of the Israeli supreme court to sit as a "high court of justice" (*bet din-gavo'ah le-zedek*). When the court is exercising its *bagaz* power, it has original jurisdiction over all claims of excessive or improper administrative or governmental power brought by any citizen. See Menachem Elon, *Jewish Law: History, Sources, Principles* (Jewish Publication Society, 1994), vol. 1, glossary.

2. Article III, sec. 1, U.S. Constitution ("The judicial Power of the United States, shall be vested in one Supreme Court, and in such inferior Courts as the Congress may from time to time ordain and establish").

3. See especially *Marbury v. Madison*, 5 U.S. (1 Cranch) 137 (1803), which reads the Constitution as imposing a duty on federal courts to overturn laws that are in conflict with the Constitution.

4. Cases in which the Supreme Court has original jurisdiction, that is, in which the Supreme Court is the first and only court in which the case can be heard, are of three kinds: cases in which a state is a party; cases affecting ambassadors, other public ministers, and consuls of foreign nations; and cases involving certain extraordinary writs. Richard H. Fallon Jr. et al., *The Federal Courts and the Federal System* (Hart and Wechsler's Foundation Press, 1996), 294–348.

5. The federal court cases brought during the election controversy included: *Bush v. Gore; Bush v. Palm Beach County Canvassing Board; Siegel v. LePore; Touchston v. McDermott; Harris v. State of Florida Election Canvassing Commission; Bush v. Hillsborough County Canvassing Board; Jones v. Bush*. The state court cases were: *Gore v. Harris; Jacobs v. Seminole County Canvassing Board; Taylor v. Martin County Canvassing Board; Brown v. Stafford; Gore v. Miami-Dade County Canvassing Board; Bush v. Bay County Canvassing Board; Palm Beach County Canvassing Board v. Harris; McDermott v. Harris; Harris v. Circuit Judges; Florida Democratic Party v. Carroll; Florida Democratic Party v. Palm Beach County Canvassing Board; Fladell v. Palm Beach County Canvassing Board; Horowitz v. LePore; Elkins v. LePore; Rogers v. Election Canvassing Commission; Gibbs v. Palm Beach County Canvassing Board; Crum v. Palm Beach County Canvassing Board; HABIL v. Palm Beach County Canvassing Board; Gottfried v. LePore; Lichtman v. Jeb Bush*.

6. *Deadlock: The Inside Story of America's Closest Election*, by the Political Staff of the *Washington Post* (Public Affairs, 2001), 21.

7. "The individual citizen has no federal constitutional right to vote for elec-

tors for the President of the United States unless and until the state legislature chooses a statewide election." *Bush v. Gore* at 529.

8. Since the founding of our country, restrictions on the right to vote have been based on race, sex, property ownership, taxation, literacy, age, and criminal record, among other considerations.

9. Although many of the reforms that frequently are credited to Jackson's Democratic Party had been initiated before Jackson became president—and were, in some cases, enacted over the objections of the Jacksonians—he and his followers were quick to assume the mantle of champion of democracy and scourge of the aristocrat. There is no doubt, however, that democracy flourished under the Jacksonian Democrats.

10. William Josephson and Beverly J. Ross, "Repairing the Electoral College," 22 *J. Legis.* 145, 161 (1996).

11. The Seventeenth Amendment, ratified in 1913, ended the practice of state legislatures selecting senators and instituted a system whereby senators would be chosen in the same way as representatives—by popular election.

12. *Brown v. Allen,* 344 U.S. 443, 540 (1953), Jackson concurring. The corollary to this power is that the Supreme Court is "infallible" only in matters over which it properly exercised its authority, and there has been considerable debate since *Marbury* over the proper role of the Supreme Court in a federalist democracy. Among those who have argued most strenuously for a limited role by the high court have been several of the very justices who voted to intervene in the Florida election case, as will be discussed in Chapter 4.

13. These two states are Maine and Nebraska. See Alexander Hanebeck, "Democracy Within Federalism," 37 *San Diego L. Rev.* 347, 389, n. 263 (2000).

14. See generally Beverly J. Ross and William Josephson, "The Electoral College and the Popular Vote," 12 *J. L. and Politics* 665 (1996).

15. 3 U.S.C. sec. 5.

16. The House has never enacted specific rules for such a proceeding. See *New York Times,* June 11, 1992, A2. Among the issues that remain unresolved by the lack of clear rules are the following: (1) Is the vote secret or open? In 1801 and 1825, the proceedings were secret. It is unlikely they would be secret today. (2) Does the House consist of the old members, including lame ducks, or the new members, including those just elected in November? In 1801 and 1825, it consisted of the old members. (3) Does each state delegation determine its state's vote by majority or plurality? In the unlikely event that the House fails to elect a president by January 20, the Speaker of the House of Representatives becomes acting president. If the Speaker is unable to qualify as acting president, then the president pro tempore of the Senate assumes the position (3 U.S.C. sec. 19). In this election, the Speaker was Dennis Hastert (R-Ill.) and the president pro tempore was Strom Thurmond (R.-S.C.).

17. Under Florida law, an automatic machine recount, which is relatively quick
     and simple, is triggered whenever the candidates are separated by 0.5 per-
     cent or less of the vote. Following such a machine recount, the candidate
     may protest and/or challenge the results:

> The Florida Election Code sets forth a two-pronged system for challenging
> vote returns and election procedures. The "protest" and "contest" provi-
> sions are distinct proceedings. A protest proceeding is filed with the Coun-
> ty Canvassing Board and addresses the validity of the vote returns. The re-
> lief that may be granted includes a manual recount. The Canvassing Board
> is a neutral ministerial body. A contest proceeding, on the other hand, is
> filed in circuit court and addresses the validity of the election itself. Relief
> that may be granted is varied and can be extensive. No appellate relation-
> ship exists between a "protest" and a "contest"; a protest is not a prereq-
> uisite for a contest. Moreover, the trial court in the contest action does not
> sit as an appellate court over the decisions of the Canvassing Board. Ac-
> cordingly while the Board's actions concerning the elections process may
> constitute evidence in a contest proceeding, the Board's decisions are not
> to be accorded the highly deferential "abuse of discretion" standard of re-
> view during a contest proceeding. (*Gore v. Harris*, 772 So. 2d 1243 (2000)
> at 1252, internal citations omitted)

     After the ballots have been counted in a precinct, that precinct's election
     board must draw up a certificate of the results, which is sent to the county
     supervisor of elections (Fla. Stat. 102.071). The County Canvassing Board
     (which is composed of the supervisor of elections, a county court judge,
     and the chair of the board of county commissioners [Fla. Stat. 102.141
     (1)]), having received the completed certificates from all the precincts, can-
     vasses and certifies the results for that county and forwards them to the
     Department of State (Fla. Stat. 102.151). If, however, the returns for a
     county show that a candidate for office was defeated by 0.5 percent or less
     of the total votes cast for such office, the board must order a recount of
     the votes cast in that race. This automatic recount is conducted by machine,
     or whatever counting method was used in the initial count (Fla. Stat.
     102.141 (4)).

     As soon as the official results are compiled from all counties, the Elec-
     tions Canvassing Commission (which is made up of the governor, the sec-
     retary of state, and the director of the Division of Elections) certifies them
     and declares the winners of all state and federal races. "If the county re-
     turns are not received by the Department of State by 5 P.M. of the seventh
     day following an election, all missing counties *shall* be ignored, and the
     results shown by the returns on file *shall* be certified" (Fla. Stat. 102.111,
     emphasis added).

     This provision appears to be in conflict with the statute immediately
     following it, Fla. Stat. 102.112, which says: "Returns must be filed by 5
     P.M. on the 7th day following the . . . general election. . . . If the returns
     are not received by the department by the time specified, such returns *may*

be ignored and the results on file at that time *may* be certified by the department"' (emphasis added). There is also a potential conflict, which became a reality in this election, between the seven-day window for a county to submit its returns and the time needed to complete a manual recount as contemplated by Fla. Stat. 102.166 (see below for details). These apparent inconsistencies were resolved by the Florida Supreme Court in *Palm Beach County Canvassing Bd. v. Harris*, 772 So. 2d 1273 (2000), using standard principles of statutory construction, and an equitable remedy was fashioned by which the November 14 deadline was extended to November 26.

Protest: Before the county canvassing board certifies the results for a specific office or within seventy-two hours after the day of the election, whichever occurs later, any candidate or political party whose candidates' names appeared on the ballot may file a written request for a manual recount (Fla. Stat. 102.166 (4)(a),(b)). If the board authorizes a manual recount, it must include at least three precincts and at least 1 percent of the total votes cast for the candidate. The person or party requesting the recount has the right to select the three precincts to be recounted (Fla. Stat. 102.166 (4)(d)). If this preliminary manual recount "indicates an error in the vote tabulation which could affect the outcome of the election," the board can order a manual recount of all the ballots in the county (Fla. Stat. 102.166 (5)).

Contest: The certification of a candidate's election by the Elections Canvassing Commission can be contested by an unsuccessful candidate for that office, qualified voter, or taxpayer by filing a complaint with the clerk of the circuit court within ten days after the last county canvassing board certifies the results of the election or within five days after the last county canvassing board certifies the results of the election following a protest, whichever occurs later (Fla. Stat. 102.168 (1),(2)). The contestant must allege one of the following: misconduct, fraud, or corruption by an election official that is sufficient to change or place in doubt the result of the election; that the elected candidate is ineligible for the office; the receipt of enough illegal votes, or the rejection of enough legal votes, to change or place in doubt the result of the election; proof that a voter, election official, or canvassing board member was bribed; or another charge that, if sustained, would show that someone other than the elected candidate actually won the election (Fla. Stat. 102.168 (3)). The circuit judge before whom the contest is brought "may fashion such orders as he or she deems necessary to ensure that each allegation in the complaint is investigated, examined, or checked, to prevent or correct any alleged wrong, and to provide any relief appropriate under such circumstances" (Fla. Stat. 102.168 (8)).

18. I will mention only those lower court decisions that impacted on the Supreme Court's decisions.

19. A stay is a judicial decision preserving the status quo until the court has

finally decided the case on its merits. In this case, there was a dispute over whether the status quo was a continuation of the ongoing count or a stopping of the count. The majority stopped the count.

20. Several issues that never made it to the Supreme Court may have contributed significantly to Gore losing the election. An investigative report by Julian Borger for Britain's *The Guardian* (London) established that Harris hired a conservative group to purge all ex-felons from the voter rolls. The group eliminated black voters with a vengeance, including some blacks whose voting rights had been restored, others who had been convicted of mere misdemeanors and were eligible to vote, and still others who were convicted in other states and may also have been eligible to vote. An election supervisor told Borger, "Yes, there were errors on the list. . . . There were instances of mistaken identity and people who should not have been on it. Something doesn't work right in the system."

Other blacks who remained on the voter list were kept from voting or having their votes counted with tactics that ranged from the use of old voting machines in minority areas (which produced high levels of uncounted votes in those areas) to the employment of police roadblocks and other forms of intimidation in black areas on Election Day. Julian Borger reported:

> On election morning, Darryl Gorham was driving some neighbours to vote in Woodville, outside Tallahassee. They turned a bend in the road about a mile before the polling station and came across a scene straight out of the segregation era: roadblocks. "There were four Florida highway patrolmen standing in the middle of the street," Mr. Gorham said. "They were stopping everybody. They had seven or eight cars stopped on the side of the road and waiting. They inspected the headlights, tail-lights, indicators, licence, registration, tags, everything. . . . I've lived in Florida most of my life, but I have never, ever seen a roadblock like that." Mr. Gorham is convinced that the white policemen were trying to slow down the flow of black voters in a historically tight election. He said: "It took maybe 15, maybe 20 minutes. But many people were taking time out from work, or going to work, and it was making them late. Some just turned 'round and went back." (Julian Borger, "How Florida Played the Race Card," *The Guardian*, Dec. 4, 2000, 3)

These tactics are now the subject of a spate of voting-rights lawsuits.

Gore, on the other hand, may have benefited from the media's early call that he had won the state—a call that came before the voting ended in the western part of Florida's Panhandle, which is on Central Time. It is impossible to know how many, if any, Bush voters stayed home after hearing the state called for Gore.

21. David von Drehle, Dan Balz, Ellen Nakashima, and Jo Becker, "A Wild Ride into Uncharted Territory," *Washington Post,* Jan. 28, 2001. The *Miami Herald* reported on Jan. 7, 2001, that Gore lost an additional 316 votes in Miami-Dade County as the result of 1,700 voters having inadver-

tently punched "the chad immediately below the one corresponding to their preferred candidate." These voters "penetrated a meaningless chad." The cause of this error was a misalignment of the ballot cards with the ballot books in the voting booth.

22.   Joel Engelhardt and Scott McCabe, "Over-Votes Cost Gore the Election in Florida," *Palm Beach Post,* Mar. 11, 2001.

23.   Pat Buchanan, interview by Charles Gibson, *Primetime,* ABC News, Nov. 9, 2000.

24.   *Deadlock,* 69.

25.   "Almost half of the Gore–Buchanan overvotes were from precincts where most of the voters were 65 or older and Democrats. Even if 1 percent of the 6,607 votes were intended for Buchanan or McReynolds—more than their combined portion of Palm Beach County's total vote—Gore would still have gained 6,541 votes, the newspaper concluded:

Are these stupid voters? Or is it a stupid voting system? There's certainly evidence here that these were not stupid voters," University of California-Berkeley Professor Henry Brady said. . . .

Three-fourths of the over-votes were punches for two candidates, most of which experts attributed to the ballot design, the paper said. The rest were for three or more candidates, which experts called voter error, not a design problem. . . .

The review of over-votes was conducted between January 17 and January 29. Last year, Brady calculated that at least 2,000 of Buchanan's 3,424 Palm Beach County votes were meant for Gore. If that were true, Gore's total gain—with the over-votes—might have been as much as 8,600 votes, the paper said.

(www.cnn.com/2001/ALLPOLITICS/03/11/palmbeach.recount/index.html)

26.   The complaint in *Horowitz v. LePore,* CL 001 0970 AG (2000), alleges that "the ballot format used in connection with the voting for President and Vice-President in the November 7, 2000, General Election was misleading, deceptive, and caused many of the voters in the election to cast votes for candidates other than the candidate for whom they intended to vote."

27.   The *Washington Post* has put a slightly different spin on her party loyalty:

LePore is a doer, not a theorist. The eldest of eight in a close-knit, hard-working Catholic family, LePore got her first job at the election supervisor's office when she was 16 through her father Joe, a former city commissioner. She started out working part-time and never left. The job suited Theresa, who prided herself on organization and order.

When her mentor stepped down in 1996 and LePore ran for supervisor herself, she declared as a Democrat because that's where the votes are in Palm Beach County. But "she is not political at all," County Commissioner Mary McCarty, a Republican, later said. "She has no use for the Republican or the Democratic Party."

There were many registered Democrats in Florida with loyalties to George W. Bush (the so-called Jeb Bush Democrats).

28.   3 U.S.C. sec. 1. Absentee ballots can, however, be cast before that day.

29.   David van Drehle, Ellen Nakashima, Susan Schmidt, and Ceci Connolly, "In Florida, Drawing the Battle Lines," *Washington Post,* Jan. 29, 2001, quoting George J. Terwilliger III.

30.   This decision was affirmed in *Fladell v. Palm Beach County Canvassing Board,* 772 So. 2d 1240 (2000).

31.   Van Drehle et al., "In Florida, Drawing the Battle Lines."

32.   *Deadlock,* 68.

33.   Peter Aronson, *The National Law Journal,* Dec. 18, 2000 (quoting cross-examination of John Ahmann, holder of several patents for components of the Votomatic).

34.   Mark Z. Barabak and Richard A. Serrano, "Decision 2000: America Waits," *Los Angeles Times,* Dec. 4, 2000.

35.   Stacey Singer and John Maines, "Many Disqualified Votes in Minority Areas," *Chicago Tribune,* Dec. 1, 2000.

36.   Jan Adlingsworth, "Voting Instructions Lacking in Some Punch-Card Counties," *Tampa Tribune,* Dec. 14, 2000. This article contradicts Chief Justice Rehnquist's assertion that "[e]ach Florida precinct . . . provides instructions on how properly to cast a vote."

37.   The Florida Supreme Court eventually deprived them of that statutory right by ruling that the interests of all the voters to have their lawful ballots counted trumped the tactical advantage sought by any particular candidate. *Gore v. Harris,* 772 So. 2d. 1243, 1253 (2000).

I have never understood why the Gore team focused so exclusively on the undervotes rather than also including the overvotes—ballots not counted because the voter had punched or dented two (or more) chads for the same office, especially since there is a close, if inverse, relationship between these two categories of uncounted ballots. For example, if a fully punched-through ballot with a hanging chad should be counted during a hand count of undervotes, then it would follow that a punched-through hole with a hanging chad would disqualify as an overvote any ballot that contained a vote for another candidate for president. Perhaps the Gore advisors suspected that they would do better in the undervotes rather than the overvotes, but there is no a priori reason to suspect that if hand-counting undervotes would help a particular candidate, counting overvotes would hurt him. Indeed, what we now know about Palm Beach County suggests that Gore was hurt by not counting both undervotes and overvotes. See *USA Today,* April 4, 2001, A1. The Gore camp decided, however, to go after the undervotes in four Democratic counties in which Gore could expect to pick up votes by a hand count of undervotes.

38.   According to one study, Gore would have been better off requesting a narrower criterion for counting ballots. See "Florida's Unchanging Les-

sons" (editorial), *New York Times,* Apr. 6, 2001, describing the results of the *Miami Herald/USA Today* study of the ballots.

39. The others were the safe-harbor and Electoral College meeting dates, about which more later.

40. See page 19, note 17.

41. Michael Cooper, "Counting the Vote," *New York Times,* Nov. 12, 2000.

42. Sec. 5 of the Fourteenth Amendment to the U.S. Constitution gives Congress the "power to enforce, by appropriate legislation, the provisions of this article."

   The principle of equality—at least for nonblacks—has been a defining element of American government since its inception. The Declaration of Independence regarded the ideal of equality as so basic and secure that a nation could be founded on it: "We hold these Truths to be self-evident, that all Men are created equal" (para. 2). However, it took a civil war and the subsequent enactment of the Fourteenth Amendment in 1868 before this principle was accorded its proper place in the Constitution. Shortly after the end of the Civil War, Congress ratified the Thirteenth Amendment (prohibiting slavery in the United States), Fourteenth Amendment (guaranteeing due process and equal protection), and Fifteenth Amendment (precluding the use of race as a basis for denying a citizen's right to vote). Together these amendments are commonly referred to as the Civil War amendments.

43. Slavery was officially ended by President Abraham Lincoln's Emancipation Proclamation, which took effect on Jan. 1, 1863.

44. See *Strauder v. West Virginia,* 100 U.S. 303, 306 (1879), asserting that the purpose of the Fourteenth Amendment was "to assure to the colored race the enjoyment of all the civil rights that under the law are enjoyed by white persons."

45. "Congressman Stevens, introducing the Fourteenth Amendment in the House characterized its basic purpose as 'the amelioration of the condition of the freedmen.'" Eric Schnapper, "Affirmative Action and the Legislative History of the Fourteenth Amendment," 71 *Va. L. Rev.* 753, 785 (1985).

46. See Chester J. Antieau, *The Original Understanding of the Fourteenth Amendment* (Mid-America, 1981), 14–17; see also *Regents of University of California v. Bakke,* 438 U.S. 265, 293 (1978), stating that although the Framers intended to bridge the gap between the white majority and the black minority, "the Amendment itself was framed in universal terms, without reference to color, ethnic origin, or condition of prior servitude."

47. For example, Senator John Sherman of Ohio asserted that all people "should stand equal before the law" (Antieau, *Original Understanding,* 16). Similarly, Senator Lyman Trumbull argued that the amendment "would put in the fundamental law the declaration that all the citizens were entitled to equal rights in this Republic" (ibid., 15).

48. *Reed v. Reed,* 404 U.S. 71 (1971).

49. *City of Cleburne v. Cleburne Living Center,* 473 U.S. 432 (1985).

50. *Skinner v. Oklahoma*, 316 U.S. 535 (1942).
51. *Harper v. Virginia State Board of Elections*, 383 U.S. 663 (1966).
52. *Shapiro v. Thompson*, 394 U.S. 618 (1969).
53. *Griffin v. Illinois*, 351 U.S. 12 (1956).
54. The most striking example of this is *Adarand v. Pena*, 515 U.S. 200 (1995); see also *Richmond v. Croson*, 488 U.S. 469 (1989); *Wygant v. Jackson Bd. of Education*, 476 U.S. 267 (1986).
55. Van Drehle et al., "In Florida, Drawing the Battle Lines."
56. *Deadlock*, 163, quoting George J. Terwilliger III.
57. See, e.g., *Powers v. Ohio*, 499 U.S. 400 (1991), Scalia dissenting.
58. Florida has long followed the clear-intent standard in all elections. As its supreme court ruled in *Boardman v. Esteva*, 323 So. 2d 259, 263 (1975):

    [T]he real parties in interest here, not in the legal sense but in realistic terms, are the voters. They are possessed of the ultimate interest and it is they whom we must give primary consideration. The contestants have direct interests certainly, but the office they seek is one of high public service and utmost importance to the people, thus subordinating their interests to that of the people. Ours is a government of, by and for the people. Our federal and state constitutions guarantee the right of the people to take an active part in the process of that government, which for most of our citizens means participation via the election process. The right to vote is the right to participate; it is also the right to speak, but more importantly the right to be heard. We must tread carefully on that right or we risk the unnecessary and unjustified muting of the public voice. *By refusing to recognize an otherwise valid exercise of the right of a citizen to vote for the sake of sacred, unyielding adherence to statutory scripture, we would in effect nullify that right.* (Emphasis added)

    In a similar vein, in *Darby v. State*, 72 So. 411, 412 (1917) (the Florida ballot initiative case), the supreme court said:

    Where a ballot is so marked as to plainly indicate the voter's choice and intent in placing his marks thereon, it should be counted as marked unless some positive provision of law would be thereby violated.

    The declaration that "[n]o vote shall be declared invalid or void if there is a clear indication of the intent of the voter as determined by the canvassing board," in Fla. Stat. 101.5614 (5), reads better as a reminder of a generally applicable principle than as a unique standard to be applied only in the narrow case of damaged ballots. The use of the comprehensive "no vote," as opposed to a narrower "no damaged ballot" or "none of these ballots," reinforces this reading. In fact, in a state that clearly provides for manual recounts (and doesn't prohibit manual counts of the initial vote), it is hard to see what other standard could apply. The statutes certainly don't provide an alternative standard.

    Fla. Stat. 101.5614 (7), which comes a few lines below the announcement of the intent-of-the-voter standard, specifically allows absentee ballots to be counted mechanically "if they have been punched or marked in a

manner which will enable them to be properly counted by such equipment," or by hand, whether or not they are capable of being counted by
machine. Presumably, all these ballots should be counted according to the
intent of the voter standard mentioned above, not just the damaged ones.
No other standard is mentioned. And if the intent-of-the-voter standard is
appropriate for counting all absentee ballots, even those that are not damaged and could have been counted by machine, then how can it be inappropriate for counting all damaged and undamaged ballots?

59. As part of their legal and political argument, Republicans pointed to the
possibility that during a manual count, some hanging chads might fall off.
Even if that claim is true factually, it could have no legal bearing on the
accuracy of a count if a fully punched-through ballot with a hanging chad
is to be counted as a valid vote, as it must be under the voter-intent standard. Thus, there is no legal difference between a fully punched-through
ballot with a hanging chad and one without. The only factual claim that
could make a legal difference would be if chads that were fully attached
could fall off during a hand count, but there was no evidence that this
could occur.

60. Von Drehle et al., "In Florida, Drawing the Battle Lines."

61. *Siegel v. LePore*, 120 F. Supp. 2d 1041 (S.D. Fla. 2000).

62. Fla. Stat. 102.166 (4)(d) and 102.166 (5)(c).

63. See note 58 for the full text of the relevant passage in the statute.

64. *Darby v. State*, 75 So. 411, 412 (1917).

65. *Boardman v. Esteva*, 323 So. 2d. 259 (1975).

66. *Beckstrom v. Volusia*, 707 So. 2d. 720 (1998).

67. Ibid.

68. Democrats, predictably led by the Reverend Jesse Jackson, were quick to
identify and broadcast the discrepancy between the high number of votes
rejected in poorer, predominantly black areas and the much smaller number rejected in wealthier, predominantly white areas. Republicans were
equally quick to counter this allegation by pointing out that Palm Beach
County, where most of the election controversy centered, is neither poor
nor predominantly black. The truth, as usual, was much more nuanced,
but it tended to support the Democrats' allegations. While many factors,
including age, education, voting experience, the form of the ballot, and the
helpfulness of the precinct's staff, undoubtedly played a part in creating
unusually high rates of voter error in some precincts, it is also generally
true that precincts in which the more accurate optical scanning machines
were employed were generally wealthier than those in which the old Votomatic machines were used. There was also a general correlation between
the percentage of minority voters in a county and that county's rate of
voter error. According to a *Washington Post* analysis of Florida's Miami-
Dade County, "precincts where fewer than 30 percent of the voters are
black had about 3 percent of ballots that failed to register a vote for president. In precincts where more than 70 percent of the voters are black, the

undervote was nearly 10 percent." "Fixing the Vote," *Washington Post,*
Dec. 11, 2000.

69. I was extremely critical of that lawyer. See *New York Times,* Nov. 18,
2000, A1.

70. See David von Drehle et al., "A 'Queen' Kept Clock Running," *Washington
Post,* Jan. 30, 2001, which lists the allowable reasons as "vote fraud, machine malfunction, substantial negligence on the part of election officials
and natural disasters—but not voter error."

71. Ibid.

72. Paul A. Gigot, "Burgher Rebellion," *Wall Street Journal,* Nov. 24, 2000.

73. Adam Nagourney and David Barstow, "The 43rd President: Resisting the
Recount," *New York Times,* Dec. 22, 2000.

74. Boies was subsequently criticized for agreeing that this deadline was significant. See Dan Balz et al., "A War Leaves Its Questions," *Washington
Post,* Feb. 4, 2001: "Still, there is a question of what might have happened
had Boies, in oral argument before the Florida high court on Nov. 20, not
agreed so readily that Dec. 12.—the date for naming Florida's electors—
was a firm deadline." My own view is that nothing different would have
happened, considering the predisposition of the majority of the U.S. Supreme Court.

75. There were two significant challenges brought against the validity of absentee ballots. First, a lawsuit was filed to disqualify either all or some of
the 15,215 absentee ballots in Seminole County, where Bush enjoyed a lead
of almost 5,000 votes among absentee ballots (*Jacobs v. Seminole County
Canvassing Board*). The complaint alleged that the Seminole County Canvassing Board allowed Republican Party volunteers to fill in missing voter
registration numbers on applications submitted by registered Republican
voters requesting absentee ballots. This action was alleged to be in violation
of sec. 101.62 of the Florida Statutes, which provides that a request for an
absentee ballot must be made by *the voter or a member of the voter's
immediate family* and that the person making the request must disclose
certain information, including the registration number on the elector's registration identification card. The complaint further alleged that the office
of the Seminole County Supervisor of Elections failed to inform the Democratic Party of the actions of the Republican Party volunteers and to afford them the same opportunity to correct defective requests for absentee
ballots from Democratic Party members. A similar suit was filed in Martin
County *(Taylor v. Martin County Canvassing Board).* Both suits were ultimately dismissed by the Florida Supreme Court in two nearly identical
rulings, both issued on December 12, 2000. Despite finding "troubling"
irregularities in conduct by the county canvassing boards, the court held
that there had been substantial compliance with the absentee voting laws
and that there was no evidence of "fraud or other intentional misconduct"
that would justify throwing out the ballots.

The second controversy involved a challenge to many of the overseas absentee ballots cast by members of the U.S. Armed Forces—the so-called military ballots. Section 101.62 (7)(c) of the Florida election statute provides: "With respect to marked ballots mailed by absent qualified electors overseas, only those ballots mailed with an APO, FPO, or foreign postmark shall be considered valid." But, for whatever reason, many of the military ballots arrived in Florida without any postmark. This created a problem because Florida law clearly requires all overseas absentee ballots to be postmarked by Election Day and received within ten days after the election. Without a postmark, it was impossible to tell whether a ballot that arrived after November 7 actually had been cast in time (*Washington Post,* Nov. 11, 2000). Several lawsuits sought to ensure that these overseas absentee ballots were included in the final count. Ultimately, bipartisan sympathy, led by Sen. Bob Dole and Sen. Joseph Lieberman, for members of the military prevented any serious challenge to these ballots from taking place (lawsuits were *Harris v. Florida Elections Canvassing Commission* and *Bush v. Hillsborough County Canvassing Board*).

76. Fla. Stat. 102.112 (1) says:

> The county canvassing board or a majority thereof shall file the county returns for the election of a federal or state officer with the Department of State immediately after certification of the election results. Returns must be filed by 5 P.M. on the 7th day following the first primary and general election and by 3 P.M. on the 3rd day following the second primary. If the returns are not received by the department by the time specified, such returns may be ignored and the results on file at that time may be certified by the department.

77. See, e.g., *Durham v. U-Haul Int'l,* 2001 Ind. LEXIS 297 (Ind. 2001) ("[W]e must attempt to determine what the legislative body intended when the statute was enacted. To facilitate this obligation courts have developed a number of rules on statutory construction, all of which are intended to give deference to the intent of the legislature"); *True v. Stewart,* 18 P.3d 707, 713 (Ariz. 2001 Ariz.) ("In construing and applying a statute, we should consider the statute's context; its language, subject matter, and historical background; its effects and consequences; and its spirit and purpose" [internal citation omitted]); *People v. Wiedemer,* 852 P.2d 424, 432 (Colo. 1993) ("The principles by which we must resolve this asserted conflict are well established. We must construe statutes harmoniously whenever possible and avoid interpretations that result in inconsistency"); *Lather v. Huron College,* 413 N.W.2d 369, 375 (S.D. 1987) ("[It is] the judiciary's vested duty to construe statutes and resolve questions of law").

78. See, e.g., Joan Biskupic, "Candidates' Legal Options Dwindle," *USA Today,* Nov. 24, 2000 ("Although little in the aftermath of the election Nov. 7 has been predictable, it would be unprecedented for the U.S. Supreme Court to accept Bush's urgent request for intervention"). This appeared on the day that the Court granted certiorari in the first of the two Supreme Court cases. See also John Aloysius Farrell and Lynda Gorov, "U.S. Su-

preme Court Enters Fray," *Boston Globe,* Nov. 26, 2000; Paul West, "Ballot Battle Shows No End," *Baltimore Sun,* Nov. 25, 2000.

79. Linda Greenhouse, *New York Times,* Feb. 20, 2001, A18.

80. I have deliberately hypothesized a case of discrimination based on sexual orientation because it is not clear that gays are a "protected group" under the federal Constitution, but they are a protected group under some state constitutions.

81. 5 U.S. (1 Cranch) 137, 177–178 (1803).

82. The majority of four judges issued a per curiam opinion in which they agreed that "we must do everything required by law to ensure that legal votes that have not been counted are included in the final election results" and decided "that the ultimate relief would require a counting of the legal votes contained within the undervotes in all counties where the undervote has not been subjected to a manual tabulation." Thus, the statewide manual recount was put in motion. Three judges dissented from this opinion. Chief Judge Wells worried that "there is a real and present likelihood that this constitutional crisis will do substantial damage to our country, our state, and to this Court as an institution." He cautioned that "[j]udicial restraint in respect to elections is absolutely necessary because the health of our democracy depends on elections being decided by voters—not by judges" and that he believed that the lower court ruling denying a recount should not be overturned unless there was clear error, which he could not find. He and the other two dissenting judges also felt that it was imperative to conclude the election by the safe-harbor deadline in December. They wrote that authorizing a recount, which they believed would not meet the safe-harbor deadline, would create "the very real possibility of disenfranchising those nearly six million voters who were able to correctly cast their ballots on Election Day." *Gore v. Harris,* 772 So. 2d 1243 (2000).

83. Fla. Stat. 101.5614 (5) (2000).

84. Indeed, Justices Breyer and Souter would have remanded the cases to the Florida Supreme Court for precisely that purpose—despite the fact that *they* had joined the per curiam opinion, which implied that such an action might violate Article II.

85. See *Hamilton v. Texas,* 497 U.S. 1016 (1990). Justice Thomas was not yet on the Court, but there is little doubt from his subsequent votes that he would have joined the majority in denying the stay in that capital case.

86. In at least two cases, the Supreme Court has granted certiorari in a death case but could not get the requisite five votes to stay the execution. The first was in *Hamilton v. Texas,* 497 U.S. 1016 (1990), and the second was *Herrera v. Collins,* 502 U.S. 1085 (1992). In both cases, there were four votes to grant certiorari, but no fifth vote to stay the execution. In *Hamilton,* the petitioner was executed before the Court could hear his case, and his case was dismissed as moot. In *Herrera,* the Texas Court of Criminal Appeals stayed the petitioner's execution in order to permit the case to be heard by the Supreme Court, but only after the Supreme Court itself re-

fused to do so. The Court decided against Herrera, and he was then executed.

In addition, at least three times in the mid-1980s, the Supreme Court had voted to hold a case (a decision requiring only three votes) pending the disposition of another case raising the same issue, but refused to stay the execution in the held case. See *Straight v. Wainwright,* 476 U.S. 1132 (1986) (four votes to hold the case pending the decision in *Darden v. Wainwright,* no fifth vote to stay execution); *Watson v. Butler,* 483 U.S. 1037 (1987) (four votes to hold the case pending the decision in *Franklin v. Lynaugh,* Court split 4–4 on stay of execution because Justice Powell had retired and no ninth justice had yet been appointed to replace him); and *Streetman v. Lynaugh,* 484 U.S. 992 (1988) (case held pending the decision in *Lowenfield v. Phelps,* but execution not stayed).

87.   *Watson v. Butler,* 483 U.S. 1037 (1987).
88.   *Hamilton v. Texas,* 497 U.S. 1016 (1990). In another case, Justice Brennan explained why four votes to hold a case pending the outcome of another, related case should be enough to stay an execution:

> A minority of the Justices has the power to grant a petition for certiorari over the objection of five Justices. The reason for this "antimajoritarianism" is evident: in the context of a preliminary 5-to-4 vote to deny, 5 give the 4 an opportunity to change at least one mind. Accordingly, when four vote to grant certiorari in a capital case, but there is not a fifth vote to stay the scheduled execution, one of the five Justices who does not believe the case worthy of granting certiorari will nonetheless vote to stay; this is so that the "Rule of Four" will not be rendered meaningless by an execution that occurs before the Court considers the case on the merits. (*Straight v. Wainwright,* 476 U.S. 1132, 1134–35 (1986), Brennan dissenting)

Justices O'Connor and Rehnquist joined an opinion by Justice Powell explaining why this case, in which four justices voted to hold, was different from a case in which four justices actually voted to grant certiorari:

> Justice Brennan correctly notes that, in the past, the Court has ordinarily stayed executions when four Members have voted to grant certiorari, and he maintains that "'a hold' is analogous to a decision to grant a petition for certiorari." . . . In my view, this last assertion is incorrect on several levels. First and foremost, the Court often "holds" cases for reasons that have nothing to do with the merits of the cases being held, as when we wish not to "tip our hand" in advance of an opinion's announcement. Second, when certiorari is granted, by definition the Court's resolution of the issues presented in that case might affect the judgment rendered below. That is not necessarily true of held cases.

Yet just four years later, O'Connor and Rehnquist disregarded this distinction and voted to execute men after the Court granted certiorari but before they could hear and decide the cases (*Hamilton* (1990), *Herrera* (1992)).

In another such case, Justice Brennan wrote as follows:

> Streetman, in his application for stay, raises precisely the question we agreed to consider in *Franklin*. Despite the fact that there were sufficient votes on this Court to hold Streetman's case for *Franklin,* there were not enough votes to grant Streetman's application for a stay. Had Streetman been convicted of bank robbery, this would be of no moment. The Court would simply hold Streetman's case until *Franklin* was decided, and then take appropriate action. But death is different. Due to the unique nature of the penalty, the relief that we could give any other type of habeas corpus petitioner is unavailable to Streetman. His case will be moot long before we can resolve *Franklin*—he will be dead. Therefore, we are presented with the same ironic situation as occurred in *Watson v. Butler,* 483 U.S. 1037 (1987), the normal and time-tested procedures of this Court are overcome by the different nature of the death penalty. Death is certainly different, but I had never believed it to be different in this way. (*Streetman v. Lynaugh,* 484 U.S. 992, 995–96(1988), Brennan dissenting)

89. Tony Mauro, "Killer Executed Though High Court Wanted to Review Case," Gannett News Service, Oct. 19, 1990.

90. In fact, the subsequent manual recount conducted by the *Miami Herald* and *USA Today* suggested that there was a relatively high level of agreement by different counters applying a fairly broad standard.

91. These are the examples selected by the Court:

> A monitor in Miami-Dade County testified at trial that he observed that three members of the county canvassing board applied different standards in defining a legal vote. 3 Tr. 497, 499 (Dec. 3, 2000). And testimony at trial also revealed that at least one county changed its evaluative standards during the counting process. Palm Beach County, for example, began the process with a 1990 guideline which precluded counting completely attached chads, switched to a rule that considered a vote to be legal if any light could be seen through a chad, changed back to the 1990 rule, and then abandoned any pretense of a *per se* rule, only to have a court order that the county consider dimpled chads legal.

92. It is rare for a justice to explain why he voted for a stay.

93. Fla. Stat. 102.166, sets forth the procedure for protest of election returns:

> 1. Any candidate for nomination or election, or any elector qualified to vote in the election related to such candidacy, shall have the right to protest the returns of the election as being erroneous by filing with the appropriate canvassing board a sworn, written protest.
>
> 2. Such protest shall be filed with the canvassing board prior to the time the canvassing board certifies the results for the office being protested or within 5 days after midnight of the date the election is held, whichever occurs later.

3. Before canvassing the returns of the election, the canvassing board shall:

   a. When paper ballots are used, examine the tabulation of the paper ballots cast.

   b. When voting machines are used, examine the counters on the machines of nonprinter machines or the printer-pac on printer machines. If there is a discrepancy between the returns and the counters of the machines or the printer-pac, the counters of such machines or the printer-pac shall be presumed correct.

   c. When electronic or electromechanical equipment is used, the canvassing board shall examine precinct records and election returns. If there is a clerical error, such error shall be corrected by the county canvassing board. If there is a discrepancy which could affect the outcome of an election, the canvassing board may recount the ballots on the automatic tabulating equipment.

4. a. Any candidate whose name appeared on the ballot, any political committee that supports or opposes an issue which appeared on the ballot, or any political party whose candidates' names appeared on the ballot may file a written request with the county canvassing board for a manual recount. The written request shall contain a statement of the reason the manual recount is being requested.

   b. Such request must be filed with the canvassing board prior to the time the canvassing board certifies the results for the office being protested or within 72 hours after midnight of the date the election was held, whichever occurs later.

   c. The county canvassing board may authorize a manual recount. If a manual recount is authorized, the county canvassing board shall make a reasonable effort to notify each candidate whose race is being recounted of the time and place of such recount.

   d. The manual recount must include at least three precincts and at least 1 percent of the total votes cast for such candidate or issue. In the event there are less than three precincts involved in the election, all precincts shall be counted. The person who requested the recount shall choose three precincts to be recounted, and, if other precincts are recounted, the county canvassing board shall select the additional precincts.

5. If the manual recount indicates an error in the vote tabulation which could affect the outcome of the election, the county canvassing board shall:

   a. Correct the error and recount the remaining precincts with the vote tabulation system;

        b. Request the Department of State to verify the tabulation software; or

        c. Manually recount all ballots.

    6. Any manual recount shall be open to the public.

    7. Procedures for a manual recount are as follows:

        a. The county canvassing board shall appoint as many counting teams of at least two electors as is necessary to manually recount the ballots. A counting team must have, when possible, members of at least two political parties. A candidate involved in the race shall not be a member of the counting team.

        b. If a counting team is unable to determine a voter's intent in casting a ballot, the ballot shall be presented to the county canvassing board for it to determine the voter's intent.

    8. If the county canvassing board determines the need to verify the tabulation software, the county canvassing board shall request in writing that the Department of State verify the software.

    9. When the Department of State verifies such software, the department shall:

        a. Compare the software used to tabulate the votes with the software filed with the Department of State pursuant to sec. 101.5607; and

        b. Check the election parameters.

    10. The Department of State shall respond to the county canvassing board within 3 working days.

94. *Washington Post,* Dec. 14, 2000.

95. Ronald Brownstein, "In Blocking Vote Count, High Court Shows Which Team It's Rooting For," in Dionne and Kristol, eds., *Bush v. Gore,* 268.

96. Quoted in Vincent Bugliosi, "None Dare Call It Treason," *The Nation,* Feb. 5, 2001.

97. *Bush v. Gore,* 121 S. Ct. 512, 513 (2000), dissenting from order granting stay of manual recounts.

98. "It suffices to say that the issuance of the stay suggests that a majority of the Court, while not deciding the issues presented, believe that the petitioner has a substantial probability of success." (Scalia)

Chapter 2

1. This unequivocal statement puts the lie to those who claim that this was really a 7–2 decision, because Justices Breyer and Souter agreed that "basic principles of fairness may well have counseled the adoption of a uniform standard." On the decisive issues—whether to grant the stay, whether to take the case, and whether to end the election without a remand—the decision was 5–4. Richard Epstein, a Bush supporter, has written that "the real decision was 5–4, not 7–2 as some conservatives have claimed." *Reason,* March 2001, 47.

2.   121 S. Ct. 525, 539 (2000).

3.   Both were far more categorical in their conclusion that this issue did not warrant review by the Court than that the Florida decision violated the U.S. Constitution. They were also categorical in their rejection of the majority's decision not to permit a recount under uniform standards.

4.   In support of this proposition, it cited a case holding the poll tax unconstitutional on equal-protection grounds. *Harper v. Virginia Board of Elections,* 383 U.S. 663, 665 (1966).

5.   The quote is from *Reynolds v. Sims,* 377 S. Ct. 533, 555 (1964), a leading reapportionment case.

6.   121 S. Ct. 525, 529 (2000).

7.   Quoted in *Bush v. Gore,* 121 S. Ct. 525, 529 (2000).

8.   Fla. Stat. 101.5614 (5) (2000). There can be no dispute that this is Florida law and that it preceded the election in this case (see page 59), despite some suggestions to the contrary. If the Florida legislature disagreed with the long-accepted interpretation of its statutes as establishing a general principle of voter intent, it could easily have enacted a law narrowing that standard or limiting it to specified situations.

9.   *Beckstrom v. Volusia County Canvassing Board,* 707 So. 2d 720 (1990).

10. There is an obvious difference between a ballot marked with the wrong pencil and a ballot which is not punched through completely. Though both may involve voter error, the intent of the former voter is unambiguous, whereas the intent of the latter voter may be subject to some doubt—in at least some instances. The crucial point, however, is that the wrong-pencil case articulated a general principle of Florida law which the majority justices ignored.

11. Every machine recount produced different results. See, for example, Dan Balz, "Bush's Florida Lead Shrinks to 300," *Washington Post,* Nov. 15, 2000, which shows that the machine recounts in Broward, Palm Beach, Volusia, and Miami-Dade counties each produced vote counts for both candidates that were different from the first counts.

12. From Mark Z. Barabak and Richard A. Serrano, "Decision 2000/America Waits: Ruling on Recount Expected Today," *Los Angeles Times,* Dec. 4, 2000:

> Stephen Zack, a Gore attorney . . . read a statement Ahmann [who holds patents for several parts of the Votomatic machine] made 20 years ago, saying that voting machines can get "clogged" when chads build up. Zack noted that it has been eight years since Miami-Dade County cleaned the chads from its machines.

From Stacey Singer and John Maines, "Many Disqualified Voters in Minority Areas," *Chicago Tribune,* Dec. 1, 2000:

> Varnette Weems, a poll clerk for precincts 263 and 266 in Miami, said she tried to shake out the chads there every few hours, although she did have one machine become clogged beyond repair. "It might have hap-

pened once or twice because some booths do get used more than other
ones," she said.

13.   Even Richard Posner, a conservative apologist for the *Bush v. Gore* decision, admitted that "[a] chad that though punched remains dangling from
the ballot by one or two corners, with the result that the vote was not
counted by the tabulating machine, may be pretty good evidence of an
intent to vote for the candidate whose chad was punched." Richard A.
Posner, "*Bush v. Gore:* Prolegomenon to an Assessment," in Cass R. Sunstein and Richard A. Epstein, eds., *The Vote: Bush, Gore, and the Supreme
Court* (forthcoming). For example, the *Miami Herald/USA Today* joint
review of the undervotes found that Bush gained 193 votes and Gore
gained 123 when only completely punched ballots—with no pregnant, dimpled, or hanging chads—were counted in twenty-two counties. See
http://www.usatoday.com/news/politics/2001-04-03-paperpunch.htm. These
hand counts were *not* included in the final certified vote count.

14.   No reference was made in briefs or oral arguments to any estimate of how
many undervotes existed by category. These statistics were not known until
the *Miami Herald/USA Today* recount.

15.   Moreover, the voting machines with the highest rates of uncounted votes
were in those counties with large minority populations. From *Los Angeles
Times,* March 12, 2001:

> Winding slowly through Florida's northern Panhandle, the muddy-brown
> Ochlockonee River neatly divides the best and the worst in America's
> troubled presidential balloting systems.
>
> To the west lies Gadsden County, which is largely poor, black and
> rural. On Nov. 7, one in eight Gadsden voters was effectively disenfran-
> chised when their ballots were rejected as invalid. The spoilage rate was
> the highest in the state.
>
> To the east lies Leon County, home of the prosperous state capital,
> Tallahassee, and two state universities. Here, fewer than two votes in
> 1,000 were not counted—the state's lowest spoilage rate.

From the *Chicago Tribune,* Dec. 1, 2000:

> A disproportionate number of rejected presidential votes in South Florida
> came from African-American and Caribbean neighborhoods, an analysis
> of election data show.
>
> One-third of the disqualified votes—22,807 in all—were concentrated
> in mostly black areas where at least 8 percent of the votes for president
> went uncounted, according to data from Broward, Miami-Dade and
> Palm Beach Counties. A few senior citizen communities in Palm Beach
> also were affected.
>
> Of the rejected votes in those problem precincts, almost 17,900 likely
> would have gone for Vice President Al Gore, data show. By comparison,
> 4,474 likely would have gone to Texas Gov. George W. Bush. The dis-
> qualified votes include "undervotes," those recorded as no vote by count-

ing machines, and "overvotes," those with two holes punched for president.

Voters interviewed in the problem districts described two sources of difficulty. A voter registration drive by civil rights groups sent many new, inexperienced or non-English-speaking votes to the polls. Some said they thought they needed to punch holes for both the president and his running mate.

But perhaps more significant for the court battles, voters in some areas described having trouble punching the stylus through the hole for Gore, most likely from the day's accumulation of chads. Gore representatives said that is a key reason that Gore continues the court fight for "pregnant" and "dimpled" chads to be counted.

16. Richard Pildes, *Democracy and Disorder*, 68 *U. Chi. L. Rev.* 695, 710 (2001), 117

17. For a discussion of the varying culpable mental states that satisfy the intent requirement for the death penalty in different states, see *Tison v. Arizona*, 481 U.S. 137, 152–54 (1987).

18. *Norvell v. Illinois*, 373 U.S. 420 (1963).

19. *Delahunt v. Johnson*, 671 N.E. 2d 1241, 1243 (Ma. 1996). As the lawyer for the Republican-controlled Florida legislature, Professor Fried took a somewhat different view:

> The decision of the Supreme Court of Florida, if allowed to stand, would set in motion a process that counted or rejected votes on an extremely wide range of standards—full perforation, various degrees of partial perforation, some degree of indentation or dimpling of the area intended to be perforated, counting only consistent dimpling, counting dimples if the voter voted for the candidates of the same party for other offices—all under the capacious and unconstraining rubric of the "intent of the voter." (Brief of the Florida House of Representatives and Florida Senate as amicus curiae in support of neither party and seeking reversal, *Bush v. Gore*, 121 S. Ct. 525 (2000))

20. *New York Review of Books*, February 2001.

21. There is, of course, nothing wrong with someone taking a different position as a judge than as an advocate or a professor, especially since in his exchange with Professor Dworkin, Professor Fried specifically noted that he had joined the majority opinion in the *Delahunt* case. He also believes the cases are distinguishable.

22. Those who argue that seven justices agreed on the equal-protection violation and two of them disagreed only on the appropriate remedy miss this point: There can be no judicially cognizable equal-protection violation where the only possible remedy produces greater equal-protection problems. Thus there can be no sharp distinction between the right and the remedy in this situation.

23. "We believe that it is better for ten guilty people to be set free than for one innocent man to be unjustly imprisoned." *Furman v. Georgia*, 408

U.S. 238, 368 (1972), quoting Justice Douglas, in Jerome Frank and Barbara Frank, *Not Guilty* (Doubleday, 1957) 11–12.

24. See note 14.

25. For example, the majority relies on *Gray v. Sanders*, 372 U.S. 368 (1963), and *Moore v. Ogilvie*, 394 U.S. 814 (1969). In *Gray*, the Supreme Court struck down a Georgia statutory scheme that weighted the votes from different counties unequally in statewide primary elections. The *Bush v. Gore* majority relied on *Gray* for its finding that Georgia's "arbitrary and disparate treatment to voters in its different counties" was unconstitutional. However, the Court in *Gray* relied on the well-established principle that "[e]very voter's vote is entitled to be counted once. It must be correctly counted and reported" (*Gray* at 380). Similarly, the Court in *Moore v. Ogilvie*, on which the *Bush v. Gore* majority also relies, struck down a discriminatory vote apportionment scheme because "[t]he idea that one group can be granted greater voting strength than another is hostile to the one man, one vote basis of our representative government" (*Moore* at 819).

26. Michelman, unpublished draft, with permission of author.

27. Michelman, n. 16, 10–11.

28. Indeed, Rehnquist vigorously enforced literacy requirements against minorities when he was a young Republican lawyer. See note 37 on 243.

29. Samuel Issacharoff et al., *When Elections Go Bad: The Law of Democracy and the Presidential Election of 2000* (2001), 8–9.

30. Additional cases, cited in this and other casebooks, law review articles, and briefs of the parties, were ignored by the majority.

31. In support of his claim, McCleskey proffered a statistical study performed by Professors David C. Baldus, Charles Pulaski, and George Woodworth (the Baldus study) that purports to show a disparity in the imposition of the death sentence in Georgia based on the race of the murder victim and, to a lesser extent, the race of the defendant. The Baldus study is actually two sophisticated statistical studies that examine over 2,000 murder cases that occurred in Georgia during the 1970s. The raw numbers collected by Professor Baldus indicate that defendants charged with killing white persons received the death penalty in 11% of the cases, but defendants charged with killing blacks received the death penalty in only 1% of the cases. . . . Baldus also divided the cases according to the combination of the race of the defendant and the race of the victim. He found that the death penalty was assessed in 22% of the cases involving black defendants and white victims; 8% of the cases involving white defendants and white victims; 1% of the cases involving black defendants and black victims; and 3% of the cases involving white defendants and black victims. Similarly, Baldus found that prosecutors sought the death penalty in 70% of the cases involving black defendants and white victims; 32% of the cases involving white defendants and white victims; 15% of the cases involving black defendants and black victims; and 19% of the cases

involving white defendants and black victims. (*McCleskey v. Kemp*, 481 U.S. 279, 286–87 (1987)).

However, the Supreme Court ruled:

> Because discretion is essential to the criminal justice process, we would demand exceptionally clear proof before we would infer that the discretion has been abused. The unique nature of the decisions at issue in this case also counsels against adopting such an inference from the disparities indicated by the Baldus study. Accordingly, we hold that the Baldus study is clearly insufficient to support an inference that any of the decisionmakers *in McCleskey's case* acted with discriminatory purpose. (*McCleskey v. Kemp*, 481 U.S. 279, 297 (1987), emphasis added)

32. Rehnquist, O'Connor, Scalia and Kennedy. Thomas was not yet on the Court, but there is little doubt, from his subsequent decisions, that he would have joined the majority.

33. The decisionmakers in McCleskey's case included the prosecutors who decided to seek the death penalty, based on their discretion alone; the jury, which considers many factors; the judge, who may override the jury's decision; and the governor, who has untrammeled discretion to commute the death sentence to life imprisonment. It was not sufficient to support an equal-protection claim by showing that each of these decision makers was more likely to authorize the death penalty in cases of a black killing a white.

34. In a speech on April 26, 2001, David Boies pointed out that in Florida itself, there is significant disparity from county to county in the imposition of the death penalty. Thus a defendant who was tried in a northern Florida county might be executed, while a defendant—similar in all respects or worse—might be sentenced to prison in a southern Florida court.

35. Variations on these sorts of laws actually existed during slavery; the practice continued even after emancipation.

36. *Powers v. Ohio*, 499 U.S. 400 (1991), Scalia dissenting.

37. *U.S. v. Hays*, 515 U.S. 737 (1995). See also *Allen v. Wright*, 468 U.S. 737 (1984).

38. Ibid.

39. Moreover, the law of Florida has long been that:

> The real parties in interest here, not in the legal sense but in realistic terms, are the voters. They are possessed of the ultimate interest and it is they whom we must give primary consideration. The contestants have direct interests certainly, but the office they seek is one of high public service and utmost importance to the people, thus subordinating their interests to that of the people. (*Beckstrom* at, 724)

40. 518 U.S. 515, 596 (1996).

41. See introduction, 4.

42. Linda Greenhouse, "Another Kind of Bitter Split," in Dionne and Kristol, eds., *Bush v. Gore*, 297.

43. Remarks of Bork at American Enterprise Institute, Feb. 13, 2001.

44. For a discussion of his colleague Richard Posner's views, see *Washington Post*, Feb. 21, 2001.

45. *Reason*, March 2001.

46. John J. DiIulio Jr., "Equal Protection Run Amok," in Dionne and Kristol, eds., *Bush v. Gore*, 321. Predictably, there are a few columnists who, shamelessly and without even a pretense of principle, will defend anything that gives their candidate a victory. They, like the Supreme Court, fail the shoe-on-the-other-foot test. Following the Florida Supreme Court's decision ordering a hand recount, William Kristol, the editor and publisher of the *Weekly Standard,* railed against "a presidency achieved by litigation and judicial fiat." He warned that "some of us will not believe that Al Gore has acceded to the presidency legitimately . . . we will . . . continue to insist that he gained office through an act of judicial usurpation. We will not move on. Indeed, some of us will work for the next four years to correct this affront to our constitutional order." But then, when the U.S. Supreme Court gave the election to the *Weekly Standard*'s candidate, its tune changed. In an editorial on behalf of the magazine's editors, David Tell railed against those who criticized the U.S. Supreme Court's decision and the manner by "which George W. Bush will have acceded to the presidency." Quoting opponents of the decision who used words eerily reminiscent of those used by Kristol to describe the Florida Supreme Court's decision, the editors said that "in our view, this goes well beyond the merely disillusional and far, indeed, into genuine irresponsibility, for many of the people making these claims are smart-smart enough to know better." It was as if these editors had failed to read the prior issue of their own magazine. Or, more likely, they simply didn't care. According to the *Weekly Standard,* judicial fiat is to be condemned when it produces a Gore victory and praised when it produces a Bush victory.

47. Michael McConnell, "A Muddled Ruling," in Dionne and Kristol, eds., *Bush v. Gore*, 292.

48. Linda Greenhouse, "Collision With Politics Risks Court's Legal Credibility," *New York Times*, Dec. 11, 2000, A1.

49. *Washington Post*, Feb. 21, 2000, A23.

50. *Harper's*, May 2001, 35, 40.

51. For one such example, see Marci Hamilton, "A Well-Reasoned 'Right to Vote' Ruling in the Eye of the Storm," FindLaw, Dec. 14, 2000.

52. Even Richard Posner, one of the Court's most peripatetic defenders, acknowledges that if he had been asked *before* this election whether the Florida courts have any constitutionally permissible role in supervising recounts of presidential elections under Florida law, he would have said yes. His quarrel apparently is with the degree to which he believes the Florida Supreme Court may have changed Florida law. See "The Triumph of Expedience," *Harper's*, May 2001.

53. "U.S. Supreme Court Justice Speaks on Constitution at LSU," University Wire, Sept. 26, 2000.

54. *Bush v. Gore,* 121 S. Ct. 525, 538 (2000), Rehnquist concurring.

55. The three justices cite *Beckstrom,* but for a different proposition, ignoring its holding that ballots that are improper because of voter error but show intent must be counted.

56. A strong inference of judicial malfeasance rather than negligence derives from the fact that the justices cited the cases, but for different propositions, demonstrating that they were fully aware of them.

57. For this crabbed reading of Florida law, the three justices relied on the dissenting opinion of a single Florida Supreme Court justice. *Bush v. Gore,* 121 S. Ct. 525, 538 (2000), Rehnquist concurring, quoting Chief Judge Wells's dissent in *Gore v. Harris.*

58. The three justices fudge this issue by saying that they would "hold that the Florida Supreme Court's interpretation of the Florida election laws impermissibly distorted them beyond what a fair reading *required,* in violation of Article II" (emphasis added). But even under their own mistaken reading of Article II, the criteria should be what a fair reading *permitted,* not what it *required.* See also text of sec. 101.5614 (5),(7).

59. In *McPherson v. Blacker,* 146 U.S. 1 (1892), the Supreme Court held that a state may choose to appoint its electors for the presidential election by congressional district (instead of by general popular vote) because the state has plenary power to prescribe the method of choosing electors.

60. Several commentators have argued, in support of the Rehnquist concurrence, that the Florida Supreme Court had refused to grant appropriate discretion to the Florida secretary of state and its local canvassing boards. See, for example, Richard Posner, "The Triumph of Expedience," *Harper's,* May 2001, 35. This administrative law argument, even if correct as a matter of policy, would not seem to rise to the level of a federal constitutional issue, even in a presidential election. Under the Tenth Amendment, and the "republican form of government" guarantee of Article IV, the states retain considerable authority regarding the allocation of power among its legislature, courts, and administrative agencies (if any). At the time the Constitution was ratified, administrative law and administrative agencies were hardly recognized by our legal system. The Florida statutory scheme for elections, as it has long been interpreted by the Florida Supreme Court, allocated to the judiciary the power to enforce the clear-intent-of-the-voter criterion if the administrative agencies refused to do so. The Florida secretary of state in this instance was also the cochair of Bush's presidential campaign in that state, creating an obvious conflict of interest and limiting the discretion any reasonable court might ordinarily allow to an unbiased administrator.

61. 357 U.S. 449 (1958).

62. Quoted in *Washington Post,* Feb. 21, 2000, A23. During the preparation of this book, my office repeatedly called and wrote Judge Posner requesting galleys of the book and article in which these arguments are elaborated. He did not respond to my requests, and so I had no choice but to base my

criticism on his statements quoted in the *Washington Post* article. After the manuscript of this book had been completed and submitted to the publisher, an article by Posner was published in the May 2001 issue of *Harper's,* and I have incorporated his arguments from that article where possible.

63. These are the words used in Benjamin Wittes, "Maybe the Court Got It Right," *Washington Post,* Feb. 21, 2001, in characterizing the views of critics of Posner's justification.

64. A variation on this "pragmatic" argument has been offered by Professor Cass Sunstein:

> OK. Maybe the best argument for the court having done what it did is not legal, but more kind of about statesmanship or politics. And so the argument could be that the court didn't really have a very good legal basis for doing what it did. But if it went the legally sound way and let the Florida system proceed to recount, then we would have had a little bit of a crisis in Florida 'cause the Legislature was all set to name its own electors. Then the Florida courts, maybe, were going to require the governor and the secretary of state to come up with a new slate if it turned out that Gore had more votes after the manual recount. The governor and secretary of state might have refused to certify, then maybe they'd be held in contempt. Well, this would be really in the nature of a constitutional crisis.
>
> We didn't get there, but if the governor and secretary of state are risking being held in contempt by disobeying the Florida courts, then we have a Florida Legislature with their own slate. That's a mess. How's that going to be sorted out in Florida and in Washington? In Washington, Congress would have to sort it out and then the partisan passions would be inflamed. We might have a Senate that is controlled by one candidate who casts the key vote. Gore maybe. And the House is predominantly Republican and that would be so messy and so procedurally complicated that it probably would be worse than what the Supreme Court did. So what some of the justices might have been thinking is that this is the only way the legal system can get its way out with minimal chaos.

(From interview on *Fresh Air,* National Public Radio, December 13, 2000)

65. Charles Krauthammer, "Our Imperial Judiciary," Dionne and Kristol, eds., *Bush v. Gore,* 208.

66. Needless to say, Krauthammer did not extend this principle to *Bush v. Gore.*

67. *Planned Parenthood v. Casey,* 505 U.S. 833, 865 (1992).

68. Speech to American Enterprise Institute, Feb. 13, 2001.

69. Fyodor Dostoevsky, *The Brothers Karamazov* (Vintage, 1991), 253.

70. Eric Foner, "Partisanship Rules," in Dionne and Kristol, eds., *Bush v. Gore* 293.

Chapter 3

1. This quote is from the chief justice's fifteenth year-end report, as reported in Irvin Molotsky, "In Year-End Report, Rehnquist Renews His Call to Raise the Salaries of Federal Judges," *New York Times,* Jan. 1, 2001.

2. "The Rule of Law as a Law of Rules," 56 *U. Chi. L. Rev.* 1175, 1180 (1989).

3. The failed nomination of Abe Fortas to become chief justice and his eventual decision to resign from the Court because he took money from an indicted stock swindler did raise the ugly specter of the thumb of financial benefit being placed on the scales of justice. Charles T. Fenn, "Supreme Court Justices: Arguing Before the Court After Resigning from the Bench," 84 *Geo. L. J.* 2473, 2495 (July 1996).

4. I will focus on the exemplary case of Judge Martin T. Manton; other federal judges who have been implicated in bribery scandals include Chief Justice J. Warren Davis of the Third Circuit (resigned 1939); Judge Alcee L. Hastings of the Southern District of Florida (impeached and removed from the bench in 1989); and Judge Walter L. Nixon Jr. of the Southern District of Mississippi (impeached and removed from the bench for perjury in 1989). It is also safe to assume that these cases represent only a small fraction of the actual occurrences of bribery among members of the federal judiciary. For more information on the impeachment of federal judges, see Todd D. Peterson, "The Role of the Executive Branch in the Discipline and Removal of Federal Judges," 1993 *U. Ill. L. Rev.* 809 (1993).

5. Deuteronomy 16:19.

6. Nor may a judge promote "the interests of one political party as against another," lest there be inevitable "suspicion of being warped by political bias." See, e.g., *ABA Code of Judicial Ethics*, as quoted in Joseph Borkin, *The Corrupt Judge* (Potter, 1962), 271. (The language may vary over time and place, but the substance is substantially similar.) Compare *Model Code of Judicial Conduct* (1990).

7. See Brad Snyder, "How the Conservatives Canonized *Brown v. Board of Education*," 52 *Rutgers L. Rev.* 383, 420–21 (2000), referring to Clement F. Haynsworth Jr.

8. D.C. Code Sec. 22-704(a) (2000), on corrupt influence:

    Whosoever corruptly, directly or indirectly, gives any money, or other bribe, present, reward, promise, contract, obligation, or security for the payment of any money, present, reward, or thing of value to any ministerial, administrative, executive, or judicial officer of the District of Columbia, or any employee, or other person acting in any capacity for the District of Columbia, or any agency thereof, either before or after the officer, employee, or other person acting in any capacity for the District of Columbia is qualified, with intent to influence such official's action on any matter which is then pending, or may by law come or be brought before such official in such official's official capacity, or to cause such official to execute any of the powers in such official vested, or to perform any duties of such official required, with partiality or favor, or otherwise than is required by law, or in consideration that such official being authorized in the line of such official's duty to contract for any advertising or for the furnishing of any labor or material, shall directly or indirectly arrange to receive or shall receive, or shall withhold from the parties so contracted with, any portion of the contract price, whether that price be fixed by law or by agreement, or in consideration that such official has nominated or appointed any person to any office or exercised any power in such official vested, or performed any duty of such official required, with partiality or favor, or otherwise contrary to law; and *whosoever, being such an official, shall receive any such money, bribe, present, or reward, promise, contract, obligation, or security, with intent or for the purpose or consideration aforesaid shall be deemed guilty of bribery and upon conviction thereof shall be punished by imprisonment for a term not less than 6 months nor more than 5 years.* (Emphasis added)

9. See note 6, above.
10. *Vasquez v. Hillary*, 474 U.S. 254, 263 (1986).
11. The Second Circuit, located in the financial center of the United States, has long been regarded as just below the Supreme Court in importance. This was especially true in the 1930s, when some of the nation's most distinguished judges sat on it.
12. Borkin, *The Corrupt Judge*, 25. Much of the material concerning Judge Manton is based on the Borkin book.
13. Gerald Gunther, *Learned Hand: The Man and the Judge* (Knopf, 1994), 503. In those days, there was an implicit understanding that at least one seat on the high court would be filled by a Catholic and another by a Jew. There were no seats for women, blacks, or other minorities.
14. Borkin, 18.
15. A Court of Appeals—comprising judges who had never sat with Manton—affirmed the conviction, and the Supreme Court denied review.
16. Gunther, *Learned Hand*, 506.
17. This is especially remarkable, since Manton's colleagues were fully aware—even before he was indicted—that he was engaged in what they politely called "cronyism":

> Manton's political associations continued after he became a judge: the waiting room in his chambers always seemed to be filled with his political friends, and his Tammany connections set him apart from his fellow judges. (Gunther, *Learned Hand*, 503.)

One reason why even the most astute of judges might not suspect corruption is that judges are generally protective of each other and rarely assume the worst about their colleagues. The same is true of many academic and professional critics: They are prepared to assume laziness, stupidity, or ideological leanings, but not outright corruption—especially in a high-ranking federal judge. Indeed, according to Judge Learned Hand's biographer, in at least one case Hand may well have suspected in 1934 that Manton had strained so hard to articulate such strange patent-misuse principles because of his friendships with old political allies, but there is no indication that he suspected Manton had been bribed. After Manton's conviction,

> Hand worried that somehow he was partly responsible for Manton's corruption, though he had not known, and had no real reason to know, that any of Manton's votes were prompted by bribes. He repeatedly speculated about what he might have done to keep Manton from temptation: if only he and Gus Hand and Tom Swan had done more to bring Manton into their circle, he would muse, if only they had not watched from a distance as Manton churned out marginal work while political hangers-on filled his anteroom. These self-tortures were unrealistic, given what Manton was like, yet to the end, Hand refused to exculpate himself entirely. (Gunther, *Learned Hand*, 509)

18. Triangulation is used to enhance the level of certainty regarding data in many academic fields. See, e.g., "Final Report and Recommendations of the Eighth Circuit Gender Fairness Task Force," 31 *Creighton L. Rev.* 9 (Dec. 1997): "We emphasize here that these multiple sources and multiple methods (known in the scientific community as 'triangulation' of data) produce the most complete, reliable, and valid body of evidence available bearing on these complex topics and issues, thus allowing considerable confidence in the findings reported below."

19. For example, there is a considerable controversy regarding President Franklin D. Roosevelt's complicity in the U.S. decision to shut the door to Jews who sought to emigrate from Nazi-controlled Europe. Much evidence is available for all to read, but there is no consensus on the standard of proof warranting condemnation or exculpation. For an account of President Roosevelt's refusal to allow the German refugees on board the S.S. *St. Louis* to disembark in the United States, see Gordon Thomas and Max Morgan Witts, *Voyage of the Damned* (Stein and Day, 1974).

20. Gunther, *Learned Hand*, 507.

21. Interview on *Fresh Air*, National Public Radio, Dec. 13, 2000.

22. It is not, however, entirely without precedent. After Justice Harry Blackmun wrote the Court's decision in *Roe v. Wade*, some critics pointed to his close connection with the Mayo Clinic and his daughter's support for abortion rights. No one charged Blackmun with anticipating any material benefit from the ruling or with partisan bias, especially since he had been appointed by a Republican president.

23. Gunther, *Learned Hand*, 507.

24. *Bracy v. Glamley*, 520 U.S. 899 (1997).

25. *Hunter v. Underwood*, 471 U.S. 222 (1985).

26. Ibid.

27. Samuel Issacharoff et al., "When Elections Go Bad: The Law of Democracy and the Presidential Election of 2000 (2001)."

28. John Locke used the term "ad hominem" to describe a "way to press a man with consequences drawn from his own principles or concessions"

(Essay Concerning Human Understanding IV, xvii, 21). Robert Bork, who was subjected to a combination of ad hominem and policy criticisms, wrote the following about the protection of ad hominem attacks under the First Amendment while he was a Court of Appeals judge: "Those who step into areas of public dispute, who choose the pleasures and distractions of controversy, must be willing to bear criticism, disparagement, and even wounding assessments." He went on to observe:

> Perhaps it would be better if disputation were conducted in measured phrases and calibrated assessments, and with strict avoidance of the *ad hominem*; better, that is, if the opinion and editorial pages of the public press were modeled on *The Federalist Papers*. But that is not the world in which we live, ever have lived, or are ever likely to know, and the law of the first amendment must not try to make public dispute safe and comfortable for all the participants. That would only stifle the debate. In our world, the kind of commentary that the columnists Rowland Evans and Robert Novak have engaged in here is the coin in which controversialists are commonly paid. (*Ollman v. Evans*, 750 F.2d 970, 993 (1984))

29. Paul D. Carrington, "Restoring Vitality to State and Local Politics by Correcting the Excessive Independence of the Supreme Court," 50 *Ala. L. Rev.* 397, 423–24 (1999), quoting Jefferson and his followers.

30. See Anthony Lewis, "What Ashcroft Did," *New York Times*, Jan. 27, 2001, A15.

31. The latter is sometimes problematic because the justices have been known to change their views quite dramatically after ascending to the bench. Justice Felix Frankfurter is often cited as an example of a political liberal who became a judicial conservative based on his views of the limited role of the judiciary in a democracy. Earl Warren is cited as a political moderate who became a judicial liberal.

32. See William Safire, "The Wicked Which and the Comma," *New York Times,* Sept. 2, 1984: "Not since Richard Nixon referred to 'the great Republican Chief Justice Earl Warren' had there been such a ruckus over a comma; had Nixon put a comma after 'Republican,' he would not have been accused of politicizing the Supreme Court."

33. A large-firm New York lawyer I knew once bragged that he had one more "big one" owed to him by a federal judge whose appointment he had supported. I would have nothing further to do with this lawyer, but lo and behold, he got his favor.

34. Although this is a hypothetical exercise, lawyers are, in fact, often asked to make these kinds of predictions, and the tools they employ include reading all the prior opinions of the judges.

35. A somewhat more pointed variation on this hypothetical would include the names and party affiliations of the litigants, but reverse them, with Bush needing the recount to win.

36. Quoted in *Reitmeyer v. Spreacler*, 431 Pa. 284, 292 (1968).

37. "The Path of the Law," 10 *Harv. L. Rev.* 457, 461.

Chapter 4

1. *U.S. v. Virginia,* 518 U.S. 515, 596 (1996), Scalia dissenting.
2. Antonin Scalia, "The Rule of Law as a Law of Rules," 56 *U. Chi. L. Rev.* 1175, 1179–80 (1989).
3. Ibid.
4. *Hubbard v. U.S.,* 514 U.S. 695 (1995), Scalia concurring.
5. *U.S. v. Virginia,* at 568. Here he quotes from his own dissenting opinion in *Rutan v. Republican Party of Ill.,* 497 U.S. 62, 95 (1990).
6. Scalia, "The Rule of Law as a Law of Rules," 1178.
7. Antonin Scalia, "Originalism: The Lesser Evil," 57 *U. of Cincinnati L. Rev.* 849, 863 (1989)
8. *Cruzan v. Director of Missouri Dept. of Health,* 497 U.S. 261, 300–301 (1990), Scalia concurring.
9. Antonin Scalia, *A Matter of Interpretation: Federal Courts and the Law,* ed. Amy Gutmann (Princeton University Press, 1997), 17–18.
10. See, e.g., Richard A. Posner, "The Triumph of Expedience," *Harper's,* May 2001; Cass R. Sunstein, "Order Without Law," in Cass R. Sunstein and Richard A. Epstein, eds., *The Vote: Bush, Gore, and the Supreme Court* (forthcoming; available at www.thevotebook.com).
11. *Morrison v. Olson,* 487 U.S. 654 (1988).
12. *Planned Parenthood v. Casey,* 505 U.S. 833 (1992).
13. Quoted in Tinsley E. Yarbrough, *The Rehnquist Court and the Constitution* (Oxford University Press, 2000), 14.
14. Scalia did write an unusual separate opinion on the stay, but it simply asserted that the majority had the votes rather than explaining how it had the legal authority to stop the count.
15. See, e.g., *General Motors Corp. v. Tracy,* 519 U.S. 278, 312 (1997), where Scalia briefly concurs with the Court's opinion but "write[s] separately to note" his particular viewpoint on a broad constitutional question that motivated his vote. See also *Lauro Lines S.R.L. v. Chasser,* 490 U.S. 495, 502 (1989), where Scalia again concurs with the majority opinion but "write[s] separately only to make express what seems to [him] implicit in [the Court's] analysis."
16. *U.S. v. Virginia,* at 601.
17. See page 74 for a full discussion of *McCleskey v. Kemp.*
18. See, for example, *Hernandez v. New York,* 500 U.S. 352 (1991), a case in which the striking of jurors because they were Latino was challenged as a violation of the equal-protection clause. In the opinion, Justice O'Connor reaffirmed her belief that an equal-protection claim must be based on discriminatory purpose and not just on a disproportionate impact on any one group. O'Connor also joined the majority opinion in *U.S. v. Armstrong,* 517 U.S. 456 (1996), where the Court stated that a claim for violation of equal protection because of selective prosecution based on race must be supported by evidence of both discriminatory effect *and* discriminatory purpose.

19. *U.S. v. Hays,* 515 U.S. 737 (1995).
20. In a 1995 equal-protection case (*Adarand v. Pena,* 515 U.S. 200, 237 (1995)), she said:

> Because our decision today alters the playing field in some important respects, we think it best to remand the case to the lower courts for further consideration in light of the principles we have announced.

In *Lanier v. South Carolina,* 474 U.S. 25, 26 (1985), a criminal case regarding the voluntariness of a confession, O'Connor concurred with the per curiam majority opinion to remand:

> I believe the [state court of appeals] on remand can consider the timing, frequency, and likely effect of whatever *Miranda* warnings were given to petitioner as factors relevant to the question whether, if petitioner was illegally arrested, his subsequent confession was tainted by the illegal arrest.

See also *Eddings v. Oklahoma,* 455 U.S. 104, 119 (1982), a death penalty case in which O'Connor defended the majority decision to remand:

> I disagree with the suggestion in the dissent that remanding this case may serve no useful purpose. . . . [W]e may not speculate as to whether the trial judge and the [state] Court of Criminal Appeals actually considered all of the mitigating factors and found them insufficient to offset the aggravating circumstances, or whether the difference between this Court's opinion and the trial court's treatment of the petitioner's evidence is "purely a matter of semantics," as suggested by the dissent.

In light of such statements, Gore lawyers were hoping O'Connor might—at the very least—vote for a remand, as Justices Souter and Breyer did. But instead she joined an opinion that concluded that "remanding to the Florida Supreme Court for its ordering of a constitutionally proper contest until Dec. 18 . . . could not be part of an 'appropriate order' " (per curiam, *Bush v. Gore* (2000)).

On the issue of whether to stay the hand count pending full briefing, argument, and decision, she also departed from her usual reluctance to grant stays, even in capital cases. See *McFarland v. Scott,* 512 U.S. 849 (1994), in which O'Connor concurred in part and dissented in part. *McFarland* was a death penalty case in which the defendant requested a lawyer for a postconviction habeas corpus petition. He also petitioned for a stay of his execution date, so that his court-appointed attorney could prepare his habeas corpus petition. O'Connor agreed that the defendant was entitled to representation while pursuing his habeas corpus petition, but disagreed that he was entitled to a stay of his execution date while that attorney was preparing to file the petition. She would have Congress amend its statutes to clear up the "clumsiness of its handiwork" and make obvious its intent to allow stays in this situation. She also shifts the blame to the defendant, who should file "a prompt request for appointment of counsel well in advance of the scheduled execution" (*McFarland* at 863). For some recent examples, see *Miller v. Arizona,* 121 S. Ct. 445 (2000); *Poland v.*

Arizona, 529 U.S. 1013 (2000); *Calambro v. Ignacio* (526 U.S. 1048 (1999); *LeGrand v. Arizona,* 526 U.S. 1001 (1999); and *Gerlaugh v. Stewart,* 525 U.S. 1131 (1999), in all of which the Court denied an application to O'Connor for the granting of a stay of execution upon her referral to the Court. Consider also that O'Connor joined the Court's majority opinion in *Clinton v. Jones,* 520 U.S. 681 (1997), where the Court refused to grant President Clinton a stay of the lawsuit against him brought by Paula Jones.

21. *Davis v. Bandemer,* 478 U.S. 109 (1986), O'Connor concurring. On the issue of deferring to state courts' judgment, consider O'Connor's statement in her majority opinion in *Engle v. Isaac,* 456 U.S. 107, 128 n. 33 (1982):

> State courts are understandably frustrated when they faithfully apply existing constitutional law only to have a federal court discover . . . new constitutional commands. . . . In an individual case, the significance of this frustration may pale beside the need to remedy a constitutional violation. Over the long term, however, federal intrusions may seriously undermine the morale of our state judges.

See also *Gregory v. Ashcroft,* 501 U.S. 452 (1991), where O'Connor, writing for the majority, held that a Missouri state law establishing a mandatory retirement age for judges did not violate the federal Age Discrimination Act because Congress and the federal courts must respect state sovereignty; *Coleman v. Thompson,* 501 U.S. 722 (1991), where O'Connor, again writing for the majority, held that the federal courts should not review a criminal defendant's federal petition for habeas corpus unless and until that defendant has exhausted all possible state remedies, thereby giving complete deference to state courts to resolve all state issues; and Sandra D. O'Connor, "Trends in the Relationship Between the Federal and State Courts from the Perspective of a State Court Judge," 22 *William and Mary L. Rev.* 801, 814–15 (1981), written while she was a judge on the Arizona Court of Appeals, in which she argues that "[i]t is a step in the right direction to defer to the state courts and give finality to their judgments on federal constitutional questions where a *full* and *fair* adjudication has been given in the state court."

22. *Deadlock: The Inside Story of America's Closest Election,* by the Political Staff of the Washington Post (Public Affairs, 2001), 163.

23. To be sure, the rule of precedent is neither rigid nor absolute, especially in the Supreme Court. While lower courts are bound by the precedents of the nation's highest court, the Court itself has the power—the freedom—to depart from its own precedents and to overrule a prior decision. But it is expected to do so only rarely and for compelling reasons, which the justices are obliged to explain and defend. A court that promiscuously ignores precedents loses respect. A justice who is perceived to be manipulating precedent in order to get the law to come out in favor of his or her personal or political predilections will not be respected. It is for that reason that

many justices, including some who joined the majority opinion in this case, have decided to follow precedents with which they personally disagree. In this case, the majority justices consciously violated the salutary approach to precedent in three different but overlapping ways. First, they ignored past precedent with which they generally agreed, but which would have kept them out of this case. Second, they sent a not-so-subtle message that they did not intend to follow the precedent established by this case in future cases, and that they did not regard this ad hoc precedent as binding on lower courts. Third, they so miscited past precedents, and wrenched them so out of their historical context, as to make a mockery out of the rule of precedent and the requirement that if past precedent is to be overruled, the Court must provide honest and persuasive reasons for breaking with the past.

24. *Adarand v. Pena* at 231 (quoting *Arizona v. Rumsey,* 467 U.S. 203, 212 (1984)).

25. In the *Adarand* case, O'Connor—writing for the majority—overruled a recent case that had failed to follow the precedent established by earlier cases. In doing so, it used the equal-protection clause to make it more difficult for government to enact affirmative-action programs. It remanded the case to the lower courts "for further consideration"—something it refused to do in the Florida election case.

26. *Dickerson v. U.S.,* 530 U.S. 428 (2000).

27. *Planned Parenthood v. Casey.*

28. Over the last ten years, Kennedy has voted with Rehnquist 81.3 percent of the time, with Scalia 74.1 percent of the time, and with Thomas 74.2 percent of the time. He has voted with O'Connor 77.4 percent of the time. And he has voted with Breyer 68.1 percent of the time, Stevens 56.7 percent, Ginsburg 68.9 percent, and Souter 72.6 percent. "The Supreme Court 1999 Term, the Supreme Court in the Nineties: A Statistical Retrospective," 114 *Harv. L. Rev.* 402, 406 table IIB (2000).

29. Robert Reinhold, "Restrained Pragmatist: Anthony M. Kennedy," *New York Times,* Nov. 12, 1987.

30. Ibid.

31. Anthony Kennedy at his confirmation hearing. *Chicago Tribune,* Dec. 2, 1987, 2.

32. See, for example, *U.S. v. Lopez,* 514 U.S. 549, 573 (199), Kennedy concurring: "Stare decisis operates with great force in counseling us not to call in question the essential principles now in place respecting the congressional power to regulate transactions of a commercial nature"; *Pacific Mut. Life Ins. Co. v. Haslip,* Kennedy concurring; and *Missouri v. Jenkins,* 495 U.S. 33, 58 (1990), Kennedy concurring, in which Kennedy attacked the majority opinion's suggestion that a federal court could require a school district to levy taxes to fund school desegregation, refused to embrace the Court's "expansion of power in the Federal Judiciary beyond all precedent" because it "disregards fundamental precepts for the democratic con-

trol of public institutions," and affirmatively recited the Court's holding in *United States v. County of Macon*, 99 U.S. 582, 591 (1879), that "[w]e have no power by mandamus to compel a municipal corporation to levy a tax which the law does not authorize. We cannot create new rights or confer new powers. All we can do is to bring existing powers into operation."

33.   *Pacific Mutual Life Ins. Co. v. Haslip.* Kennedy then went on to cite the precedents of capital cases:

> As we have said in the capital sentencing context:
>> "It is not surprising that such collective judgments often are difficult to explain. But the inherent lack of predictability of jury decisions does not justify their condemnation. On the contrary, it is the jury's function to make the difficult and uniquely human judgments that defy codification and that 'build discretion, equity, and flexibility into a legal system.' " *McCleskey v. Kemp*, 481 U.S. 279, 311 (1987) (quoting H. Kalven & H. Zeisel, *The American Jury* 498 (1966)).

34.   The per curiam opinion does seek to distinguish people from things, but as pointed out in Chapter 2, even with regard to decisions made by people, more uniformity can always be achieved.

35.   See also *City of Boerne v. Flores*, 521 U.S. 507 (1997); *Hubbard v. U.S.*, 514 U.S. 695 (1995).

36.   *New York Times*, Feb. 20, 2001, A18.

37.   When Rehnquist was a law clerk to Justice Robert Jackson in 1952, he wrote a memorandum to his boss in favor of state-supported segregation in the public schools: "I realize that it is an unpopular and unhumanitarian position, for which I have been excoriated by my 'liberal' colleagues, but I think *Plessy v. Ferguson* was right and should be reaffirmed. Snyder at 441." *Plessy* had ruled that the equal-protection clause permitted state-supported segregation, whose purpose was to keep the races separate, so long as the segregated facilities were "separate but equal"—an obvious impossibility, given our relatively recent history of slavery. In another memorandum, he advised his boss that "[i]t is about time the Court faced the fact that the white people in the South don't like colored people" (see David G. Savage, "The Rehnquist Court: Bill Rehnquist Was Once Considered an Extremist. Now His Views Almost Always Become the Law of the Land," *Los Angeles Times Magazine*, Sept. 29, 1991, 12). Rehnquist concluded that "the Constitution does not prevent the majority from banding together, nor does it attain success in this effort" (see George Lardner Jr. and Saundra Saperstein, "A Chief Justice-Designate with High Ambitions," *Washington Post*, July 6, 1986). In other words, if the majority doesn't like a particular racial or ethnic minority, it is entirely constitutional to segregate them.

    When one of these damning memoranda surfaced during the confirmation process, Rehnquist had the audacity to deny that its contents reflected *his* own views, attributing them instead to the dead justice for whom he had worked (see Stuart Taylor Jr., "Opposition to Rehnquist Nomination Hardens as 2 New Witnesses Emerge," *New York Times,* July 27, 1986). But the late Justice Jackson's longtime secretary blasted Rehnquist for having "smeared the reputation of a great justice" who did not harbor such segregationist views, especially after serving as the chief prosecutor at the Nuremberg war crimes trials and witnessing at first hand the consequences of racism and segregation (see Ronald J. Ostrow and Robert L. Jackson, "Bias, Candor Again Issues as Rehnquist Faces Senate," *Los Angeles Times,* July 29, 1986). Several of Rehnquist's fellow law clerks were also outraged by his blame-the-dead-man defense and confirmed that the segregationist views expressed in the memoranda were typical of those expressed at that time by Rehnquist.

A decade and a half later, when Rehnquist was promoted to chief justice, several of these issues reemerged, along with some new ones. It was discovered that Rehnquist owned a home with a restrictive covenant barring the leasing or sale of his Vermont house to "any member of the Hebrew race" (see "Justice Knew of Deed in '74," *New York Times,* Aug. 6, 1986). The Senate Judiciary Committee also revisited Rehnquist's early history as an enforcer for the "Republican Party Ballot Security Program," which was a euphemism for a heavy-handed effort—largely successful—to harass minority voters away from the polls during 1960s elections (see "Rehnquist on Hot Seat: Kennedy Cites Race Ban on Home Deed," *Chicago Tribune,* Aug. 1, 1986). Rehnquist's testimony about his bigoted past—he denied or minimized nearly every charge—was so questionable that the *New York Times* editorialized as follows: "A Chief Justice can be less than inspiring or less than an ardent civil libertarian, but he cannot be less than a champion of truth" (see "The Past in Mr. Rehnquist's Future," (editorial) *New York Times,* Aug. 3, 1986). What the polite editors of the *Times* were saying, in their understated language, was what several senators had already concluded, namely, that Rehnquist had lied under oath at his confirmation hearings, in an effort to deny his bigoted background.

Several law professors used even stronger language: The chief justice of the United States had committed "perjury." See Michael E. Parrish, "The Chief Justice Plays the Race Card," *San Diego Union-Tribune,* Dec. 15, 2000, quoting University of Chicago law professor Philip Kurland as stating that "Rehnquist did not tell the truth to the Judiciary Committee on his first nomination and did not tell the truth on the second one either"; Joseph L. Rauh Jr., "Historical Perspectives: An Unabashed Liberal Looks at a Half-Century of the Supreme Court," 69 *N.C. L. Rev.* 213, 242 (1990), in which the author recounts testifying at Rehnquist's confirmation hearing about the 1952 memo and concludes that "[t]he evidence appears incontestable that he was not [telling the truth]"; Brad Snyder, "How the Conservatives Canonized *Brown v. Board of Education,*" 52 *Rutgers L.*

Rev. 383, 451 (2000), citing the following legal scholars who have concluded that Rehnquist's account cannot be totally accurate:

> Richard Kluger, *Simple Justice: The History of* Brown v. Board of Edu-
> cation *and Black America's Struggle for Equality* (1976) AT 603–10 &
> n.* (casting doubt on Rehnquist's account); Gregory S. Chernack, *The
> Clash of Two Worlds: Robert H. Jackson, Institutional Pragmatism,
> and* Brown, 72 *Temple L. Rev.* 51, 55 n. 21 (1999) (examining Justice
> Jackson's jurisprudence and the dilemma that *Brown* posed for Justice
> Jackson); Bernard Schwartz, *Chief Justice Rehnquist, Justice Jackson,
> and the* Brown *Case,* 1988 Sup. Ct. Rev. 245, 245–67 (giving weight
> to Justice Jackson's unpublished draft opinion in *Brown,* stating that
> segregation was unconstitutional, and concluding that the memo in
> question stated Rehnquist's views); Mark Tushnet and Katya Lezin,
> *What Really Happened in* Brown v. Board of Education, 91 *Colum. L.
> Rev.* 1867, 1880, 1911 n. 190 (1991) (arguing that Jackson was "deeply
> ambivalent" about race and that Rehnquist's account may be partially
> truthful).

See also Tinsley E. Yarbrough, *The Rehnquist Court and the Constitution*
(Oxford University Press, 2000), 1–6.

38. Recent important cases in which the Supreme Court used strict scrutiny
analysis to strike down state and federal preferences for racial minorities
include *Adarand v. Pena; City of Richmond v. Croson,* 488 U.S. 469
(1989); and *Wygant v. Jackson Bd. of Educ.,* 476 U.S. 267 (1986).

39. *Sugarman v. Dougall,* 413 U.S. 634, 649–50, 657 (1973). In this case,
Rehnquist was the sole dissenter from the opinion holding that discrimination against aliens requires strict scrutiny under the equal-protection
clause.

40. In dissenting from a decision that declared state discrimination against illegitimate children unconstitutional under the equal-protection clause
(*Trimble v. Gordon,* 430 U.S. 762, 785 (1977)), Justice Rehnquist (then
still an associate justice) offered the following interpretation of that
clause:

> Every law enacted, unless it applies to all persons at all times and in all
> places, inevitably imposes sanctions upon some and declines to impose
> the same sanctions on others. But these inevitable concomitants of leg-
> islation have little or nothing to do with the Equal Protection Clause of
> the Fourteenth Amendment, unless they employ means of sorting people
> which the draftsmen of the Amendment sought to prohibit. I had thought
> that cases like *McGowan,* in which the Court, speaking through Mr.
> Chief Justice Warren, said that "[a] statutory discrimination will not be
> set aside if any state of facts reasonably may be conceived to justify it."

41. *Califano v. Boles,* 443 U.S. 282, 284 (1979), applying this principle in a
case approving the limitation of certain Social Security benefits to married
women, thus creating a discriminatory effect on illegitimate children.

42. *Trimble v. Gordon*, 430 U.S. 762 (1977).

43. See, for example, *Bowers v. Hardwick*, 478 U.S. 186, 190 (1986), in which Rehnquist joins Justice White's majority opinion upholding the constitutionality of a state law criminalizing sodomy because "many states . . . still make such conduct illegal and have done so for a very long time"; *Jones v. U.S.*, 526 U.S. 227, 254 (1999), Kennedy dissenting, in which Rehnquist joins Kennedy's dissent arguing that Congress has the authority to make bodily harm an element in a carjacking statute and concluding that "the majority's sweeping constitutional discussion casts doubt on sentencing practices and assumptions followed not only in the federal system but also in many States. Thus, among other unsettling consequences, today's decision intrudes upon legitimate and vital state interests, upsetting the proper federal balance."

44. *Fry v. U.S.*, 421 U.S. 542, 550 (1975) (quoting *Maryland v. Wirtz*, 392 U.S. 183, 205 (1968), Rehnquist dissenting.

45. *U.S. v. Lopez*. See also *National League of Cities v. Usefy*, 426 U.S. 833; Michael Dorf, "Instrumental and Non-Instrumental Federalism," 28 *Rutgers L. J.* 825 (1998).

46. William H. Rehnquist, *Grand Inquests* (Morrow 1992), 10.

47. *M.L.B. v. S.L.U.*, 519 U.S. 102 (1996).

48. *FCC v. Beach Communications*, 508 U.S. 307 (1993), 313–14, quoting from *Vance v. Bradley*, 440 U.S. 93, 97 (1979).

49. *Holder v. Hall*, 512 U.S. 874, 897–902 (1994), Thomas concurring (footnote omitted).

50. *New York v. United States*, 505 U.S. 144, 187–88 (1992).

51. Professor Dorf lists Thomas, along with Rehnquist, as members of the hard anti-Federalist bloc. See Dorf, "Instrumental and Non-Instrumental Federalism," 826.

52. *U.S. Term Limits, Inc. v. Thornton*, 514 U.S. 779, 849 (1995), Thomas dissenting.

53. *McPherson v. Blacker*, 146 U.S. 1, 25 (emphasis added), quoted by Justice Stevens in his dissenting opinion in *Bush v. Gore*.

54. Scalia in *Planned Parenthood v. Casey*. Although Scalia's statement was made in the context of the abortion controversy, it aptly characterizes the issues at stake in election cases as well.

55. See Richard Posner, "The Triumph of Expedience," *Harper's*, May 2001, 39.

56. Quoted in Alan M. Dershowitz, "Of Justices and 'Philosophies,'" *New York Times*, Oct. 24, 1971.

57. They also may have shared an outrage at the Florida Supreme Court for acting in what they believed was a partisan manner, but this outrage appears quite selective, and I doubt it would have moved the justices if the Florida Supreme Court had shown partisanship toward Bush. In any event, outrage—even justified outrage—is not a proper basis for Supreme

Court intervention into a matter which the state has constitutional authority.

58. Christopher Marquis, "Job of Thomas's Wife Raises Conflict of Interest Questions," *New York Times,* Dec. 12, 2000; Bob Woodward and Charles Lane, "Scalia Takes a Leading Role in Case," *Washington Post,* Dec. 11, 2000.

59. Evan Thomas and Michael Isikoff, "The Truth Behind the Pillars," *Newsweek,* Dec. 25, 2000.

60. Edward Lazarus, Findlaw, Feb. 16, 2001. The other conservative justice Lazarus was apparently referring to was Chief Justice Rehnquist. See page 169.

61. See Daniel Schorr, "The Supreme Fix Was In," *Christian Science Monitor,* Dec. 15, 2000; Mary McGrory, "Supreme Travesty of Justice," *Washington Post,* Dec. 14, 2000.

62. J. O. Brown, W. E. Farmer, and M. E. O'Connell, M.E., "The Rugged Feminism of Sandra Day O'Connor," 32 *Indiana L. Rev.* 1219, 1222 (1999).

63. *Washington Post,* July 8, 1981, A1.

64. Justice O'Connor served on the Superior Court of Arizona (the trial court) from 1975 to 1979, before being appointed to the Arizona Court of Appeals.

65. See Brown, Farmer, and O'Connell, "The Rugged Feminism of Sandra Day O'Connor," 1222 n. 26.

66. See, for example, Edwin M. Yoder Jr., "Justice O'Connor's Unfortunate Letter," *Washington Post,* Mar. 19, 1989; "The 'Christian Nation' Fallacy," *St. Petersburg Times,* Mar. 17, 1989; and Al Kamen, "Justice O'Connor to Brief GOP Donors at High Court; ABA Code Bars Speeches to Political Groups," *Washington Post,* May 1, 1987. See generally, Alan M. Dershowitz, "Justice O'Connor's Second Indiscretion," *New York Times,* April 2, 1989.

67. O'Connor's reply included the following: "You wrote me recently to inquire about any holdings of this Court to the effect that this is a Christian Nation. There are statements to such effect in the following opinions: *Church of the Holy Trinity v. United States. Zorach v. Clauson. McGowan v. Maryland.*" In addition to the impropriety of a justice lending the Court's judicial imprimatur to a controversial political proposal, Justice O'Connor's case citations are just plain wrong. The last two cases do not contain any statements of support for the claim that "this is a Christian Nation." Indeed, their entire thrust is to the contrary. The first case, decided in 1892, does contain such a statement in passing, though certainly not a "holding," since the case involved an interpretation of an immigration statute, not a construction of the First Amendment's prohibition against the establishment of religion. No Court decision over the last ninety-seven years lends any support to the claim that we are a "Christian Nation." There are statements that we are a "religious peo-

ple," but they are invariably followed by assurance of "no partiality to any one group."

68. Not only was Justice O'Connor's letter used in that partisan political campaign to increase the number of Republican voters, but its miscitation of cases became the basis of the religiously exclusive resolution enacted by the Arizona Republican Party. That resolution begins, "Whereas the Supreme Court of the United States has three holdings to the effect that this is a Christian nation . . . " It then cites the decisions provided by Justice O'Connor and declares that we are "a Christian nation" and that the Constitution created "a republic based upon the absolute laws of the Bible, not a democracy."

69. Tom Wicker, "Sage Advice from R.N.," *New York Times,* Apr. 15, 1988.

70. Robert Novak, "Court That Really Swings," *Chicago Sun-Times,* Dec. 21, 2000, 39.

71. Even that would not constitute a complete defense, since it is improper for a judge to participate in any case where she may have a personal interest in the outcome, even if that interest has no effect on her decision.

72. Elizabeth Olson, "O'Connor: Poise, Stamina and Grit," *Washington News,* Sept. 12, 1981.

73. Neil A. Lewis, "Democrats Readying for Judicial Fight," *New York Times,* May 1, 2001.

74. The former clerk requested anonymity. His information was corroborated by the Novak column cited *infra* note 75.

75. Novak, "Court That Really Swings."

76. Robert Novak, "Sniping at Cox's Success," *New York Post,* May 30, 1999.

77. Jeffrey Rosen, "In Lieu of Manners," *New York Times,* Feb. 4, 2001.

78. He has been called "a knee-jerk right-winger" by law professor Pamela Karlan. He has "carried an aura of partisanship" from the beginning of his tenure on the Court (Yarbrough, 44).

79. Clarence Thomas's Senate confirmation hearings became a nationally televised spectacle after Anita Hill, a former employee, accused him of sexually harassing her. Thomas's denial and Hill's subsequent graphic testimony nearly derailed his nomination to the Supreme Court, although he was eventually confirmed by the full Senate in a vote of 52–48.

80. "Senators Against: Questions About Charges, Qualifications," *Washington Post,* Oct. 16, 1991.

81. Reported in Frank J. Murray, "Election Could Reshape Court," *Washington Post,* Oct. 16, 2000.

82. Two related vignettes, reported in David Savage, "In the Matter of Justice" *Los Angeles Times,* Oct. 9, 1994, reveal how differently Thomas can act to friends and enemies even in small matters. Senator John C. Danforth, his biggest supporter during the confirmation hearings, called Thomas and asked him to meet with a group of his summer interns. "He had them come over the next day. He took time with every one of them. . . . That's the real Clarence Thomas," said Danforth. William L. Robinson, the dean

of the District of Columbia Law School, also wanted to bring some students to meet his old friend. But Robinson, a black civil rights lawyer, had disagreed with Thomas about some legal issues. Robinson called Thomas's chambers repeatedly. "He wouldn't even call me back." That, too, is the real Clarence Thomas. It depends on which list your name appears.

Thomas told an interviewer that he roots for the Dallas Cowboys because they are hated by Washington fans, and he also likes the Los Angeles Raiders "because everybody hates them." He is on record as believing that those who disagree with him hate him. He himself seems to be consumed by hatred, despite his fervent Christianity. He played his favorite song, "Onward, Christian Soldiers," during recesses in his confirmation hearings.

83. Yarbrough, *The Rehnquist Court and the Constitution*, 44.
84. David Savage, "In the Matter of Justice" *Los Angeles Times,* Oct. 9, 1994.
85. According to Professor Mark Tushnet of Georgetown University Law Center, Thomas has put in the "least impressive performance of any justice since Whitaker"—a marginally competent justice who resigned in his fifth year upon realizing he was not up to the job. Thomas quickly became a staunch opponent of a woman's right to choose abortion, leading many observers to conclude that he had fixed views on this issue long before he was appointed as a justice. Yet during his confirmation hearing, he swore that "I cannot remember personally engaging in" any discussion of *Roe v. Wade.* As Jeffrey Toobin observed in "The Burden of Clarence Thomas," *New Yorker,* Sept. 27, 1993, 47.

> Since it was the most famous Supreme Court case of his generation, this statement drew widespread skepticism at the time. In any event, it appears clear that Thomas had made up his mind about the fate of Roe before he arrived on the Court; without even discussing the issue with his law clerks, he decided that the case should be overturned. "There was no point in talking about Casey," the source says. "There was no doubt whatsoever on where he was coming out. There was no discussion at all." Thomas joined Justice Scalia's dissenting opinion, which urged that Roe be overturned.

This has led Professor Pamela Karlan to conclude: "I think he perjured himself about *Roe*" (Savage, "In the Matter of Justice," *Los Angeles Times,* Oct. 9, 1994).

There have been other allegations of untruthfulness regarding Thomas, beyond his testimony about *Roe v. Wade* and his denial of Anita Hill's allegations, including that he lied in a highly publicized speech about his own sister being a lazy, undeserving "welfare queen"; see Clarence Page, "Thomas's Sister's Life Gives Lie to His Welfare Fable," *Orlando Sentinel-Tribune,* July 25, 1991. Thomas's assurance to schoolchildren in the wake of *Bush v. Gore* that partisan politics played no role in the decision should be evaluated against this history.

86. The primary financial backer of the Claremont Institute—whose previous speakers included Rush Limbaugh and Newt Gingrich—was Richard Mel-

lon Scaife, a right-wing Clinton-hater who had financed an investigation into Clinton's activities. See Joan Lowy, "Thomas Urged Not to Lecture to Conservatives," *Pittsburgh Post-Gazette*, Feb. 2, 1999.

87. David G. Savage, "Thomas Urged to Cancel Speech to Conservatives," *Los Angeles Times,* Feb. 2, 1999. Thomas postponed the speech for three weeks.

88. Shortly after being sworn in, he raised eyebrows among his fellow justices when his wife threw a party for him at the high court with an invitation list that read like a who's who of Republican politics. Ibid.

89. These include the Georgia Public Policy Foundation, National Empowerment Television, Concerned Women for America, and other stridently right-wing Republican groups.

90. Fiftieth Anniversary Tribute to the Free Congress Foundation, April 26, 1993.

91. Two such cases are *Lamb's Chapel v. Center Moriches Union Free School District,* 508 U.S. 384 (1993), and *Bray v. Alexandria Women's Health Clinic,* 506 U.S. 263 (1993); see generally Toobin, "The Burden of Clarence Thomas."

92. Thomas's wife is a full-time Republican activist, having worked for the House Republican Conference. In 1996, she was involved in digging up dirt on President Clinton and served as an aide to House Republican leader Dick Armey. Despite her husband's nonpartisan job, she "remains in the thick of the fight," according to an associate, and always "wants to bring the battle to the Democrats" and "go the extra mile" (Toobin, "The Burden of Clarence Thomas"; see also Jess Bravin et al.,"*Bush v. Gore* Has Personal Angle for Some Supreme Court Justices," *Wall Street Journal,* Dec. 12, 2000).

   The couple's life has been described as "one of shared, brooding isolation." Or, as Thomas himself put it: "We travel everywhere together like a pair of nuns." This includes driving his wife to her political job every morning. (Jeffrey Toobin, "The Burden of Clarence Thomas," *New Yorker,* Sept. 27, 1993)

93. A federal appellate judge, Gilbert S. Merritt of the United States Court of Appeals for the Sixth Circuit, said he saw a serious conflict of interest for Justice Thomas in deciding a case that could throw the election to Governor Bush.

   "The spouse has obviously got a substantial interest that could be affected by the outcome," he said in an interview from his home in Nashville. "You should disqualify yourself. I think he'd be subject to some kind of investigation in the Senate."

   Judge Merritt, who has long association with the Gore family and was considered a leading contender for the Supreme Court early in the Clinton Administration, said he would not launch a formal complaint against Justice Thomas.

But he urged Justice Thomas to remove himself from the case in order
to prevent any violation of a federal law—he cited Section 455 of Title
28 of the United States Code, "Disqualification of Justices, Judges or
Magistrates"—that requires court officers to excuse themselves if a
spouse has "an interest that could be substantially affected by the outcome of the proceeding."

Judge Merritt offered his views about Justice Thomas after someone
in the Gore campaign provided the *New York Times* with his name and
telephone number. Judge Merritt said he had had no direct contact with
the Gore campaign.

(Christopher Marquis, "Challenging a Justice," *New York Times,* Dec. 12,
2000)

94. Toobin, "The Burden of Clarence Thomas."
95. Ibid.
96. "I was drunk with anger, out of control with hostility toward what I saw
as the oppression around me," he told Holy Cross students (Savage, "In
the Matter of Justice Thomas," *Los Angeles Times,* Oct. 9, 1994). He is a
man given to extremes in his politics and his emotions—and this was before
the contentious confirmation hearing, which he characterized as a "high-
tech lynching" (Toobin, "The Burden of Clarence Thomas"). Former Senator John Danforth, Thomas' most ardent supporter, has reported that
during the hearings "Thomas was reduced to uncontrollable fits of weep-
ing, vomiting, hyperventilating, and writhing on the floor." Before the Hill
allegations "he suspected that people were tyring to kill him." (Yarbrough,
44)
97. Toobin, "The Burden of Clarence Thomas."
98. Yarbrough, *The Rehnquist Court and the Constitution,* 44.
99. Toobin, 46.
100. During Antonin Scalia's first day on the high court bench back in 1986,
he so monopolized the oral argument that Justice Lewis Powell declaimed
in a stage whisper, "Do you suppose he knows the rest of us are here?"
Since that time, the brash justice has established a reputation as the Supreme Court's reigning bully, interrupting oral arguments with his sharp
tongue and sometimes even insulting other justices with his acid pen. He
has shown "intellectual contempt for most of his colleagues." (Yarbrough,
43) In the process, he has alienated several of his colleagues, but he remains
the darling of the political right—the justice who, along with Clarence
Thomas, serves as a model for future appointments by President George
W. Bush.
101. As David Boies put it: "Justice Scalia would not have voted for Gore even
if his son had been *my* partner." ("Votes and Voices" symposium, Cardozo
Law School, April 26, 2001)
102. *Harper's Magazine,* May 2001, 39.
103. A *Washington Post Magazine* article by Garrett Epps focused on Scalia's
disappointment with Bill Clinton's election and reelection:

By 1996 Scalia was allowing his bitterness to show. In a much-criticized speech to a prayer breakfast in Mississippi, he cast himself in the role of the lonely religious dissenter ridiculed by a trivial, secular culture. "We must pray for the courage to endure the scorn of the sophisticated world." And in the wake of Bill Clinton's landslide reelection that year, friends and associates of Scalia began to hint that the justice would consider a conservative draft as the Republican presidential candidate in the year 2000.

The presidential talk was far-fetched and almost silly. But it underscored that much of Scalia's unhappiness was due to presidential politics. In 1986, when he took his seat on the court, he and other conservative jurists looked confidently forward to an unbroken string of Republican nominations to the court, which would solidify right-wing dominance and make coalition-building unnecessary. But in another of history's surprises, two-party politics reemerged. Bill Clinton, not George Bush, named the last two justices. (Garrett Epps, "Nino to the Rescue," *Washington Post Magazine,* Feb. 25, 2001)

104. Ibid.
105. Quoted in Henry David Rosso, *ACLU: Rehnquist, Scalia Disregard Bill of Rights,* U.P.I., Sept. 7, 1986.
106. "Court Appointees Must Be for the Constitution," *Dallas Morning News,* June 29, 1986.
107. Scalia has pointed to his vote to strike down a flag-burning statute as proof that his judicial philosophy is not a cover for his political preferences. He has argued that he doesn't particularly like sandal-wearing, long-haired flag burners. That misses the point. No one who supports freedom of speech necessarily likes all those who exercise it. By lowering the level of abstraction from support of free speech to approval of flag burning (or Nazi propaganda or pornography), Scalia makes it appear that this case caused a conflict between his personal views and the result demanded by the Constitution.

He has also pointed to his vote in a case involving the right of an accused child molester to confront his accuser but the *Wall Street Journal* has—commendably—made the issue of false allegations of child abuse a cause célèbre of the right.
108. George Lardner Jr., "Nixon on Appointing Rehnquist; On Tape, He Exults Over 'Hard-Right' Nominees," *Washington Post,* Oct. 30, 2000.
109. In an op-ed article for the *Los Angeles Times* on Dec. 28, 2000, entitled "Justice May Be Blind, but It's Not Deaf," I urged any law clerk who has information about possible improprieties by any justice to come forward and disclose it.
110. Second review of Florida vote is inconclusive, *New York Times,* May 11, 2001, A29.

Chapter 5

1. Jeffrey Rosen, "The Supreme Court Commits Suicide," in E. J. Dionne Jr. and William Kristol, eds., *Bush v. Gore: The Court Case and Commentary* (Brookings Institution, 2001), 311–16.
2. *The Nation,* Feb. 5, 2001.
3. Randall Kennedy, "Contempt of Court," in Dionne and Kristol, eds., *Bush v. Gore,* 336–38.
4. Scott Turow, "A Brand New Game: No Turning Back from the Dart the Court Has Thrown," in Dionne and Kristol, eds., *Bush v. Gore, 304.*
5. *New York Times,* April 21, 2001, 1.
6. Cass Sunstein in "What We'll Remember in 2050," in Dionne and Kristol, eds., *Bush v. Gore,* 340.
7. Anthony Lewis, "A Failure of Reason," in Dionne and Kristol, eds., *Bush v. Gore,* 299–301.
8. *Harper's,* May 2001, 37.
9. Chief Justice Rehnquist, then an associate justice, recused himself in the Nixon tapes case. The vote was 8–0.
10. Victor Williams, "Third Branch Independence," 5 *Seton Hall L. Rev.* 854 (1995).
11. Several years ago, I brought charges against a federal district court judge who committed no crime or (arguably) any impeachable offense. He had announced from the bench that I would no longer be allowed to argue cases in his courtroom because he disagreed with what I had written in a book. The book, *Reversal of Fortune,* was about the Claus von Bülow case, and in it I criticized several members of the Rhode Island judiciary, not including him. Although I had never appeared in his court or even met him, he issued his decree of exclusion from the bench. The Judicial Conference agreed with my charges and condemned him in the strongest terms. This condemnation ended any chance that he would ever be promoted, and his career as a judge suffered considerably from that rebuke. See David Margolick, "A Glimpse at the Secrets of Penalizing Judges," *New York Times,* July 14, 1989, A1. Were a justice of the Supreme Court—or even the entire Supreme Court—to commit a similar offense against a lawyer or a litigant, there would be no place to go for relief.
12. See page 156.
13. Speaking to a group of high school students the day after the case was decided, Justice Thomas defended the decision and the decision-making process, saying, "Don't try to apply the rules of the political world to this institution. . . . We have no axes to grind, we just protect [the Constitution.]" In an exchange with reporters regarding Thomas's telling statements, Chief Justice Rehnquist heartily agreed: "Absolutely, absolutely." See Bill Rankin, "Was It Politics? That, Too, Is in Dispute," *Atlanta Journal and Constitution,* Dec. 14, 2000. Justices from the dissenting minority have also played down the decision, preferring to defend the Court in the face of

public criticism. See Linda Greenhouse, "Election Case a Test and a Trauma for Justices," *New York Times,* Feb. 20, 2001, which describes speeches by Breyer, Scalia, and Ginsburg defending the Court as nonpartisan.

14. Shortly after the decision, my colleague Laurence Tribe, who was one of Gore's lawyers, appeared on television to urge all Americans to "rally around" the decision even if they disagreed with it. Normally that occurs, but it did not in this case.

15. *Planned Parenthood v. Casey,* 505 U.S. 833, 868 (1992).

16. See, e.g., Charles Fried et al., " 'A Badly Flawed Election': An Exchange," *New York Review of Books,* Feb. 22, 2001, where Fried says, "Vehemence in dissent is traditional, but fouling your own nest always seems desperate."

17. For a discussion of this concept, see Alan M. Dershowitz, *The Best Defense* (Random House, 1982).

18. From "Judicial Independence," a speech to the Federalist Society National Convention, Nov. 12, 1999.

19. Alan Dershowitz and John Ely, "*Harris v. New York:* Some Anxious Observations on the Candor and Logic of the Emerging Nixon Majority," 80 *Yale L. J.* 1198 (1971).

20. See Larry Kramer, "The Supreme Court v. Balance of Powers," *New York Times,* March 3, 2001, 13.

21. This reality is what has led Bruce Ackerman, a professor of law at Yale, to propose that the Senate should "simply refuse to confirm any Supreme Court nomination until the next presidential election."

Ackerman elaborated on this view in an article in the *American Prospect:*

> This is not the first time in history that the Supreme Court has made a decision that called its fundamental legitimacy into question. But on past occasions, the normal operation of the system provided a remedy. As the wheel of mortality turned and justices were replaced, the Court regained credibility as an independently elected president and Senate appointed new members. But this time, the president has not been independently elected. He is in the White House as a result of an unprincipled judicial decision that brought the electoral contest to a premature end. If such a president is allowed to fill the Court, he will be acting as an agent of the narrow right-wing majority that secured his victory in the first place.
>
> In our democracy, there is one basic check on a runaway Court: presidential elections. And a majority of the justices have conspired to eliminate this check. The Supreme Court cannot be permitted to arrange for its own succession. To allow this president to serve as the Court's agent is a fundamental violation of the separation of powers. It is one thing for unelected judges to exercise the sovereign power of judicial review; it's quite another for them to insulate themselves yet further from popular control. When sitting justices retire or die, the Senate should refuse to

confirm any nominations offered up by President Bush. ("The Court
Packs Itself," *American Prospect,* Feb. 12, 2001)
Despite the powerful logic of Ackerman's argument, the Senate is unlikely
to refuse to confirm *all* nominees, regardless of their qualifications. But it
might be possible to persuade enough senators to oppose all partisan nominees who lack greatness. See page 203.

22.   Judicial restraint was, of course, practiced much earlier and even discussed
        by Oliver Wendell Holmes, among others. But Brandeis and his successors
        more fully developed it as a systematic judicial philosophy. See Alexander
        Bickel, *The Least Dangerous Branch* (Yale Univ. Press, 1986).

23.   We will never know how true Brandeis would have been to his judicial
        philosophy of judicial restraint had he lived in a different era—an era in
        which conservative legislatures were enacting conservative laws that were
        inconsistent with his political, ideological, or personal views. Indeed, he
        constructed a judicial philosophy that was sufficiently flexible to allow a
        considerably greater degree of judicial activism when legislatures restricted
        freedom of speech and conscience then when they restricted freedom of
        contract or property rights. This prioritization reflected Brandeis's political
        and ideological views, but it was also consistent with the special status of
        freedom of speech and conscience in our Bill of Rights.

        Justice Oliver Wendell Holmes seemed true to his judicial philosophy
        most of the time. But he was rarely tested until very late in his life.

24.   This is not a recent development. Back in the early 1970s, I wrote a series
        of articles for the *New York Times* about the confusion between judicial
        and political philosophy in which I made the following point:

        What the President [Nixon] meant by "judicial" philosophy is far less
        clear. "Now I paraphrase the word 'judicial,'" he said, and "by judicial
        philosophy I do not mean agreeing with the President on every issue."
        A justice, he continued, "should not twist or bend the Constitution in
        order to perpetuate his political and social views."

        After assuring his audience that the nominees shared his judicial phi-
        losophy and that they were conservatives ("but only in a judicial, not in
        a political, sense"), the President went on to give an example of what a
        conservative judicial philosophy means to him: "As a judicial conserva-
        tive, I believe that some Court decisions have gone too far in the past in
        weakening the peace forces as against the criminal forces in our society.
        The peace forces must not be denied the legal tools they need to protect
        the innocent from criminal elements."

        The President's law-and-order attitude is not a "judicial philosophy."
        It is just the sort of "personal political and social view" that the President
        emphasizes should not be perpetuated by a Supreme Court justice.

        A judicial philosophy deals with the roles of the Court as an institu-
        tion. It is responsive to questions such as: What precedential weight
        should be given to prior decisions? What power should the Court exer-
        cise over the other branches of the federal government and over the

states? What tools of judicial construction should it employ in giving meaning to a constitutional or statutory provision? A judicial philosophy—if it is truly judicial rather than "political" or "social"—does not speak in terms of giving the peace forces "tools" to "protect the innocent from criminal elements."

A "conservative" judicial philosophy is one that respects precedent, and that avoids deciding cases on constitutional grounds whenever a narrower ground for a decision is available. Most importantly, a judge with a conservative judicial philosophy abjures employing the courts to effectuate his own political or social program—he is a decider of cases rather than an advocate of causes. (Alan M. Dershowitz, "Of Justices and 'Philosphies,'" *New York Times*, Week in Review, Oct. 24, 1971)

25. As Professor Randall Kennedy has aptly said, "Those who abhor what the Court did should say so and say so loudly and directly." "Contempt of Court" in Dionne and Kristol, eds., *Bush v. Gore*, 338.

26. The major area in which substantial rights were considerably expanded by the Warren Court—often over the vigorous dissent of conservatives—was the civil rights of racial minorities under the equal-protection clause. As Professor Larry Kramer has correctly observed: "Warren Court activism was largely confined to questions of individual rights, mainly racial equality and the treatment of criminal defendants [and such individual rights] actually affect only a small portion of what government does." The Rehnquist Court's aggressive activism has been designed "to strip the federal government of many of its most long-recognized powers under the Commerce clause. It has struck down congressional legislation dealing with violence against schoolchildren and women, with discrimination based on age and religion, with copyright protection and much more. No court in the history of our nation has been as aggressively activist as the current Rehnquist court in reallocating authority between the federal and state government as well as among the branches of the federal government, grabbing from Congress and for itself the power to determine the reach of the 14th Amendment and the Commerce clause." *New York Times*, Dec. 12, 2000.

27. The Senate is 50–50, but the deciding vote is cast by the Republican vice president.

28. Obviously, some women and minorities are likely to reflect liberal ideologies, but they are still very much a minority on the federal bench.

29. Pro-choice advocates will, of course, argue that precisely because there is so much division of view—religious, moral, political—among people, each woman must be allowed to decide the abortion issue for herself. While I personally agree with this argument, I understand the counter-argument that where human life is concerned, we do not let people make individual choices. No one would suggest that a pregnant woman be allowed to wait to make the "abortion" decision until the moment after birth, when she can be certain that her child will be "normal." The state

takes that choice from her, because a born child is plainly a human being whose own interest in life must be protected. For those who believe
that a fetus is just as human as a born child, there is no difference between these cases: A pregnant woman may not choose to "kill" the "human
being" in her womb.

30.   *ACLU Position Paper: The Right to Choose* (fall 2000).
31.   A point similar to the one I am making was made in a recent essay:

> Seventy-five years ago, we believed firmly enough in a rock-solid, un-
> changing Constitution that we felt it necessary to adopt the Nineteenth
> Amendment to give women the vote. The battle was not fought in the
> courts, and few thought that it could be, despite the constitutional guar-
> antee of Equal Protection of the Laws; that provision did not, when it
> was adopted, and hence did not in 1920, guarantee equal access to the
> ballot but permitted distinctions on the basis not only of age but of
> property and of sex. Who can doubt that if the issue had been deferred
> until today, the Constitution would be (formally) unamended, and the
> courts would be the chosen instrumentality of change? The American
> people have been converted to belief in The Living Constitution, a
> "morphing" document that means, from age to age, what it ought to
> mean. And with the conversion has inevitably come the new phenomenon
> of selecting and confirming federal judges, at all levels, on the basis of
> their views regarding a whole series of proposals for constitutional evo-
> lution. If the courts are free to write the Constitution anew, they will,
> by God, write it the way the majority wants; the appointment and con-
> firmation process will see to that. This, of course, is the end of the Bill
> of Rights, whose meaning will be committed to the very body it was
> meant to protect against: the majority. By trying to make the Constitu-
> tion do everything that needs doing from age to age, we shall have caused
> it to do nothing at all.

The author of this perceptive essay was Antonin Scalia (*A Matter of Interpretation,* 47). It is too bad he contradicted its essential thrust in *Bush
v. Gore,* when he joined an opinion writing the equal-protection clause
anew and making it do what he and the other members of the majority
believed needed doing in order to reach a partisan result.

32.   President Reagan may have overplayed his hand by nominating Robert
Bork, but the ensuing confirmation battle made it virtually impossible for
President Clinton to nominate any activist liberal justices, even if he had
wanted to. Even some of his lower-court nominations were either rejected
or not voted on.

33.   "The Wages of Crying Wolf: A Comment on *Roe v. Wade,*" 82 *Yale L. J.*
920, 947 (1973).

34.   The high court was divided into three camps. The hard right—comprising
Rehnquist, Scalia, and Thomas—could be counted on in most cases to rule
in favor of governmental power and against individual rights, unless the
government was seeking to enforce liberal programs, such as affirmative

action, and the individual rights were those of white Christians. The soft right—comprising O'Connor and Kennedy—generally agreed with the hard right on policies but was less willing to overrule prior decisions, especially in highly visible and politically charged matters. The moderates—Breyer, Ginsburg, Souter, and Stevens—could generally be counted on to rule in favor of the rights of racial and religious minorities as well as women, but often not criminal defendants, except in capital cases and other special situations. The old liberal wing had ended with the retirements of Brennan, Marshall, and Blackmun, though Stevens sometimes echoed Blackmun's center-left views on certain issues.

35. Thomas received "the worst result of any Supreme Court nominee since the ABA entered the rating business in 1955" with its Standing Committee on the Federal Judiciary. Thomas was deemed "qualified" (the second of three rating levels) by twelve committee members and "unqualified" by two members, with one abstention. The other justice who received less than a unanimous "well qualified" rating is O'Connor, who was rated at least "qualified" by all fifteen members of the ABA panel but "well qualified" by only a few, probably because of her lack of experience. See "Thomas: The Least Qualified Nominee So Far?" *National Law Journal*, Sept. 16, 1991.

36. Both Rehnquist and Thomas were believed by some respected individuals to have been less than forthright at their confirmation hearings. The *New York Times*, after reviewing Rehnquist's testimony about his bigoted past, said this: "A chief justice can be less than inspiring or less than an ardent civil libertarian, but he cannot be less than a champion of truth." "The Past in Mr. Rehnquist's Future," *New York Times*, Aug. 3, 1986, A22. See page 242, note 37. Several senators and law professors believed that Thomas had been less than truthful in discussing his views on abortion and in his denial of Anita Hill's charges. See generally Tinsley E. Yarbrough, *The Rehnquist Court and the Constitution* (Oxford University Press, 2000), 2–26.

37. The Republicans were not the first to select justices based on their political or ideological reliability. Franklin D. Roosevelt had a litmus test—his nominees had to support his New Deal. But beyond that single issue, Roosevelt nominated justices across the ideological spectrum, as did Presidents Truman, Eisenhower, and Kennedy. President Johnson picked a crony (Abe Fortas) and a symbol (Thurgood Marshall), both of whom had extraordinarily distinguished careers as lawyers.

Richard Nixon, who made law and order into a political issue, was the first president in modern history to try to pack the Court with mediocrities who mirrored his politics. Warren Burger, a judge of no distinction, became chief justice and then persuaded Nixon to nominate his "Minnesota twin," Harry Blackmun, who began his career on the high court as a reliable Burger clone, but then moved considerably to the left. Nixon then tried to nominate two mediocre lower-court judges—Clement Haynsworth and G. Harrold Carswell—as part of his "southern strategy," but when these nominations failed, he was forced to select credentialed candidates. He didn't even know the name of one—he called him "Renchberg"—but he was advised that Rehnquist was a reliable right-winger. The second was Lewis Powell, an extremely distinguished practicing lawyer from Virginia with a strong conservative background.

Gerald Ford selected John Paul Stevens, a nonideological choice. When I had dinner with Ford several years ago, he told me the selection of Stevens was the act of which he was most proud in his presidency. President Carter filled no Supreme Court vacancies.

President Reagan was determined to avoid Nixon's initial mistakes by appointing right-wing ideologues with credentials. He succeeded with Scalia, failed with Bork and Ginsburg, and was then forced to nominate a reliable Republican with few enemies or problems, Anthony Kennedy. He also selected the first woman to serve as a justice and in doing so, had to dig deeply to get beyond the hundreds of eminently qualified women and select an obscure judge from the Arizona intermediate appellate court with a strong Republican Party background and an endorsement from William Rehnquist.

President George Bush selected a mediocre, and very young, right-wing ideologue to replace Thurgood Marshall. In nominating Clarence Thomas, he described him as the most qualified person for the job. I don't know a single lawyer who believed that was the case, or who believed that Bush thought that was the case. Then he nominated David Souter to replace William Brennan. The little-known Souter surprised Republicans with his moderate views, giving rise to the conservative mantra "No more Souters."

President Clinton selected two moderate centrists, one of whom—Stephen Breyer—had been nominated to the Court of Appeals with the blessing of both Edward Kennedy and Strom Thurmond, and the other of whom—Ruth Bader Ginsburg—had a reputation for being a procedurally oriented, highly technical judge with strong views regarding women's rights but little else.

38. There has never been ideological symmetry between Republican and Democratic nominations. Right-wing ideological extremism has been a virtue in the eyes of Republican presidents such as Nixon, Reagan, and Bush. Left wing ideological extremism has been a disqualification for Democratic presidents. Indeed, nearly every liberal justice has been an accident, with the possible exception of Thurgood Marshall, who was put on the Court more for his race and his professional accomplishments than his ideology.

39. Robin Toner, "Interest Groups set for Battle on a Supreme Court Vacancy," New York Times, April 21, 2001, A1.

40. Ibid, describes the opinion of Ralph G. Neas, president of People for the American Way.

41. Conservatives are pushing the names of some extremely right-wing members of the Federalist Society for the Courts of Appeals. See Neil A. Lewis,

"Bush to Reveal First Judicial Choices Soon," *New York Times*, April 24, 2001, A17.

42. "Bush Set to Grant Courts a Conservative Tilt," *USA Today*, March 23, 2001, 3A.

43. Ibid.

44. Ibid.

45. Robin Toner, "Interest Groups Set for Battle on a Supreme Court Vacancy," *New York Times*, April 21, 2001, A1.

46. Ibid.

47. To some degree, the abortion issue may be seen as a surrogate for other liberal-conservative splits, but it is not a precise surrogate, since some judges have particularly strong views on abortion but not on other issues.

48. Quoted in Dershowitz "Senate's Role: It Need Not Allow the President a Partisan Victory," *New York Times*, October 24, 1971, Week in Review, 1.

49. Linda Greenhouse, "Another Kind of Bitter Split," in Dionne and Kristol, eds., *Bush v. Gore*, 297.

Index